BY RICHARD MERYMAN

Hope: A Loss Survived
Louis Armstrong — a Self-Portrait
Andrew Wyeth
Mank: The Wit, World, and Life of Herman Mankiewicz
Broken Promises, Mended Dreams

BROKEN PROMISES
MENDED DREAMS

RICHARD MERYMAN

Little, Brown and Company
Boston   Toronto

FIRST EDITION

Library of Congress Cataloging in Publication Data

Meryman, Richard, 1926–
Broken promises, mended dreams.

1. Alcoholism—Treatment—United States—Case studies.
2. Alcoholics—United States—Biography—Case studies.
3. Women—United States—Alcohol use—Case studies.
I. Title.
HV5279.M46   1984   362.2'92088042   84-11283
ISBN 0-316-56784-1

MV
Designed by Patricia Girvin Dunbar

Published simultaneously in Canada
by Little, Brown & Company (Canada) Limited

PRINTED IN THE UNITED STATES OF AMERICA

As if I asked a common Alms,
And in my wondering hand
A Stranger pressed a Kingdom,
And I, bewildered, stand —
As if I asked the Orient
Had it for me a Morn —
And it should lift its purple Dikes,
And shatter me with Dawn!

— Emily Dickinson

CONTENTS

PART ONE
Chapter One 3
Chapter Two 22

PART TWO
Chapter Three 53
Chapter Four 83
Chapter Five 108

PART THREE
Chapter Six 143
Chapter Seven 168
Chapter Eight 194
Chapter Nine 216
Chapter Ten 231
Chapter Eleven 248

PART FOUR
Chapter Twelve 269
Chapter Thirteen 291
Chapter Fourteen 318

Author's Note 347
The Twelve Steps of Alcoholics Anonymous 351

PART ONE

CHAPTER

1

THE DAY was Sunday, April twenty-fifth, and Abby Andrews was returning from a week alone on Martha's Vineyard. Gazing down from the small plane at the vast flatness of the sea, she watched two tiny ferryboats meet and pass — heading, separate and unswerving, toward opposite horizons. "That's Martin and me," she thought.

The plane tilted downward to descend into Boston and the seat belt sign flashed. But Abby disliked the confinement of the strap. She did not care to be part of a herd — "All together now . . ." Glancing quickly at the stewardess, she hid the unfastened buckles beneath her purse. Then, with the tiny mirror in her compact, she began her own landing checklist. Lipstick okay. Eyeliner okay. But the eyes were bloodshot. Leaning her head back against the seat, opening her mouth slightly as her forefinger pulled down each lower lid, she skillfully applied four drops of Murine. Martin used to say it was her eyes that first attracted him — because they were so clear, so level. "Amazing" was his word, and she'd been pleased. He'd liked her voice, too. "Full," he'd said, "but soft around the edges."

With the mirror she examined the area around the eyes and thought, "The crow's-feet are on the march." And why, she wondered, was her skin always so dry? The Sahara. Well, better living through chemistry. Pouring moisturizer onto her palm, she rubbed it over the offending lines and down

3

into the dark hollows under her eyes. Then, squeezing blush from a tiny tube onto the tip of her forefinger, she smoothed it onto the pale skin stretched over the high cheekbones.

Next, with a few brisk strokes, she brushed her chestnut hair — the bangs across the forehead and the easy curls reaching down to the shoulders. But why was her hair so dull? Nothing seemed to help that. Then, finishing the ritual, she removed an atomizer of perfume from her open purse. Turning her head toward the shelter of the window, Abby quickly sprayed the inside of her mouth.

The plane was on the ground. Standing up to leave, she adjusted her flannel pants and tucked in the silk shirt, pleased by the knowledge that its delicate green stripe repeated the green plaid of her knee socks. Adjusting the milky, yellow agate necklace around her neck, Abby thought, "For the best performance by a supporting actress . . ."

As she crossed the cement runway toward the terminal, Abby could feel the queasiness starting up in her stomach. There had been a time, she thought, when that would have been the anticipation of seeing Martin — the excitement that soon she would be complete again and safe, that she was going toward her happiness. But instead it was the panic — the reason she had run away to Martha's Vineyard — the feeling that she was going under for the third time, that the person inside her was sinking, suffocating. Why was Martin doing this to her? Treating her like an inept and foolish child, taking over everything, constantly correcting and countermanding, never letting her be good enough. Was he trying to drive her crazy? He kept telling her things were true, when she knew they weren't true. Like *Gaslight.* And the more helpless she felt, the more helpless she became. "He's going to destroy me," she thought.

In the waiting room Martin stood against the far wall, wearing his customary three-piece, gray pinstripe suit, in his hand a briefcase. He had on his half-glasses; he must have been working. As always, seeing him suddenly, she noticed that his long, plumpish face didn't fit the slender athlete's body. She'd once teased him about that, asking, why didn't he put his face on a diet? Martin hadn't liked that. Well, right now *she* didn't like that police lineup look on his face: pick out the naughty little girl. Maybe she could jolly him into a good mood. Maybe, for once, they could have a peaceful, friendly ride home. With a grin in her voice, she said, "You would have really laughed. This man, sounding like forty gloomy trolls, came over to me in the airport and . . ." But Martin's face, with its dark mustache, was looming over her for the hello kiss — and for his sneaky little sniff. Abby held her breath and turned away her mouth, giving him her cheek.

They walked down the tunnellike corridor of the terminal. The butterflies were growing in Abby's stomach. She felt the jitters crawling again like spiders along her nerves. Her body was clammy. Her hands had begun to shake, and she hid them in her pockets. While Martin waited for her suitcase, she excused herself and headed into a ladies' room. In the privacy of a stall, seated on the toilet, she opened her purse. Among the packs of cigarettes, lighters, bite-sized Mr. Goodbars, Murine, wintergreen Lifesavers, lipsticks, compact, dark glasses, makeup, vial of Valium, wallet with snapshots of Frederick and Judy and Evan — was a Milk of Magnesia bottle. From it Abby gulped a raw, burning mouthful of vodka. She winced with distaste and thought, "Goddamn him for making me do this."

Then she sighed with relief and thought, "Now things will be okay." She took another gulp and sat waiting for that warm ball in her stomach to spread out through her needy body, muffling her shivers, smoothing the sharp edges, filling up the holes. "Normal women," she thought, "don't carry around booze in their purses and drink on airport toilets." But her other voice, always so reasonable, so reassuring, told her, "You've never in your life been like other people. And they don't have to deal with Martin. They don't get the jitters. If they knew what it was like, they'd understand."

5

In the car going home, Abby sat silent, waiting, watchful, intensely aware of Martin with his right hand, as always, at the top of the steering wheel, his left hand in his lap, the thumb hooked into the safety belt across his chest. She could see right now from his hurt, mad expression that the next words from his mouth would be sarcastic hints for self-improvement — unconnected to any tenderness or sensitivity. And then she would defend herself, and they would be at it again, and there would be no real hope.

Presently, Martin's eyes flicked away from the highway and glanced over his glasses toward Abby. "You look completely burnt out," he said. "Had your nose in the sauce?"

Abby twisted toward him, hands clenched in her lap, voice controlled. "It so happens I almost missed the plane and haven't had any breakfast. I feel like I've been in a Waring blender set on chop."

"I thought you went away for a rest?"

Abby leaned back again in the seat, aware, irrationally, of the pleasant smell of leather in the car. She ran her hand through her hair. The muscles along her jaw were hard. But her voice was conciliatory. "If you say I look terrible, okay," she said. "But please believe me. Deep down where it matters, I *am* rested. I absolutely *had* to be alone and have a little time of peace by the ocean. I was going crazy at home trying to do everything you wanted, and I just couldn't cope anymore. You *said* you understood. But now I'm all right again. Truly!" She reached across and touched his leg. Her voice was earnest. "Life's going to get better now. I promise."

"I've heard that before."

Abby retreated into silence — wondering how she could ever swim against this tremendous tide.

Martin's eyes remained unswervingly on the road, his face set and grim. When he spoke again, his voice was cutting, punishing. "How much did you drink?"

Abby drew in a deep breath. He was determined to have his scene. "You've forgotten all those phone calls," she an-

6

swered patiently. "I told you. I slept late. Read a lot on the beach. Took naps and cooked fish every night. Sometimes I did have a drink before dinner. Now please. It's really nice to be home. Don't ruin it all."

"Just a drink. Right."

Abby felt her heart beating faster. "You have so much contempt for me, Martin. If only you could admit it, maybe we could talk and be closer."

Martin said wearily, "It's hopeless. When will I ever learn to keep my mouth shut."

Abby spoke flatly, looking away from him out the window. "Something's got to change between us."

As they followed the turnpike through the beginnings of Worcester, Abby looked out over the small industrial city and wondered if this man, this place, was to be her whole life. Would that be her epitaph? Born, lived, died in Worcester — and graduated from Worcester Academy — to everybody's great relief. Thank God for Middlebury College — away from her mother's evil eye. But away from her father, too. A small lump rose in her throat and for a second she closed her eyes. He had approved of Martin. Parents did. Mr. Upright, the town catch who married the town character. The girl his parents didn't like.

Abby glanced again at Martin, his shoulders slightly hunched as he drove. He was still pretty good-looking, she decided. Had all his hair, but it was too fine to control, which irritated him. She liked the mustache, though somehow it didn't suit that file-card mind of his, everything in perfect order. But he was a very good stockbroker; she had to give him that. How ironic that she had loved him, married him, for the very qualities that drove her crazy now: books in shelves by size and color, not subject. If she returned one to the wrong spot, he was immediately rising from his chair, saying, "It doesn't go there. It goes on the third shelf. Can't you see?" But for a long time it had been wonderful — exhilarating — to feel so safe and organized and in her own proper slot. The cockeyed bits of her life were pulled together at last. Everything seemed possible. And she was loved. Which, she had thought, meant that he understood her — and loved her anyway.

"What happened?" Abby wondered, shaking her head almost imperceptibly. What had gone wrong between them? Was it the kids? He used to call her a motherholic. He liked that word — ignoring the slight detail that *he* was a card-carrying workaholic. Why couldn't he understand her now? Hear her. When she needed him so desperately. When she could *still,* if he was nice to her, get that old feeling — her heart lifting and expanding toward him — a yearning — in spite of everything. But God help her if she ever showed it. He'd drive his Mack truck right through that opening.

Abby lit a cigarette and inhaled the smoke deeply. Would Martin have his Sunday golf date this afternoon? He *always* did. His version of church. So she'd be alone. But maybe it was too late and he'd missed the golf. If she asked, he'd hit her with more sarcasm. If he did play, she'd be alone maybe four hours. But would the children be home? How would she get rid of them? Abby felt her heart contract. What kind of a mother was she, thinking that? She *loved* her children. But why didn't she *feel* it? She was depraved. She really was. She'd known it the day she couldn't take Communion, couldn't desecrate the Sacrament. Feeling that awful embarrassment in front of God, the shame hot under her skin. Now her mind shifted and another voice, deep inside her, asked again, "Will I be alone?"

As the car turned down their suburban street, Abby thought how nice it seemed, how quiet. The trees somehow protective. The New England saltbox looked so settled with its shingled roof, dormer windows, lawn and flower beds across the front. Like a haven. "How deceptive," she thought, dreading going inside. She was too exhausted, too nervous, to cope with anything. If only she was back on Martha's Vineyard.

Martin carried her suitcase upstairs to their bedroom while

Abby stood idly leafing through the mail on the chest in the small front hall — and listening for sounds of children. There were none. She felt a little twist of hurt. Why weren't they home to welcome her? Then Martin came down dressed for golf — green cotton pants and tan windbreaker, half zipped. She asked where the children were. Judy had taken Frederick to the K mart to buy some jeans. Evan was off somewhere. Abby felt another jab of pain. *She* should be with Frederick getting those jeans, not Judy, the fifteen-year-old mother.

Martin, his mouth a narrow line, asked, "What are you going to do?"

"Unpack, I guess. There's probably some wash to be done. Woman's work."

"Be good," Martin said, and left. She was alone.

Abby stood in the hall soaking up the heavenly stillness. Nobody was there, hitting her with thousands of demands. Nobody could get at her. She was in charge. Of course, she really *should* get busy on her routines — pick up the crumpled sneakers and comic books that were always on the floor of the den, empty the wastebaskets, clean the cat hairs off the pillows, start a load of laundry. "But a drink now would be nice," she thought. "I deserve a little welcome-home treat. I'll start the housework tomorrow. Anyway, they don't respect what I do around here."

Already Abby was moving almost mechanically to her left, into the living room, around to the liquor cupboard just inside the door. In front of the cupboard she paused. Maybe she wouldn't have a drink right now. She didn't *need* it. And if she had one, plus another later, Martin might be able to tell, and she'd be in trouble. But just *one* wouldn't hurt. Abby opened the cupboard door. "You know you're going to do it," she told herself. "You've got two or three hours with nobody to check on you. So what the hell."

She took out the half gallon of vodka and slowly turned it in her hands, studying it like a scientific specimen. The price label was pasted exactly at the level of the vodka — one of Martin's tricks to check on her. Well, the joke was on him. That was why she had her hidden bottles, her private stock, so she would always be sure of a drink, with another behind it, and would never have to worry.

Picking a glass from a cupboard shelf, she turned and paused, letting herself enjoy the feel of burnished wood and subtle patterns in this room she had assembled. In front of the fireplace there was the grouping of the amber-and-mustard-striped couch facing chairs covered in light greens and pale oranges. Above the mantel was the painting of purple-red bougainvillea, bought on that glorious trip to Haiti. By the fireplace leaned the polished brass fire tongs used by her father. In the left-hand window the angel-wing begonia, with its sprays of blossoms like red candy, was still alive after eight years. On the walnut coffee table was the huge bowl of seashells she had collected and bought. She thought how much she loved them — coming to her from the still deep of the ocean — a piece of nature various and beautiful, perfect in design, no worked edges.

For a moment her spirits lifted with the remembered happiness of Martha's Vineyard and those barefoot walks with Martin along the empty beach — *"their* beach." The sublime desolation, the ribbon of sand leading to the sky between gray-ochre bluffs and white foam, the crashing, mesmerizing surf, sweeping in, sliding away, stranding the tiny shells she collected till her bulging hand hurt. She could remember the peacefulness within her then, a stillness so deep she could hear Martin's silent feelings, could fill up with his pleasure — which was hers, too.

Abby continued down the length of the room, past the antique pine blanket chest on the inside wall, and stopped in front of the upright piano between two windows at the far end. She slid back the door in the piano's varnished front. Reaching a slender, silk-clad arm into the interior, she extracted a fifth of vodka. Wrinkling her nose as she filled the glass, she thought, "Carbona, undiluted." She returned the bottle to its hiding place and headed back toward the kitchen, planning to add ice and cranberry juice. In the front hall she stopped. That was so much trouble. Quickly, she gulped from the glass and climbed the stairs from the front hall to the large corner bedroom.

The afternoon sun flooded through the windows across the beige pile rug. Violently, she yanked the venetian blinds closed. She took the telephone off the hook and opened her suitcase on the king-sized bed. Unpacking, sipping her drink, she walked back and forth to her bureau, between the windows to the left. On top of it were framed photographs — the three children posing for a Christmas card, the wedding picture, eighteen years ago when she and Martin were twenty-four and twenty-seven. She had been staging fashion shows for Boston department stores, and they had met at a party, and made jokes about "across a crowded room." Abby thought, "How little I knew." There was also her mother and father's wedding picture. "They didn't know much, either," Abby added to herself. That was the way she liked to think of her father — young and barrel-chested, square handsome face, those bright eyes — everything happy. She didn't like to think at all about her mother, tall, heavy, with that impatient voice. "Stand up straight or you'll be round-shouldered. Take your hands *out* of your hair." The one really terrific thing her mother had ever done was to move permanently to California.

On Martin's bureau, opposite the foot of the bed, was a package of his shirts back from the laundry. Impulsively, she arranged them in his drawer, the way he liked them, with the cardboards pulled out. After tilting the glass up for the last swallow, she undressed, put on her nightgown, and got into bed. Leaning back against the three down pillows, feeling caressed and sealed away, she exhaled a reverential sigh. She lit a cigarette and positioned on the coverlet a silver clamshell, forever full of butts. She leaned in the other direction and clicked on the electric blanket, a necessity winter and summer. Then she snuggled down between the fresh sheets, pulled up the quilt to add the right ounces of weight, and plumped a pillow to enfold her head.

But the vodka had not done its job. She lay exhausted and sleepless, neither drunk nor sober, her stomach burning, adrenaline tingling unpleasantly through her body. Maybe she needed some more. Alcohol used to calm her, make her feel fluent and wise, valuable and popular. Why couldn't she get that high anymore? Now Abby began worrying that if she went to sleep, something would wake her up. The phone might ring downstairs, a child might come home without a key and buzz the doorbell.

Where were her children? she wondered. Maybe it didn't matter. Nothing she said to them ever made any difference. Frederick was sassing at school — and he was only ten. And Judy hated her. Evan was hanging out with those creeps. She felt so helpless, so inadequate. How could she be afraid of a seventeen-year-old boy? But he knew how to torment her — withdrawing behind his sullenness, leaving her to stew in her anger and frustration. Maybe Martin was right. He had said the children would grow up hating her. What a god-awful, sadistic thing to say. That son of a bitch. Why couldn't he be nice to her. Like the early days. So she wouldn't need to drink.

Turning restlessly in the bed, Abby remembered her early dreams of motherhood — how wise and skillful she was determined to be, how much she was going to love and be loved. "God, it's so *hard*," she said to herself — and thought about that moment beside Evan's crib, looking down at his miniature fingers curled below the perfect, rosebud mouth. She remembered her rush of pleasure and expectation and hope. He was a boy and he was *hers* and his life would be wonderful. Then she had bent down and gently rubbed his back, feeling his entire small being pulse beneath the spread of her hand.

She heard a circular scratching on the closed door — Frederick's private signal. Her spirits lifted. Here was some hope — somebody who needed her and loved her unconditionally. She still had a chance with Frederick. "Come in, Frizzer," she called.

He stepped silently into the room. "Hi, Mother. Are you okay?"

"I'm fine. But I have this terrible headache. I couldn't get to sleep last night, and when I did, I had nightmares. I'm really glad to see you." She moved over and he positioned his wiry little body on the bed beside her. Her heart swelled as she looked up into his face — the tender lips, big ears, large brown eyes so concerned, expectant, trusting. Abby thought, "He's my comforter. He's untouched."

"Maybe if I put on a record you like . . ."

"No, thanks. But it's sweet of you to offer."

Frederick began asking about Martha's Vineyard, proud of his total recall of their trip last year. He wanted to know if that super dune was still there — the one he used to run down.

"Yes, it is," Abby answered, putting her hand quietly on his leg, feeling its sinewy energy. "I remember you ran down so fast, I thought your legs couldn't keep up and suddenly you'd be a boy gliding without a glider." She smiled tenderly, and at the same time thought how much she wanted to be alone again and sink back and shut her eyes. But she could not bring herself to send Frederick away, to be like her own mother in bed with a headache, saying, "Abby, dear, please leave me alone." She could remember the guilt for causing her mother such pain.

Frederick said, "Mother, you look sad."

"Not as long as you're here, Frizzer," she said, patting his leg.

He was quiet again, and then said, "I think I'll go ride my bike and I'll come back and see you in a little while. Maybe you'll feel better then."

Alone again, Abby let herself sink back into the bed's embrace. Soon, however, her cocoon was pierced by sounds of Evan and Judy downstairs. She gave herself ten more minutes, and then dragged her body out of bed and into her robe. Even a rotten mother had to spread *some* motherhood around. She followed the sound of the television down the stairs and walked left through the dining room into the small, book-lined den. Two figures were slumped in the love seat facing the glowing screen. "I can remember," Abby thought, "when people sat and read in front of fires." She called above the noise, "Hi, guys. Let's hear it for the vagabond mom."

They looked around. "Hi, Mom." "Hi." They stood up to accept her kisses. Abby liked Judy's looks — an evolving version of her own — the same chestnut hair but straighter, the same squarish, symmetrical face, but guarded eyes, and a mouth on the edge of annoyance. Evan had his father's full face, but his own round eyes looked out at the world with an inborn surprise, a natal innocence. She wondered now, as she often did, how his jeans stayed up on those vestigial hips and bottom. She patted her children's shoulders and touched their backs and noticed an unpleasant stiffness in herself, as though the real emotions between them, so complex and fraught, made this little scene a fake.

She went back through the dining room into the kitchen to begin dinner — enough chili for six children. And to prove that all was well and there was nothing to hide, she casually poured herself a scotch and water. Presently she summoned the children and called Frederick, who was roller-skating on the sidewalk out front. The thought of food repelled her, but, dutifully, she sat with them at an empty plate. As she sipped her drink, Judy and Evan exchanged knowing glances. Abby felt sudden anger. How dare they question what she did! They didn't know what her life was like! Would they tell Martin about the drink?

Evan, plying his spoon back and forth to his mouth like a robot, suddenly stopped, his blue eyes appraising. He said, "Can I ask a question?"

Abby knew that opener, that ingratiating tone of sweet reason mixed with the merest nuance of challenge. "He's going to do it to me," she thought. "I haven't been with him ten minutes and he's starting in. I can't handle it." She leaned against the high back of the chair. "Certainly," she said.

"I know that sometimes noise really bothers you when you're napping, and you complain a lot about my electric guitar — so you'll be really pleased to hear that they make amplified earphones. Billy's got a pair and they're super."

"How much are they?"

"Forty-five dollars."

Abby could feel her chest tightening. She was such a horrible mother, the least she could do would be to . . . but she did not like being used. "The only time you ever come to me," she said, "is when you want to get something."

Evan laid down his spoon. His voice was tinged with anger. "Mom, I'm serious. Why can't you do this for me? You always do stuff for Frederick. Last week you got him a paint set that cost twenty-six dollars. And don't tell me that it will all even out. You did it for him, and you won't do it for me. It's not fair."

Abby felt a worm of doubt. Maybe she wasn't fair. "Well," she said, "it's true that I'd appreciate a little peace in this house. But I don't . . ."

Judy cut in. "Jerk," she said impatiently to Evan. "Look at her eyes. Can't you see you won't get anywhere now? Tomorrow, tell her she said yes. She won't remember."

Abby stared hard for a moment at Judy's tight, sour face. Then she said, "I'm sitting right here in full possession of my faculties, which include hearing. If you're going to talk about me so insultingly, as though I'm the village idiot, have the courtesy to wait till I've gone." Judy stared down at her hardly touched dinner.

"Leave Mom alone," said Frederick loudly. "She's tired." The circle of faces turned toward him, startled. Taking another sip from her drink, Abby inquired, "How did the history paper go?"

"I don't want to talk about it, Mom," Judy said.

Wanting to show interest, but afraid she might have to

help and wouldn't be able to, Abby asked, "Are you having trouble with it?"

"I'm not in the mood to talk about it. Don't you ever feel that way?"

Fighting down her frustration and impatience, Abby wondered whether *everything* was a hot subject in this family. She asked, "Haven't you finished it yet?"

Her words rushing, blurted out, as though a small dam had burst, Judy answered unhappily, "I start writing and I think, 'Oh, God, what's everyone going to think of it and shouldn't I add this other stuff and make it colossally, incredibly good?' And half of me is saying, 'So what! Just finish it.' And I don't know what to do."

Guilt and panic ached in Abby's chest. She clenched her teeth. How could she help these children, when she couldn't even help herself? Maybe a little pressure on Judy. "You better write something good," she said, her voice accusing. "You're already on thin ice in that class."

Judy's hands clenched into fists on the table. Her voice was loud, her mouth twisted. "You always want *me* to be perfect. But it's okay for *you* to say, 'I can't cope,' and bail out and go to bed." Suddenly she was shouting. "Can't you see you're making us all miserable!"

Here it was. The most dreaded attack. Rage exploded through Abby, stiffening the skin of her face, pressing inside her brain, flooding out all thought. With the crash of a gunshot, she smashed her open palm down onto the table top — and a detached, distant corner of her mind saw Judy's face flinch as though buffeted by the sound waves. Abby could hear her heart pounding. She yelled, "I don't need this! When you're in *my* house, you play by *my* rules — and that means no sass. Think that over!"

She sat gripping the edge of the table with both hands. The children watched her, hypnotized. Tears streamed from her eyes as she gasped for breath. She wiped under her nose with the back of her hand. Then, head down, hair hanging forward, she said softly, "I don't belong in this house. I don't belong here."

In one sudden motion she spun away from the table, the chair legs screeching on the tile floor, and ran wildly up the stairs, slamming the bedroom door behind her. She stood in the middle of the room, panting, desperate. How could she have lost control again! Everything was hell. She might go crazy. She might explode into a thousand pieces. Cease to exist. She had to escape. Could she go on another trip? No. Too soon. She was trapped. Well, if they thought she drank a lot before, wait till they saw her now!

Abby opened the lid of the low antique chest under the window beside her bureau. It was full of winter sweaters and mittens and wool socks, and the smell of mothballs was unpleasant in her nose. At the left rear corner, accessible only by folding the lid all the way back against the wall, was a tall, square compartment with a lid of its own. From it, Abby pulled a pint of vodka, unscrewed the top, put the bottle to her mouth, tilted it up, took a long swallow, shivered, took another mouthful, wiped her mouth with her hand, and returned the bottle to its hideaway. She felt better, but still needed another quick fix. She lay on the bed with the telephone and dialed Annie O'Reilly.

At least she still had two friends, Abby comforted herself. Two good ones she had known since kindergarten. Annie O'Reilly and Jan Cummings. They would still laugh and drink with her, let her feel normal. They didn't have, far back in their eyes, that flicker that said the person *knew* and no longer took her seriously. But she didn't need any of those fair-weather friends. She'd finally realized how uptight they were, how stuffy and boring. She talked on the phone with Annie for a comforting hour about the Vineyard week, about Annie's stalled divorce proceedings, about Martin's latest outrages.

After hanging up, she lit a cigarette and leaned back against the pillows and began reading a book — *The Cinderella*

Complex. But she could not concentrate. That happened so much now. She put the book face down on the rust-colored coverlet and looked across the room at the blanket chest. Feeling reassured by aid and comfort so close at hand, she reflected with pride that this was the best of all the hiding places. Martin had never found it. God, what battles they had fought over her bottles. He would come home and accuse her of being drunk and check the bottles in the cupboard, and then go berserk. She could see in front of her now his red and pop-eyed face as he screamed, "The bottle! Where's it hidden! Where's the bottle!"

Of course, she never told him. So he would tear the house apart, searching. But there was that time when he went *really* bananas and grabbed her by the arms, fingers digging down toward the bone, and threw her across the bedroom into the blanket chest. Lying on the floor, terror bursting her chest and her head, body trembling and sweating — she had shrieked, "Get out! Get away from me! Get out!" But she had been smiling in her mind. Inside the chest, only a foot away from her head, in the chest, was a bottle.

Now, sitting in bed, Abby felt a sense of mortal doom spreading through her like a vapor she could not exhale. She started to perspire. The muscles of her thighs and arms were twitching. "What's the matter?" she wondered, and answered herself, "Everything's the matter!" She began pacing the room, wringing her ice-cold hands. Her stomach was nauseated. Her temples throbbed, and her eyes seemed to press out from her head. Fighting to hold herself together, she thought, "I want to run . . . I can't run . . . I want to lie down . . . I want air." Frantically she pulled up the blinds and opened the window. The sunshine had turned black! "I've got to warn everybody," she thought. As though plugged into electricity, her whole body began quivering. She staggered to her purse, and fumbled a Valium from the bottle. Then two. She swallowed them dry, and huddled on the bed, waiting for the shivering to ease, wondering if she was going to die.

There had been terrifying symptoms six months ago — a sudden pounding of the heart, dizziness, shortage of breath. The doctor had said it was a minor fibrillation. But he was wrong. It was serious heart trouble. Her psychiatrist friend had listened to her and prescribed Valium. And it had worked. There hadn't been any more symptoms, just the slight embarrassment of telephoning the psychiatrist and saying the Valium bottle had fallen from the medicine chest and broken, or that she had left it behind in a hotel, and could he please phone the druggist.

But now, thank God, the Valium was taking hold, the delicious, floaty numbness was easing through her. Sitting up to get her book again, seeing her legs sticking out from the tangled robe, Abby felt a stab of sadness and disgust. Her legs were so thin, so blotchy with bruises. Every time she bumped against something, she was instantly black and blue. Why was that? Did she have some blood disease? And she used to have terrific legs. But if she gained any weight, she'd be fat.

Martin's tread sounded downstairs, going from room to room. He always did that — looking for her — probably scared of what he'd find. Soon he arrived at the bedroom and stood there for a moment, hands in his pockets, studying her — "as though I'm some crazy person," she thought. He came over and sat on the bed. She could tell he was fresh from a shower. His hair was still damply in place, not yet flopping down onto his forehead. And he smelled of cleanliness, of health. What did she smell of? she wondered. Martin's eyes were wary, but kind. "Are you hungry?" he asked. Yes, she was. Her voice was small. He went down to the kitchen and returned in a while with creamed chicken — "nursery food," as she called it. He put on his light blue pajamas, and they ate sitting in bed, side by side, watching television.

But loneliness weighed on her, and she thought how sad it was that she felt so separated. She picked up her book again. Soon, her eyes still on the book, she reached blindly across the bed and groped for Martin's hand. Still not looking at him, her voice pleading, she said, "Be nice to me."

Martin turned toward her, moving closer. "I am nice to you," he said. With the tips of his fingers he began massaging her scalp through the thick hair. After another silence, he added, "Nicer than you know."

Smiling at him, Abby said, "I put your shirts away."

"That's good."

"Do you love me?" she asked, pressing her head luxuriously against his fingers.

"Yes, Abby, I love you," he answered, a faint weariness in his voice. "But there are times when I don't like you very much."

He was doing it to her again, giving her a morsel and taking it away. But she felt too lonely and weary to be mad. Pulling along a pillow, she moved close to him and rested her head against his shoulder, feeling the hardness of it. "I'm afraid I'm not a very good wife," she said.

Taking off his glasses, he turned to her and slid an arm behind her neck and hugged her to him. He kissed her on the forehead, saying, "I'm willing to take the bitter with the sweet."

She snuggled her chin into the hollow of his neck and said, "We've had some good times together. Do you remember that crazy night in New York when that cab driver took us to a diner in New Jersey for breakfast?"

"I was wearing a tuxedo and you were in that pink evening dress."

"I remember you with your arm half out the open window and your hair blowing back like a boy's in a rumble seat. And I've always remembered what you said that night. You told me I was teaching you to soar."

With his attention half on the TV screen, Martin nodded. "That was true," he said. "You were." He was quiet for a moment. "Do you remember what you said? You told me you wanted to grow old with me."

Still nestled against his neck, Abby said, "Things will get

better, Martin. They really will. I just don't know what's the matter with me."

. "I only wish you could be happy," Martin said. They sat in silence. Then Martin bent over, kissed Abby again, clicked off the television set, and rolled away from her to go to sleep.

That was Sunday.

CHAPTER

2

ON MONDAY, Abby slept late. She awoke weighed down by weariness and a nebulous foreboding. Something had gone wrong yesterday. What was it? She'd let the kids get to her again. She used to enjoy her kids. What had happened? God, she was sick of feeling blah. Even a year ago, with a little willpower, she could usually pick up the pieces and run forward into battle. Now, just getting out of bed was doing battle.

Abby dozed another hour. Ordering herself to get out of bed, she pulled on a pair of jeans and a sweat shirt, and hobbled down through the empty house to the kitchen. Why were her joints always so sore in the mornings? She could hardly walk on her feet. Was it arthritis? They couldn't cure that! She made coffee, lit a cigarette, and wondered why she felt so listless, so drained. She shuffled anxiously about the room, overwhelmed by the decisions that faced her. Should she clean up the breakfast plates? Abby lifted the lid of the dishwasher. It was full of clean dishes. That was too much trouble. And she really ought to mop the kitchen floor. But that meant climbing the stairs, getting the vacuum cleaner, and dragging it downstairs to pick up the crumbs. It was *such* a job. She wasn't up to it. And besides, the cupboards needed organizing. But she didn't have the energy. Maybe she should just fix a casserole for tonight's dinner. But what kind? She couldn't deal with that.

On the table was today's job list from Martin. Large at the top was written, "Please Do." She read the first item: "Call the repair man about the dryer." Her heart sank. The repair man would ask questions she couldn't answer. Putting down the list, she drifted away from the table, telling herself to get busy, do *something.* But a cold beer would taste *wonderful* right now. She opened the refrigerator. There was no beer. Damn Evan! Well, if she was a good housekeeper, she'd go out right now and do the week's grocery shopping.

Blanking out her mind, putting herself on automatic, she drove the ten blocks to the Safeway. Inside the door, at ranks of nested shopping carts, she froze. This was impossible. She couldn't face it. But she *would* like a beer, and they sold it cold in the deli department. She forced herself. Then, comforted by a six-pack safely in the cart, she meandered slowly up and down the aisles, looking vacantly at the food, demoralized by the enormity of the decisions. "Let's see, Frederick likes pork and Judy likes chicken, or is it the other way around? Or should I get steak? The sirloin is awfully expensive and I'll use up my house allowance and won't have enough for a bottle tomorrow. But the top round may be tough and Martin will complain. Should I get the Italian coffee and grind it, or maybe they'd grind it here because the grinder at home makes that awful noise. Or should I get the Colombian? Somebody was saying that's good. What were they saying about it? Or maybe . . ."

Occasionally, almost at random, Abby dropped something into the cart —,until suddenly, in the distance down an aisle, she glimpsed a woman she knew. Immediately, Abby joined a checkout line and stood there fidgeting, jiggling the cart with one hand. Then, at last, she escaped the store and settled into the safety and quiet of her car. Sighing with relief, she drank a can of beer. That would get her through the drive home. At the house, after pulling into the garage, she had another can. That would help carry in the bags. In the kitchen a third can was for putting away the groceries.

But when the telephone rang, the sound still raked her

nerves. She pulled herself together and answered it — fighting to sound normal. It was a school mother calling to ask Abby to work at the bazaar. Pouring regret into her voice, Abby said she had a doctor's appointment that day. She hung up and unplugged the phone — and noticed the clock. Hell! She had a lunch date! "I can't arrive shaking like a nervous wreck," she thought. Using the bottle in the piano, Abby poured herself a vodka and grapefruit juice.

A friend who was marketing a line of blouses wanted Abby's opinion on designs, and they met in a local Italian restaurant. Abby drank two whiskey sours, until the designs, the waiter, the food, the friend — everything — floated at the end of a disjointed distance. Her head hummed. Her joints ached. Her eyes felt like pinpricks. The light from the nearby window seemed white, and she kept shading her eyes with her hand, and then put on dark glasses. The hum in her head moved out into her whole body, and each syllable and movement had to be manufactured one at a time. Afterward, in her car, driving with elaborate care, Abby wondered, "Why did I get so blitzed? There was no need. Was I frightened of her? She must have thought I was on some drug. I've got to call up tomorrow and make an excuse — say the doctor gave me a medication."

At home Abby went immediately to bed and to sleep. She was awakened by Martin shaking her roughly, asking if she had forgotten there was a dinner party tonight. Abby answered, "I can't handle it. I'm not well enough to go."

"For once, you're not going to have the flu or a sick child," Martin told her harshly. "This is the birthday party of the chairman of the church board, and you're *going*. And don't choose tonight to put on one of your performances." He turned and went downstairs to ask Judy to make dinner.

Abby thought, "He always assumes the worst about me. Assume, assume." Couldn't Martin see how sick she was? She'd be lucky to last till nine-thirty. He was such a hypocrite, pretending tonight was for the greater glory of the church. It was all business — getting new clients. Abby got out of bed and opened the top of the blanket chest. Taking a swig of warm vodka, almost gagging, she thought, "Oh, God, why am I doing this?" Then she noticed the bottle was now empty. She returned it to its hideaway, thinking she must get another one tomorrow.

On the way downstairs in her robe, Abby thought, "I'll fix him." At the liquor cupboard in the living room, she noisily filled her favorite opaque drinking glass with ginger ale and carried it into the kitchen, where Martin sat watching Judy cook spaghetti. Abby took two ostentatious gulps from the innocent drink, set it down on the counter, and went into the adjoining bathroom. Leaving the door slightly ajar, she watched through the crack. Martin moved quickly across the room, put his forefinger into the glass, and then into his mouth. "I'll bet he feels really silly," she thought with satisfaction.

The party was at a restaurant, and the cocktail hour went well for Abby. She liked her looks — the black, long-sleeved dress stitched with maroon and blue rosettes. Sipping a glass of white wine, feeling virtuous, she discussed child psychology with two women, and was reassured. Even to herself she sounded like a good mother. Next she talked to a couple just back from the ancient city of Machu Picchu, in the Andes. She listened, fascinated, to their word picture of the vast ruin, terraced into the barren side of a peak almost above the clouds.

At dinner her partner was a lawyer she considered dull, but she felt tolerant now — toward herself, toward him. Magnanimously she thought, "This man is not so bad. Did you expect Louis Nizer?" But while he talked, her gaze wandered. Charlie Brook was looking at her, and she surreptitiously waved a finger at him. He smiled and waved back. He had wanted to marry her. Why had she broken that off? He was so kind and understanding. Not like Martin, who'd changed so much.

After dinner, Abby switched to brandy. Circulating,

talking, laughing, she let men keep filling her glass. She kept hoping this next drink would bring the wonderful, winging high — that feeling of marvelous fluency and intelligence, the certainty that she was valuable and popular and belonged, the knowledge that anything was possible and nothing mattered. But for months and months she had been feeling the way she did now — neither drunk nor sober — just anxious and blah. Maybe a little more brandy . . .

Every time she got a refill, every time a man put his arm around her, every time she moved, Abby felt Martin's eyes on her. Keeping track. Monitoring. Her goddamned chaperone. But she couldn't really blame him, after all the disasters. Maybe she'd better slow down. She didn't want to wake up tomorrow with no memory of anything and Martin livid and not talking to her. She didn't want to call up people and fish around and find out that she'd done a solo version of smash dancing. Or made cracks about some woman's Orphan Annie perm. Or puked and passed out in a bathroom and been smuggled out the back door like a corpus delicti. Or all of the above.

At midnight, in the car going home, Martin suddenly broke the charged silence. His voice, delivered in a slight singsong, festered with sarcasm. "Want to tell me again how much you were going to hate this party? Of course you got loaded. When haven't you? You must have told that boring story about your mother's birthday present ten times. You should bottle yourself as a sedative."

Abby, profoundly lonely, clamped her lips closed. Her mind, however, was racing, exalted to an almost cosmic speed and clarity. She thought, "He's done it once too often. He's pushed me too far. Now I really am going to leave. I only got home yesterday, but everybody's lucky I've stayed around this long, because I'm going to Peru and see Machu Picchu and I'll take Frederick. I'd like to go to Peru with Frederick."

At home she briskly climbed the stairs while Martin followed wearily behind. In the bedroom she unzipped her black dress and methodically hung it from a coat hanger over the top of the closet door. Elaborately ignoring Martin, her face set, she put on brown gabardine pants. Walking to the bureau, she selected a wash-and-wear shirt and a rust-red sweater. After holding several necklaces up to her neck, she chose the loop of agate beads. She drummed her fingernails on the bureau top for a moment, and then clamped over her wrist a Mexican silver bracelet, a present from their honeymoon. Concentrating totally on the mirror, she brushed her hair with hurried strokes, cocking her head to left and right. "God, my eyes look awful," she thought, detachedly. "Like two holes burned in a blanket." Then, all sinew and bone and fury, her eyes narrowed, she swung around to face Martin. He was sitting on the edge of the bed in his pajamas, watching her with a small, quizzical, irritating smile. His legs were crossed and with one hand, over and over, he rubbed the arch of his foot.

Abby's rage was triply menacing because it began quietly, suppressed, like the still sea before a hurricane. Her voice was measured, very controlled, lowered an octave, throaty, as though from some sound chamber too large for that body. Bent slightly forward, eyes fixed on his, she said, "This is it. I can no longer endure you. You are so condescending, so superior. You think you are so damned smart. Well, you're just a miserable prick. No, you're better than that. You're a *smart* prick. So cunning, so clever, so pious with your glad-handing and wonderful generous personality — and the Jack the Ripper at home destroying me. You phony son of a bitch."

A hum vibrated in her head, bearable as long as she kept her eyes on Martin's. "You convince me that you are so reasonable, that I am wrong, that I am a mess, that if only I would shape up, everything would be fine. You keep me constantly explaining myself, constantly trying to measure up, constantly atoning. Whatever I do, it could have been done a little better." She lifted her voice into falsetto. "Now, Abby, I think we've got to have more practice with the Cuisinart before you can solo!"

Martin, still rubbing his foot, interrupted, his voice ultracalm and reasonable. "I don't see why I have to stand silently by while you overload the motor."

Abby ignored him. Her voice was getting louder, harsher, all edges now — the storm moving in. Her hands were clenched into fists. "I constantly have to worry whether I will or won't disappoint you, whether I've said the right or the wrong thing. All you want from me is an excellent performance. I'm just a decorative accessory in your life. Be charming. Look well."

Martin leaned backward onto his elbows, his light hair straggling down over his forehead. "Here we go again," he said, with the put-upon weariness that always enraged Abby.

Abby rushed on. "You don't care about my feelings. But you don't know anything about emotions. You wouldn't know an emotion if it kicked you in the balls, you Germanic bastard."

Suddenly, Martin snapped forward, his forefinger jabbing the air, his voice staccato. "Stop it right now, Abby. You are deliberately stamping on our marriage, viciously trampling in hobnail boots on something beautiful. I married you out of the highest idealism, believing it was right and good, and I . . ."

"Right and good!" Abby shouted. "I take everything back. You're *not* a smart prick. You're a self-righteous, pompous prick. What about. *love?* Can't you see that nothing is happening between us? You are not interested in anything I think or say." She paused for breath. Then she wailed, "Martin, I *need* you. I am starving to death."

His control split. "Wrong!" he bellowed. "You are drinking yourself to death! You are killing yourself! And you are killing me!"

Suddenly, like an echo, there was a wild pounding on the door. Judy's voice yelled, "Goddamn it! Shut the hell up! You're not the only people living here. I've got a test tomorrow."

"Okay, Judy. Okay," Martin called. "Go to bed."

Abby turned away to the bureau and bent over it, bracing herself on her arms. "Oh, my God," she said. "Look what we're doing to our children." But the hum in her head was building again to a roar, like a train rushing toward her in a tunnel. It drowned out that terrible thought, and all she could hear was Martin's words, the ultimate, cruelest assault.

She wheeled back toward him, her voice vibrating with controlled rage. "Here we are at your last refuge, calling me a drunk just because I have a zest for life — for people — for conversation. Thank God *I* didn't grow up in a straitjacket, afraid to let go." Now she was yelling. "If you think I'm an alcoholic, you're a workaholic. You didn't marry a majordomo to run your house. You married *me!*" She was screaming now, bending over him, hitting herself on the chest. "Can't you *ever* hear how lonely I am? How abandoned I feel?"

"I see," Martin said, gazing up at her, maddeningly calm, a little smile on his mouth. "That's why you go away on trips and leave everybody. Because you're lonely. But maybe you're just crawling under a rock to drink? Which is it, Abby?"

She paused for a second, startled. How did he find out? Nobody saw her. But, oh, God, she hated that smug look. She yanked the chair away from the head of the bed and sat facing Martin. Looking into his eyes again, seeing a tiny flicker of fear, the roar in her head receded. As she spoke — her voice low, urgent — the muscles around her mouth contorted with contained fury. "This is what you do to me. You turn everything around. Make me feel crazy. I leave because I need a rest, and you say I do it to drink. The truth is I can't stand you, and tonight I'm *really* going to put miles between us. I'm going to Peru. You won't be sad. You'll be completely in charge. You'll have Judy all to yourself."

Martin leaned back, recrossed his legs, and began rubbing his other foot. He said casually, "Go ahead, Abby. Go to Peru. I can't stop you. I don't really want to stop you."

Abby thought, "That's a strange reaction. Why isn't he trying to stop me?" As she went to the closet for her suitcase, she thought again, "It's odd that he's not mad." She felt diminished, almost defeated. She opened her suitcase on the floor in front of the bureau and started packing. She thought, "Let's see, it's April here so it'll be fall in Peru. I'll need heavy sweaters and mittens in those mountains."

Aloud, she said conversationally, "You know, Martin, your priorities are all screwed up. There was a time when you could have been a brilliant money manager. A really creative analyst. But you sold out for security. Now you are a complete and total pawn, kissing the asses of a bunch of clients who are constantly second-guessing you. You never put the family first. You never make me feel I'm more important than a golf game or your desk. If you quit work when other husbands do, the work will still be there the next day. It wouldn't leave."

Behind her, Martin answered, "You silly bitch. Where do you think the money comes from that you're so happy to spend. You've got a terrific deal, but you can never look at the positives. I've told you many times, Abby — when *you* look at a rose garden you only see the thorns."

"Shit!" Abby said. Then she thought, "I wonder if I could borrow Annie's raincoat, the one with the zip-in fur liner. That would be just the thing." Turning toward the door she told Martin matter-of-factly, "I'm taking Frederick with me." She crossed the hall to Frederick's room, sat on his bed, and gently rubbed his back, waking him gradually as she always did. She said, "Sweetheart, how would you like to go to Peru?"

"What?"

"I'm going to Peru tonight and it would be a wonderful trip for us to take. Never mind about school because they'll agree that the experience of going to Peru is much more valuable for you, and I would really love to have you go with me."

Frederick, looking up in the semidarkness, said, "Do you really mean it? How long will we be gone?"

"About two weeks."

"Okay, I'll get dressed."

Abby went back into the bedroom.

Martin was standing in the middle of the room, arms at his side, eyes cold. "There is no way in the world that you are going to take that kid," he said. "You are stinko."

Abby stopped in the doorway. Clenching her hands, she said, "You have taken everything else from me. You've taken my love and abused it. You've tried to take my mind away. But you're not taking my child. He's the only one you haven't turned against me."

Martin did not move. "I can't stop you from doing something crazy," he said. "But you're not going to take any chances with my son."

The feverish clarity in Abby's head shattered. The hate stabbed into her brain. The agony, the panic, was almost unbearable. She looked wildly for a weapon. A book. She threw it at his head and missed. She flung herself at him, legs and fists flailing. Easily he sidestepped and shoved her sprawling across the bed, where she lay on her back, the sweater wrenched up around her chest, shirt out of her pants. She wept silently, tangled hair swirled around her head, eyes squeezed closed, her mouth a dark hollow. Then she lifted her open hands and hid her face.

Looking down, his body limp, Martin said dully, "I think we're both crazy."

Frederick appeared in the room, still in his pajamas. "I'm sorry," he said. Instantly, Abby rolled onto her side toward him. He looked from his mother to his father and back at Abby. Tears turned his eyes enormous. "I can't go to Peru with you, Mother," he said. "I'm too frightened. We don't speak Spanish and I'm afraid we might never get home. I really want to go to Peru with you someday, but I can't go right now."

Martin said, "That's all right. Go back to bed. I'll come kiss you good night in a minute." Before Abby could speak, Frederick turned and disappeared. Abby got off the bed. "I'm going anyway," she said, and went into the bathroom to put herself back together. Then, with elaborate dignity, she carried her suitcase out the door, and ducked into Frederick's room ahead of Martin. She bent over the pale face on the pillow and said, "Don't worry, there'll be another time." She kissed him on the forehead, saying, "I love you, Frizzer." He was silent.

Downstairs she telephoned for a taxi. She looked at her watch. Two A.M. Annie wouldn't mind. She telephoned Annie O'Reilly, and, ignoring the grogginess of the voice on the line, announced that she was flying to Peru, where it was cold, and she would like to borrow Annie's coat. Could she swing by in a cab on the way to the airport, where, if necessary, she was going to live until she got on a plane.

After a long pause Annie told her, certainly, come right away, but they could let the cab go and have some Bloody Marys and some giggles and then she'd take her to the airport herself. Abby thought, "Isn't that nice. Martin would never be kind like that."

When the cab delivered Abby, Annie was waiting in the doorway — a short, thin woman with a narrow face, large, striking brown eyes, and fine brown hair pulled back into a ponytail. They sat in the kitchen — Abby very animated in her gabardines and rust sweater, Annie, a small figure bundled in a terrycloth robe, yawning between quick smiles. The red Bloody Marys sat in front of them on the round white table. Abby was saying, "Can you imagine, after all you know, that Martin actually . . ."

But soon Annie interrupted, "You look exhausted, Abby, and absolutely white as a sheet. Why don't you go to bed and I'll pull the shades down and put you under the comforter, and then I'll get on the phone and make a reservation and wake you an hour and a half before the plane."

Abby thought, "Somebody is taking care of me. Isn't she wonderful. I'm safe here."

Twelve hours later, at 4 P.M., Annie woke her saying, "Here's some hot tea and English muffins and I've called Martin and everything's fine, nothing to worry about. You just stay here and rest all you want. When you're ready, I'll take you home or wherever you want to go."

Abby folded her right arm across her eyes and stared into the mottled constellations beneath her lids. Still floating up from sleep, her mind was open, its defenses down. In it flashed the words, "The jig is up." Now they knew the truth. They knew how much trouble she was in. She'd finally screwed up enough, and they were going to pay attention.

But by nine o'clock there had been more tea, aspirin, a long, hot shower, fresh clothes from her suitcase. She had regrouped, but her memory was like a gray fog. There had been a fight with Martin. Terrible things had been said. But what were they? Well, whatever, he deserved them. Had she asked Frederick to go to Peru? How could she have done that? He was only ten. How was she going to get out of this mess?

Abby strolled downstairs, and Annie came to her immediately. They sat in the kitchen again and drank coffee while Abby talked and Annie listened, brow furrowed with sympathy, but the tiniest smile sometimes flitting on her lips. Abby was saying, "This time I have pulled a real horror show. I was actually going to Peru. What if you hadn't been here?" She went on to explain that, of course, she had been so worn out that very little alcohol sent her right over the top. But really, it was all the fault of Martin, who so distorted everything. She wouldn't have behaved that way if he hadn't pushed right to the limit.

"You know," Abby said, "he actually tells me I'm an alcoholic and he's been after me for two years to go into Riverside for treatment, like I'm a candidate for a torture camp in Tibet. I think he wants a divorce. If he gets me into a drunk tank, he can tell the judge, 'See what I have to put up with?' Well, I'm here to say that nobody, especially Martin, will *ever* get me alive into Riverside." Then, knowing instinctively that people backed down when asked *the* question, Abby said, "Do *you* think I'm an alcoholic, Annie?"

Annie took a drink of coffee before answering. "Once in a while," she said carefully, "you do get outrageous. Who doesn't? But you have no idea how terrific and funny you are when you don't drink. I just wish you knew it."

Abby was miffed. That was not the right answer. Had even Annie turned against her?

That day, Tuesday, Abby stayed with Annie and spent the night. She was still too angry, she said, to deal with Martin. The next morning, Wednesday, Annie drove her home after Martin was safely at work. As they neared the house, a headache pulsed across Abby's forehead. This time she was *really* in a tight spot. Frederick had never seen her like that. Now *he* knew. Now she didn't belong *anywhere*.

At home, Abby dropped her bag in the front hall. She felt nervous, uneasy, adrift. Thank God Martin wasn't there. They'd be fighting again, or she'd be giving him the silent treatment. So why did she want to talk to him? Maybe he'd forgive her, and she'd feel better. Abby went directly to the phone and dialed his office. Waiting for him to come on the line, she considered her strategy — maybe a rueful joke — "They don't let people on the plane who have hair on their tongue." No. Contrition would be more appealing. She said, "Oh, Martin, I'm really, really sorry. I'm not doing well at all."

He answered, "Yes, it was really awful, Abby. I don't know what to say."

"I know you've heard this before, Martin," she said. "But

honest to God, it won't happen again. I've got to cut down on my drinking. I haven't had a thing since Monday night. I'm going to limit myself to two drinks a day. But you've got to realize how unhappy . . ."

Martin interrupted her. "Listen, Abby, we're going to have a talk about this when I get home. I have to keep my head clear for an executive committee meeting in five minutes. And dinner will have to be late because I promised Roger Albritten I'd stop by and talk about his portfolio. And I'm leaving for Chicago early tomorrow morning. But we'll have a chance this evening, so try to take it easy, and I'll talk to you later."

The hurt made Abby wince. Their marriage, her needs, came second to a goddamn committee meeting. If only once he would say, "I'm coming home right now, and we're going to talk about all this till we're blue in the face."

Abby hung up and stood looking around the den — at the comic books, the sneakers, the casually discarded sweater, the dirty glasses and plates. Well, Abby decided, no matter how mad she was at Martin, this was the day to lie low. *No* drinks. She'd be a model homemaker. She picked up the den, vacuumed the downstairs, cleaned up the basement laundry room, which had been annoying Martin, opened his mail and sorted it, and, to satisfy a special quirk of his, polished the water spots off all the chrome faucets. She cooked the children's dinner — Fettucini Alfredo — Evan's favorite dish. While they ate, she made them laugh with silly jokes. What does an exploding sheep sound like? Sizz Boom Baa.

When Martin came home, she broiled him a steak. Then they took their places for their talk — Martin on the living room couch in his gray pinstripe suit, legs straight out, his body a bit too upright to be comfortable. This was the Martin that Abby knew well — the expert problem-solver — look at the data, use your brain, follow the printout, always bet on reason and logic. But for a long time the confidence in Martin's eyes had been dulled — clouded by bewilderment and bitterness and desperation. She was his one great failure. Enough, perhaps, to make him feel not quite a man.

Abby sat in the wingback chair. Wearing corduroy jeans and a fluffy sweater, one hand trailing a cigarette toward the floor, she was a picture of ease and beauty with her chestnut hair smoothly brushed, the symmetrical face carefully made up, an indulgent smile on her wide, expressive mouth. But inside she felt a nightmare of panic, an Abby fleeing down endless corridors, slamming doors behind her. Maybe this time had been the last straw. Maybe whatever hold she had on Martin had been broken.

Getting in the first word, Abby said, "Martin, I definitely had too much to drink at that party. I hadn't eaten all day and the dinner was terrible and I thought I was going to collapse — and I knew you'd be embarrassed if I made you take me home. So I tried to pull myself together with a medicinal brandy, and it put me right over the top."

Martin sighed. "Abby, it wasn't *a* brandy. Your glass was full every time I looked at you."

"You're absolutely right. I was just sipping it. If you think I'm lying, I'll go right to the phone and call the bartender and . . ."

Martin held up his hands to stop her. "That's not the point. It's the whole past five years. You have two drinks and a look comes into your eyes and a certain tone comes into your voice — and I think, 'Oh, God, no. Not again, It's too late.' A curtain has come down and you are on the other side of it and you are a totally changed person. I feel utterly helpless and it's another evening off to the races. It's terrifying."

As he spoke, Abby was mystified. He'd said that a lot: "A curtain comes down." What did he mean? And she never got drunk on two drinks. "Martin," she said with genteel outrage, "please stop trying to convince me that I'm either crazy or an alcoholic — or both."

Martin folded his arms in front of him, like a first line of defense. "Abby, other men's wives aren't pulling the scenes you are — they don't turn up bombed at PTA meetings.

They're not passed out when the school telephones that their child is sick. When a daughter says, 'I don't want any applesauce,' other mothers don't say, 'Well, have some anyway,' and dump it on the girl's head. Normal women aren't roaring bitches in the middle of the night, blasting their husbands and leaving for Peru. How much longer do you think I can stand all this?"

Abby fastened on the last sentence. It was finally happening. He was going to leave.

Martin was saying, ". . . and you don't seem to care what you're doing to your health."

Abby took a long pull on her cigarette and tapped off the ashes into the dish on the little table. "Martin," she said, very businesslike, "I've already agreed that things are getting a bit out of hand. I think I *should* stop drinking — I mean drinking hard liquor. From now on I'll stick to white wine spritzers."

"If you cared about me and the kids, you'd stop completely."

"Martin," Abby answered, pleading now, "I'll give up anything else. I'll do anything you want. But you can't ask me to stop. You don't understand that I'm *very* shy. Dealing with people is extremely hard for me. With alcohol, I can be the real me. Do you remember how awful I was that time I quit for six weeks? Life was completely gray, no colors. I went to parties and didn't belong. A person who doesn't drink doesn't belong anywhere. *You* drink. *You* know. It's the oil in the crankcase. Look at Marion Sullivan after she came out of Riverside. A walking lobotomy."

"Marion was a walking lobotomy when she went *into* Riverside. Does Bill Mason strike you as unhappy? He hasn't changed since Riverside. If anything, he's better."

"That's because Bill is such a strong-willed, bright person."

"Aren't you? That's what you and Bill have in common."

Abby was leaning forward now, elbows on her knees, hands clasped, eyes earnest and innocent. She answered, "Bill went into Riverside because Sally was about to divorce him and he was going to lose his job and there would have been a public scandal. I'm glad Riverside was there for Bill. If they could fix *him* up, it must be the best place in the country, and I'd go there if I ever went anywhere. But Bill drank a fifth of Black and White every day between five and eleven. I don't drink anywhere *near* that much. I don't *need* it the way he did. I don't get drunk at every party. Remember the night at our house when he got off on that anti-Semitic tirade? Everybody was shocked. I don't do anything like that."

"No," said Martin, "but you drove my car into a tree by the Caswell's driveway."

"Yes, but everybody thought that was funny."

"Was it funny when you drove six children to Boston drunk out of your mind? Was it funny when you were caught shoplifting at Filene's? Was it funny when you slapped Ken Burton, who is merely a director of my firm?"

Abby sat back, an ache in the center of her chest. "Do you want to know why I drink?" she asked. "It's because I can never measure up to you. You never do anything wrong. You are always in the right place at the right time, always saying the right things. That's why I drink. Because you're too perfect."

Martin's face slowly turned red. Abby watched, frightened, as he lifted his right hand. Had she gone too far this time? Someday he was going to hit her. But he only brushed the hand across his mouth and mustache, wiping away sudden sweat. When he spoke, she could hear the disgust, the frustration, hot in his voice. "That *is* such bullshit," he said. "You need help, Abby."

"You'll never get me into Riverside alive," she answered angrily. "When the time comes to quit drinking, I'll quit. But nobody's going to tell me when or what to do. It's *my* decision. I'm in charge of my life. Not you. If I want to drink myself to death, that's my privilege."

Martin stood up — as Abby knew he would. It was the next step in this ritual dance they had been repeating for years. And now he was going to take his parting shot. He shook his head slightly and said, "Don't you feel any responsibility to your children? They're terrified of you. They never know what you're going to do next. Haven't you noticed they never bring any friends home? They're afraid of what they're going to find."

A small pulse was beating beside Abby's right eye. "Does it ever occur to you, Martin, that they don't invite friends because you're such a crab-ass?"

Martin stood silent. His face had turned pale, white around the lips. "Now he would go," she thought, "to avoid the really big fireworks." But he did not move, and her heart tensed. "You're going to have to stop," he said, very evenly, "because you're going to lose everything. I'm not going to put up with this crap much longer. My work is going downhill. I can't concentrate on anything — except what might be happening at home. And I don't have the strength to watch you kill yourself, and maybe somebody else in the process."

Looking up at him, Abby's heart hurt, and the skin tightened over her whole body. She said, "Well, our marriage isn't so terrific anyway." Martin walked rapidly out the door and up the stairs. "Chicken!" Abby yelled as he disappeared.

Abby stayed motionless — impaled — in the wing-backed chair. "If Martin leaves me," she thought, "he'll be the loser in that bargain because I will certainly get the children — I'm their *mother* — and Martin will pay handsomely. I'll show everybody how gutsy I am. I can go into any court and convince the judge of anything. I know it!"

She lit another cigarette, exhaling the smoke in one long breath. Moving the ashtray to the coffee table, she leaned forward, elbows on her knees, eyes unseeing. She took another long pull on the cigarette and picked a bit of tobacco off her tongue with her little finger. Could Martin be right? Was she really an alcoholic? Abby focused on the liquor cupboard. How could that innocent fluid ruin her life? Nonsense.

But an image of herself kept intruding into her mind — a blowzy, beat-up Abby, looks long gone, alone, ignored, a nothing, thrown away. Maybe she really would cut down on her drinking. Anything, rather than go to Riverside. At least Martin hadn't tried to sell her on AA. Abby wrinkled up her nose, remembering the meeting she had been tricked into attending. Everybody introduced themselves by their first names and said they were alcoholics. And then they had been so rude. They laughed when she said, "My name is Abby, and I don't know what I am." But the poor souls had no other life. No theater, books, music. And such infantile signs on the walls — "Easy Does It" — "Go Slow." Like on somebody's driveway. "Let Go and Let God." How incredibly naive. But that was okay for them. By the time they got to that point, it was all they could grasp. Al and Caroline were there. So that's what happened to them; they died and went to AA.

Abby leaned back and her attention wandered. That fireplace was clean. A *real* home would have ashes in the fireplace. She crossed her legs and absently rubbed the leather pump on her foot, drawing an odd reassurance from its feel of textured softness. "Quality and taste," she thought. Her attention returned to the fireplace — to memories of the fires they had in their first house, the one they renovated themselves — her hair looking elderly with flecks of white paint. No money. But the same goals. She and Martin on the same team. The feeling that she was an extension of him. And he of her.

Every day there had been the anticipation of five-thirty when Martin would come through the door — the nice feel of his kiss — he didn't have his mustache then. The fire would be going and they'd have drinks sitting side by side on the sofa. She'd covered that sofa with denim herself. Did a good job, too. They would sit there. Close. Martinis in champagne glasses. She didn't click his glass with hers. She rubbed it. And she had a name for the feeling then: "the warm fuzzies." It was a sense that everything was right, and would always be right. A sense of completeness, of roundness. They would talk about their day — how the market did — which interested her. They would discuss whether to paper the bathroom or paint it with enamel — or could they teach themselves to put up tiles. They would congratulate themselves on their life, on finding each other, and Martin would put his hand on her leg. Her emotions, as though in some pool at the bottom of her being, would sometimes rise up into her throat, pushing happy tears ahead of them in behind her eyes. She would wonder if he could feel her feeling this?

"Why can't it be that way now?" Abby asked herself. She had to admit it. Mostly she felt nothing. Just blah. Looking at the barren fireplace again, she thought grimly, "Well, there's no lack of ashes inside me."

She checked the watch on her bony wrist. Ten o'clock. Martin would be safely in bed, watching TV. Maybe a little brandy would be nice. But he might smell it and go into orbit. He'd tell her again she was killing herself. But a Valium wouldn't hurt. She couldn't endure lying there in the darkness, so alone, feeling that nobody else in the world was awake, sure that she would never sleep again. She pulled her purse up from the floor, took two of the yellow pills from the bottle, collected saliva in her mouth, and swallowed them. She had to have *something* to relax her. Make her able to face Martin. Keep her glued together so she wouldn't shatter into little pieces — so many pieces that all the king's doctors . . . If only Martin could understand that she wasn't killing herself, that she was drinking to stay alive!

Figuring she had a half hour before drowsiness set in, Abby made the rounds of the children. Judy was sitting in bed, knees up, reading a book.

"Good night, Judy."

"Good night, Mom."

"Shouldn't you be doing your homework?"

Judy answered in that brisk and cheerful voice Abby knew was a brush-off. "It's all done. It went real easy tonight."

Abby stood irresolute, feeling exasperated, helpless, foolish. Should she hassle Judy? To hell with it. Evan sat in his room plinking on his guitar — the amplifier was banned after Martin came home — and he did not look up. "Good night, Mom." Abby glanced around the room and gritted her teeth at the unmade bed, the old, half-full bottles of soda, the food dried on plates. She closed the door and stood motionless in the hall, worrying, feeling helpless again. Evan was hanging around with the two crumb-bum Crawford boys, who people said were selling pot. Well, Evan was bound to smoke it sooner or later. Just a phase, and maybe they'd all grow out of it. She wouldn't tell Martin anything. Only suspicions. And he'd blame it all on her. "His mother's son," he'd say. If she accused Evan, he'd accuse her right back. "I couldn't handle that," she thought.

Frederick was in bed. She asked, "Did you clean your teeth?" He said he had. Abby sat down on the bed and with her forefinger began curling the lock of hair lying across his smooth forehead. Suddenly he turned over on his stomach. "Rub my back." Reaching under his pajama top, Abby moved her fingers on the velvet skin, giving him the special fingertip tickle he loved. "Sweetheart," Abby said, "you must have thought I was really peculiar night before last. The doctor gave me some medicine and I had a drink and the combination made me a little nuts. It'll *never* happen again. I hope you weren't scared."

"No," he said, and was silent. After Abby kissed him good night, he said, "You dream about me and I'll dream about you."

Leaving the room, she thought, "How can I not break his heart."

When she got into bed in her flowered flannelette nightgown, Martin had already turned off the television and was on his side, facing away from her. She lay on her back, looking up at the ceiling and the branching cracks she had named the Mississippi, the Hudson, the Snake, the Shenandoah. If only Martin would listen to her, really listen. If only he would ask her, "How can we team up and solve our problems?" Abby wept silently, trying not to shake the bed, feeling the tears running down the sides of her face, over her ears.

She reached her foot across the vast distance of the king-sized bed and touched Martin's foot. He did not respond. "Why has he gone so far away?" she wondered. "Why has he left me so alone?" As she used to do in the beginning of her marriage, Abby slid across the bed to say good night, fitting herself against Martin's back, her head behind his on the pillow. Once upon a time they would have snuggled now and giggled and played tickle-and-slap games, and, often as not, made love. "You know," she said, "if we could be on the same team, maybe I could get myself together."

He lay still, his body unyielding as wood. He spoke away from her. "Abby, I just *can't* get into another big discussion. I'm leaving tomorrow for Chicago and I'm exhausted."

She rolled back away from him, furious, a sick ache in her stomach. He had switched her off, the son of a bitch. She'd opened up and he'd switched her off.

The next day was Thursday, April twenty-ninth. Abby slept late. Triumphant at waking with no hangover, she told herself proudly, "See, I don't *have* to drink." She called Jan Cummings and invited herself to lunch. Jan, happily married, was a wide-hipped, round-faced woman with a quick mind and an ironic smile. Jan suggested daiquiris. Abby thought, "It's a little early in my new regime, but I've been very good and I don't want to be a wet blanket. What harm can one do? But only one." She sat at the kitchen table watching raptly as Jan measured the rum, squeezed the limes, spooned in the sugar, added pulverized ice and churned the mixture in a blender. From the freezer, Jan brought two frosted champagne glasses and poured out the frothy drinks.

Abby's heart expanded as a single drop of condensation rolled down the side of her glass. Ceremoniously, she clicked her glass with Jan's and took a long sip, filling her mouth with the tart sweetness, swishing it gently through her teeth, cradling it on her tongue, washing it across her taste buds. "Delicious," she said, feeling the warm glow coming on and taking another gulp.

When that daiquiri was finished, she thought, "One more wouldn't hurt. That was *so* good." Jan poured a second. Drinking a little slower, Abby gave herself over to the gentle hum of a beginning high. But then it sagged. Her head felt heavy. Maybe she needed a third one. A tiny voice reminded her, "But you said you wouldn't have any more." Well, she was just going to, and that was that. Abby kept drinking all through the chef's salad. Afterward, walking to her car, she said, "I don't understand how anybody can say I drink too much because neither one of us is falling down or weaving or anything. Have those drinks hit you?"

"No," said Jan, who had stopped after three drinks.

At home, like a tiny flame deep inside, there was a sensation Abby could not reason with — the feeling that she still had not had enough, that she must have more. She told herself, "I shouldn't waste those daiquiris. I'm not there yet. Perhaps something stronger this time. Scotch. No. Bourbon. Yes. He knows I hate that and he won't check the bottle." She poured the brown fluid into a glass of milk, took a sip, grimaced, and carried it into the living room, where she put a Scott Joplin ragtime record on the stereo.

She sat in the wingback chair, sipping, sinking into the hypnotic tinkling of the piano. Gradually the familiar trance carried her into wonderful sensations of love and safety mingled with memories of her father — sitting in his lap rearranging his white hair and getting him to laugh. And when he laughed, he shook her up and down and joggled her and made her laugh, too. She heard his voice singing "Over Here, Over There," and she could still feel her hand in his as they toured the woolens mill he managed — the long clackety

44

lines of weaving machines — and she felt again her pride that he remembered all the workers' names and asked the questions important to their lives. She could still feel his hand in hers the moment that he died of pneumonia when she was seventeen. And she could hear herself yelling at her mother and the nurse, "If nobody's going to close his eyes, I will." On the tip of her forefinger was the soft sensation of his lids when she reached out and touched them shut, and in her mind was the surprise at the way they snapped down over the blank stare. Putting the drink on the little table at her elbow, Abby rose and danced slowly to the music. Deep inside she wailed, "How could he be gone when I need him so." Tears streamed down her face as she swayed.

Suddenly Judy was there in the doorway, her face expressionless. Abby went rigid — but her voice was all naturalness. "Hi, sweetie, home from school?"

"Hi, Mom."

"Judy, would you fix supper tonight, I'm just not up to it."

Turning quickly away, Judy said in the hall, "So what else is new."

Abby thought, "Everybody's got a zinger around here. Oh, well." She made herself another milk and bourbon, and piled the stereo with Schubert. Hours later she awoke stiff and cold on the floor, her head shattering, her body immobilized by weakness. The room was dark. The red eye of the silent stereo still glowed. She managed to sit up and switch it off. Near her head stood the bottle of bourbon. "Ugh," she thought. "How repulsive. How did it get here? God, there's a lot gone." She hid it beneath the pile of records and thought, "How could this have happened again? The children must have seen me." She dragged herself onto the sofa, pulled the pillows over on top of her, and slept.

On Friday, the sound of the children in the kitchen woke her at seven. She crept up the stairs, undressed, went to bed and back to sleep. At ten she got up. Shaky, fragmented,

45

feeling kicked in the stomach, she listlessly pulled on her blue robe. The dryness in her mouth and throat was painful. Her headache was like a nail in her skull. Taking five aspirin in the bathroom, she looked into the mirror and saw a total stranger — bleak, mocking eyes in a puffy, red face, deep lines, a cold sore on one lip. Her robe lay on her shoulders as though on the crooks of canes. She turned away, frightened. Telling herself that she *had* to stay healthy, she managed her daily handful of vitamin pills. Down in the kitchen making coffee, she bumped the measuring spoon against the machine, dumping the grounds on the counter. Her nerves shrieked. "Oh, shit!" she said aloud.

Drinking the first mug of coffee, Abby leaned heavily on the counter and stared out the window at the apple tree and the pale pink buds, poised, waiting to explode on the first hot day of May. Then it would be time for the first rum collins of the summer, and the fat 747 bees would be buzzing among the white blossoms. By August, the blossoms would be crab apples — August when Frederick was born — a last-minute caesarean — and she'd let the doctor talk her into a hysterectomy at the same time. "A once-in-a-lifetime package deal," she thought bitterly.

When she had arrived home from the hospital, the leaves of the apple tree were yellow-brown in the hot, stagnant air. Crab apples were rotting on the ground and dangerous-looking yellow jackets sucked up the cider. Thinking, "How can it be blooming one minute, and yellow and dying the next," she had stood under the tree weeping and looking down at a boy's pink Day-Glo plastic bat.

Now, in the kitchen, Abby turned away from the window and poured herself another mug of coffee. Every joint ached. Exhaustion possessed her like an illness. Sapped of all strength, she dragged herself to the solace of the wingback chair — the last safe corner on earth. She had no will to move, no will to speak. There was not one thing in life to do but sit. The machinery had ground to a halt. Holding her coffee mug in both hands, as though to warm them, she thought, "Well, now I'm going to die. But they'll manage. Everything will still go on." She thought about all those unfeeling people who had so casually botched her life. If only they had seen behind her facade, which was so thin, and found the gentle, vulnerable person who lived there. Surely they would not have done what they did. "I had so much promise," she thought.

Then, like an automaton, Abby stood up, went to the cellar and returned with a bottle of wine. Back in the chair, she leaned forward, elbows sharp on her narrow knees, a cigarette in one hand, the bottle and a glass on the coffee table beside the silver cigarette box she had won in a tennis tournament. The robe fell away and she stared uncaring at her blotched and bony legs. Sipping glass after glass of wine, she felt nothing but a deepening torpor. She could hear the Abby who lived in the dead shell of her body screaming, "Help me, somebody! Please help me!" — and the sound reverberated in the emptiness inside her.

Occasionally there would be terrible flashes of reality — the horrific damage she was doing to her family and to herself — and the pain would be unbearable and she would snap back into her numbness, into her sense of unutterable separation, as though dangling in a vast, dark space. Then she would plunge downward into the nothingness beneath her. And the voice would frantically scream, "Wake up! Live!" But, terrified of living, she longed for death.

In the middle of the morning, Martin called to say he was taking a morning plane on Saturday. Lifelessly, she told him to do what suited him.

"What's going on?" he demanded. "Shall I come right home?"

Fear brought energy into Abby's voice. "No. No. Everything's fine. Come Saturday."

At noon Annie hurried through the unlocked door. She stood looking down at Abby and said, "I just came by for a

47

second to tell you it's happening. We're going to court and I'm meeting my lawyer this afternoon and I'm really scared. What's the matter with you, Abby?"

With excruciating slowness, Abby laid down her cigarette, looked up, and said with fatalistic calm, "I have a fatal illness. I'm going to die."

"What are you talking about?"

"I didn't tell you this before because I didn't want to worry you. It's my heart. I know there's something very wrong and I'm going to die."

Annie, frowning, said, "You can't do this to me, Abby. I've got too much ahead of me. I think you've had a lot to drink and I think you should go to bed and sleep it off. I wish I could stay and talk about it, but I can't."

Watching Annie leave, Abby thought, "Something is always more important to them than I am." But nothing really mattered anymore. Each time a bottle was empty, she would think, "I'm too tired. I don't feel like drinking any more." Then she would decide, "Maybe another would get me going," and she would make the basement trip again. All afternoon she sat comatose. Once, head down, hands in her lap, she wept. Once she threw her head back and screamed into the silence, "Oh, Christ! Help me!"

When the children came home from school, she was still there, legs up on the coffee table, bottles hidden behind the sofa. She gave Judy money and sent them out for pizza. She was there when the children went to bed. Then Judy in her nightgown came down and kneeled in front of Abby and took her limp hands. "Mom," she said pleadingly, "you can't sit here all night. You've got to go to bed. You'll feel better in the morning." Abby looked at her blankly. Judy, still gripping her hands, stood up and began tugging at them with small jerks. "Come on, Mother." Abby rose obediently and Judy led her up the stairs by the arm. While Abby undressed with the weariness that melts the bones, Judy turned down the covers of the bed. Then she helped her mother into the bed and pulled the covers back over her. Resting a hand gently on Abby's hair, she kissed her forehead — Abby's own good-night ritual in Judy's childhood.

On Saturday morning, sick at heart, ill in body, Abby lay in her nest too frightened to move. Everything outside the bed was beyond endurance. She could no longer fight off the sickness and exhaustion, the desolation and guilt, no longer keep going in a life that only seemed to get worse. She was sure now that she was insane. Only a crazy person would do what she had been doing. Annie telephoned to apologize for not staying and listening. Did Abby want her to come over now? "No," Abby said. "I'm globally depressed, and the only thing that can help me is Valium. Gobs of it."

A half hour later, Annie and Jan, fright on their faces, rushed into the bedroom. Like a poorly jointed doll, Abby snapped upright in bed. Sitting there in her flowered nightgown, her mind empty, she opened her mouth. Disembodied words came out. "Don't say anything. I'm going."

The two women looked at each other. "Going where?" Jan asked. "Going to die?"

"I'm going to Riverside," Abby said.

The decision had still not registered on her conscious mind. She looked at her two friends, who were laughing crazily. Or were they crying? They had tears on their cheeks. Abby thought, "What in the name of God is the matter with them? What did I tell them? Did I say that? I really *am* crazy. Well, okay, I *will* go to Riverside." Amazed at herself, she felt a kind of awe — an enormous relief.

But that second voice — now roused and terrified — could not imagine a life without alcohol. "What have you done?" it demanded. "You can't go through with this!"

The first voice came back, manipulating, reassuring. "You've shut them up at last. Wouldn't you like to see Martin's face when he hears this! He was planning on putting you away himself. And maybe they can teach you there how to drink."

49

So she compromised. She announced, "I have two stipulations. First, you are *not* to tell Martin until *after* I am in Riverside. I could not stand hearing him say, 'Well, thank *God*.' Second, I will *not* go to Riverside unless I go *today*." They would never get her in there with those long waiting lists. But now they couldn't claim she'd refused help. She said, "This is your lucky day, folks. But the special is only on for one day."

PART TWO

CHAPTER

3

TWO HOURS later on that Saturday, Abby was sitting in a bronze Pinto on her way to the Riverside Treatment Center for Alcoholism, near Cambridge, Massachusetts. A chirpy, cheerleader voice was saying, "Really, Mrs. Andrews, this is just the best thing you ever did for yourself." Her family doctor had pulled strings, and a place had been made available. But Abby wanted the doctor's nurse to take her there, not her friends. Riverside was her *own* decision. Nobody was going to have the satisfaction of putting her away. And she was afraid of tenderness. Its touch might shatter her control and turn loose her pandemonium.

Dropped off on the sidewalk, Abby stood looking at the three-story brick building set well back from the street, rectangular in front with three wings radiating out at the rear. Her stomach burned, sour with fear — though she'd taken every precaution. A low-profile outfit. Tan twill pants, man-tailored blue shirt, brown Shetland sweater, a bandanna hiding her hair. A half-hour makeup job — so nobody would guess why she was coming to Riverside. And at the last minute, a fortifying trip to the piano, so her hands wouldn't shake.

To the right of the treatment center, at the peak of a tall, white flagpole, a languid American flag was still lit by the sinking sun. Abby thought, "Perfect Hollywood. Little Orphan Annie sentenced to the Big Slammer." Here she was, a friendless child, terrified, defeated, bereft — a permanent twilight falling across her life. Never any alcohol again. Inconceivable! But what if they couldn't make her stop drinking? Well, maybe she wasn't an alcoholic. No alcoholic would voluntarily do this. Abby headed toward the big glass front door. She'd show everybody! She was going in on her *own!*

Inside, Abby was directed to the business office to sign the admission papers. She made an elaborate show of reading every word. She was no drunken psycho who'd sign away her right to leave this place. A pleasant-faced nurse introduced herself as Sally, and said, "I'm glad you're here."

Sally picked up Abby's suitcase and led her to the elevators. At the third-floor nurses' station, positioned at the junction of three long corridors, Abby sat down beside the curving counter, her bony ankles crossed deep under the chair. Sally knelt in front of her and looked directly into her eyes, asking, "How are you doing?" Abby answered, "Okay," and knew it had not been a casual question. Sally took her temperature and blood pressure, and Abby thought, "They're really serious here." Now she felt queasy, on the edge of throwing up. This place was *not* going to work. It was money down the drain. "If I'd gone to Hawaii," she thought, "I'd feel a helluva lot better."

In a small room behind the counter, Sally issued her a yellow name tag in a plastic cover. Pinning it onto her sweater, Abby thought, "At least it doesn't say, 'Hello! My name is Abigail.' " Then Sally filled out an elaborate health form and another questionnaire on Abby's drinking history — when she had her first drink, did she get drunk, any alcoholism in her family. Then, still carrying the suitcase, Sally led her down the left-hand corridor. Fixed to the pale green walls were handrails. Abby thought, "The people here must be really out of it. I don't belong in this place." Then she realized the women's rooms were mixed in with the men's. "What would my mother think?" she said to herself.

In Abby's room Sally put the suitcase on the bed and said, "I'm afraid I have to go through your things. May I open your bag?" Surprised, Abby nodded. Then, watching the efficient fingers winnow through her underwear, probe the flowered nightgown, press the embroidered throw pillow brought from her bed at home — she flushed with humiliation.

Suddenly, Sally, holding Abby's purse, was saying briskly, "I'll have to take these." In her hand was the Valium bottle.

Abby's heart jumped. Her skin felt even hotter. This nurse thought she was some kind of junkie! And a sneak. But she took them *everywhere*. Keeping the panic from her voice, Abby said, "They're only for sleeping. I *have* to get my rest. My doctor prescribed them."

Sally smiled. "Our staff doctor will be examining you soon, and he will give you whatever medication he thinks you need."

Turning to go, Sally said, "If you'll wait here, the doctor will be with you soon. Call me if you need anything. We're here to help you."

"The hell you are," Abby thought, watching the Valium bottle leave the room. She stood looking around the room. She hadn't known it would be like a hospital — crossed with a motel. The hospital bed projected into the middle of the room. Along the inside wall, parallel to it, was a long, low, blond wood bureau with a long mirror above it. The rest of the walls were bare. On the other side of the bed were two large windows, and under them, like a sill, was a combination heating and air conditioning unit. One of the panels was loose, projecting out several inches. "This is a sloppy ship," Abby thought. Opposite the foot of the bed was a small, formica-topped, gray table and a straight-back wooden chair. Abby smiled grimly. "Sparta, here I come."

She strolled into the bathroom. Standard motel. But the room was a single, thank heavens. Suppose she'd gotten a real *drunk* for a roommate. At the bureau Abby took off the

55

bandanna and brushed her hair. Why did it look so dull? Maybe a rinse would help. Her eyes were dull, too. And her skin was so dry. She should unpack. But that would commit her to this place. She distributed onto the bureau top a few cosmetics, her hairbrush, pictures of the children; put the embroidered pillow on the bed; hung a few clothes in the closet — just enough to deceive the nurses. She hoisted the almost full suitcase onto the top closet shelf. Then, sitting down on the bed, hands between her knees, she stared out the window into the dusk, oblivious to the city lights, the flowing stream of lights along the roadway, the dark band of the Charles River below. She thought how cut off she felt — even from herself — in a green-walled box, floating in space. How could this be happening to her? Abigail Andrews in a drunk tank! She choked back the sobs gathering in her throat.

She wondered if Judy and Evan would be glad she wasn't home. She could feel the tears in her eyes now, and she forced her mind into practicalities. In her note to Judy, had she remembered everything? "Tell Dad not to forget Frederick's dentist appointment. Tell Linda to get somebody else for hot dog day at school." Had she bought enough food at the supermarket? Then, beginning to feel fluttery inside, she thought, "Oh, let *them* worry about the food."

Abby checked her hands, noticing vaguely that her wrists were awfully thin. Well, her hands still weren't shaking. But she needed another drink right now. She must not lose control. People would think she was sick. "Dummy, you are sick," she thought. But how could they cure her when she didn't know what was wrong? Abby rose and stood in front of the window, biting her lower lip. Gazing out over the vast expanse of the city beyond the window, she thought, "There must be thousands of people out there in worse shape than I am."

The doctor knocked and came into the room — a short, smooth-faced man, a cherub in glasses carrying a clipboard.

He sat on the chair and introduced himself. "I'm Doctor Richardson." Abby sat facing him on the wide window sill, her right forefinger coiling a lock of hair. He asked, "How is your general health?"

"Excellent," Abby answered, the wide mouth in a confident smile. This doctor, an expert, would see how different and extremely together she was — only lightly dipped in alcohol. Soon he would be saying, "There has been a terrible mistake, Mrs. Andrews. You're not an alcoholic."

While he gave her a physical examination, he asked questions. "How much do you drink on the average?"

"Sometimes nothing, like today." The doctor shot her a shrewd look. Abby thought, "He doesn't believe me. How does he know?" She continued, her voice businesslike, "On the average I guess about three or four drinks a day." Since the doctor was asking about alcoholic drinking, Abby told herself, social drinks with friends did not count. But he should see that she was honest. "On rare occasions," she added, "I have quite a lot more."

Dr. Richardson asked about hallucinations.

"None," Abby said.

"Any anxiety attacks?"

"No."

"Blackouts?"

"What are those?"

"A blackout is a complete, permanent loss of memory for a given period of time, during which the alcoholic acts and talks relatively normally."

"No," Abby answered. "No blackouts."

"What pills do you take?"

Abby's voice was still brisk. "Occasionally, when I wake up in the night, I take a five-milligram Valium to help me get back to sleep."

"Uh-huh," Dr. Richardson said. "Count backwards from fifty by sevens as fast as you can."

She did it easily — "Fifty, forty-three, thirty-six . . ."

She reached twenty-two and thought, "Well, now he sees how well I can do it." She stopped, saying to him, "That ought to be enough."

"No. Just keep going."

She thought, "Oh, he's tougher than he looks," and felt a flash of fear and anger. But then she thought, "When I have explained myself in detail, he'll understand. Clearly he's preoccupied with all the really *sick* people."

As he left, Doctor Richardson gave Abby a psychological questionnaire to be completed by the next day. Abby threw the paper onto the bed. "I'll do it later," she told herself. There was a knock at the door — Sally telling her to come down to the nurses' station for her medication. The doctor had prescribed a tranquilizer, Librium, for two days to help her through alcohol withdrawal and prevent the d.t.'s — and Dilantin for possible convulsions during Valium withdrawal. Abby was relieved. She would have some help. But d.t.'s! Convulsions! My God! And *withdrawal!* She hadn't bargained on *that!*

After her temperature and blood pressure were checked, Sally explained the treatment routine. On Monday Abby would attend an orientation meeting, and on Tuesday or Wednesday she would be assigned to a therapy group of about a dozen patients. Her group — which would be the heart of her treatment — would meet with their counselor twice a day at nine-thirty and one-thirty. Three times a day, after each meal, there was a lecture on chemical addiction. So the schedule was meal, lecture, group; meal lecture group; meal, lecture. Television was available in the small lounges from seven-thirty to ten-thirty. All patients must be in their rooms by midnight. Phone calls were unrestricted. No visitors for a week. No smoking in the rooms. Patients could go for walks outside as long as they stayed on Riverside property and were accompanied by another patient. "Well," Abby thought, "at least it's not a jail. But almost."

Then Sally took Abby on a tour of the floor. At the end of each of the three corridors was a small lounge used by the residents of the corridor. "More motel," Abby thought, taking in the wood and sponge-rubber sofas and easy chairs, the plastic-topped table and its chairs. Returning to the nurses' station at the hub of the three corridors, they crossed through the elevator bank into the large lounge across the full front of the building. Sally explained that it was used by all of the two hundred patients from both floors. The corresponding room below on the second floor was the lecture hall.

Abby stood nervously in the doorway, feeling heads turn toward her, eyes focus on her, the new girl. Street kids — only a little older than Evan — in tight jeans and sloppy tee shirts were lounging on the window sills, playing pool and Ping-Pong, laughing and yelling. They were too noisy. They made her head hurt. They wouldn't like her. And the rest of the room: it was a skid row cruise ship. Rough, dry slacks. Rump-sprung housedresses. Beards. Skinny arms. Biafra stomachs. And coffee mugs everywhere. And cigarette butts. Ugh! She couldn't stay in this place. "I'm not one of these people," Abby thought.

Sally led Abby past the Ping-Pong table, through a door, and into a small kitchen. Patients were rummaging in a huge refrigerator, pulling out juice and sandwich makings. Well, at least there was a big coffee maker and — this was something *good* — a freezer full of ice cream bars. Sally introduced her to the "wing leader" of her corridor, a sort of proctor elected by the other patients. He was a short, blond man in his fifties, smooth-faced with wide, surprised eyes and a pedantic voice — a lawyer, he was quick to tell her — and Abby was surprised. His name was Sam, and he invited Abby to have dinner with him. On the first floor they stood in the cafeteria line as Sam explained the eating schedule. Breakfast was at seven-thirty, lunch at eleven-thirty, and dinner at five-thirty. Everybody had to come to all meals and sit ten minutes, whether or not they ate. Patients living on the second floor ate twenty minutes later. There was very little mingling, he said, between the two floors.

The line snaked into the dining room and past a cafeteria

59

counter. The dishes of food repelled Abby, and she took only a bowl of canned peaches and a cup of coffee. Sam sat across from her at one of the long tables, and Abby answered his questions politely but absently while she covertly looked around. Down the table a gray wren of a woman with steel-rimmed glasses arranged a paper napkin doily under her plate of pressed meat. Next to her was a gaunt man with laborer's hands, his movements shaky and hesitant. At the far end of the table was a middle-aged man in a Shetland sweater and striped Oxford shirt. "There's somebody who might like me," Abby thought.

Across from her, a plump-faced girl in her early twenties was saying, "I can give up alcohol, but I can't give up cocaine." Abby thought, "My God, some of them are drug addicts." Would they say anything to her? Ask her questions? Several people did smile at her and say, "Hi." Abby inwardly recoiled. She did not want to be one of these people, to be sick, to be somebody who belonged at Riverside.

After dinner, while the patients attended a lecture, Abby went to her room and played her tape machine. But the music did not help. She longed to be home where she could do what she wanted, where she could have a drink. All these rules here! She fled the solitude. Going to the small corridor lounge, she sat apart in a corner chair, leaning back, legs in the tan pants crossed, head down, trying to lose herself in a detective novel. But soon she was staring into nothingness, thinking that it was May now, and she was going to miss the blooming of the apple tree, that feeling of the two of them poised together, waiting for the haze of whiteness to unfold. She would miss sitting under her tree, enveloped by the perfection of the blossoms, in her ears the hum of bees drinking the new nectar. She would miss that first sip of the first rum collins of the summer. She could taste its delicious sweetness.

At ten she reported to the nurses' station for her medication. Then, betting that the Librium would make her sleep, she went to bed. But at midnight she was still awake, damp with sweat, the sheet sticking to her thin legs, tangling as she tossed and turned. Her heart was pounding, and from time to time muscles twitched in her arms and legs. Vague premonitions swept her. Loneliness spread like pain through her body. She felt as though a hole had been cut in the middle of her chest and there was no way she could stopper it and keep out the fears and anxieties and guilts swirling in and out of her.

This, she knew, was her punishment for her sins: to lie awake night after night in this strange bed in this sterile place, separated from alcohol and pills, from everything familiar, stripped of every person and thing able to protect her from herself. And each day her most secret person would be laid out to be cut open and the entrails read; and she would see them, too, and know the truth. She would find out that she was insane. Then she would shatter. The future opened up before her eyes — a lifetime in institutions looking at pale green walls. A sentence of death.

On Sunday morning, May second, after three hours of restless sleep interrupted by a nurse checking her with a flashlight, Abby's stomach was nauseated and the occasional twitching of her limbs had increased. She reported for her medication and tests. Her blood pressure had soared — 210 over 150. The nurse said her pressure would return to normal in two or three days when the alcohol had left her bloodstream. This was typical of alcohol withdrawal. But Abby was still frightened. She'd heard of people dying from withdrawal. And she had a weak heart. She could be dead at any moment.

The sight of breakfast brought her close to vomiting, and she sat with an empty tray, hands trembling. Why wasn't the Librium doing a better job? She returned to her room and lay down on the bed. A band of tension was cinched around her chest. Through the window she could see the May sun on the budding trees. Soon those gatherings would

61

start on the patio at Annie's house. That part of her life was gone forever. Everything was going to be different, something she did not know, something gray, half dead. She would never laugh again.

Jolts of panic set her heart pounding. "I've got to get out of here," she cried out to herself, jerking her body upright on the bed and swinging her feet to the floor. But the nausea rose up toward her throat and the muscles in her legs jerked and jumped. "I can't go anywhere like this," she thought, rolling back. "I'll wait till I'm better."

There was a knock on the door — a nurse saying that Martin was on the telephone. Abby's stomach contracted. Eyes wide, she called out, "Tell him I'm too sick." But then she wanted to hear his voice, make contact with her life away from this desert island. "Wait. I'm coming."

The call was on a pay telephone in the main lounge. Her hand holding the receiver shook. With her other hand she scratched an itch on her side. In the receiver Martin's voice, full of solicitude, said, "Oh, Abby, how are you?" Abby's face collapsed. Her mouth trembled. Fighting back the tears, her jaw rigid, she could not speak.

"Are you all right?" came his voice.

Finally she said, softly, "Oh, Martin. What's happened to me?"

"Abby, I love you. I miss you."

Instantly, Abby was angry — and felt more comfortable. "If he loves me so much," she told herself, "why is he letting me stay here and go through such hell?"

"When I got back to the hotel," Martin continued, "my box was full of messages. I thought something terrible had happened to you. But it was Annie calling with the news. You're doing the right thing, Abby."

She said nothing, feeling judged. Martin, the final arbiter, was once again deciding what was right and what was wrong.

"What's it like so far?" he asked.

"It's not Club Med."

"Look, Abby, I'm going to come right there so we can talk."

She could hear the anxiety in his voice. "Are you afraid I'll pack up my bongos and come home?" she asked. The inside of her nose was itching, and with two fingers she squeezed her nostrils together.

"Abby, I'm pinning all my hopes on Riverside. It would be just crazy to come home now, after you've finally admitted you're an alcoholic and are taking the proper steps to . . ."

"Well, I'm not so sure I'm an alcoholic," Abby interrupted, resentment filling her voice. "I'm not like *any* of the people here. I can't live through this. I never told you about my heart, but . . ."

"Don't be ridiculous!"

A long silence — angry, helpless, sad — hung between them. Then Abby said, "There's no point in your coming here. I can't see any visitor for the first week. But I have to ask you to send me some money. Special delivery. I have to buy treatment books and a note pad."

"Okay," Martin said. His voice perfunctory, he added, "Hang in there. It's all for the best."

"Don't worry. I'll be okay."

They hung up and Abby stood indecisively by the phone. She could not endure any more calls. There were too upsetting. But she *should* telephone her mother in California. No. Anything but that. Anything but listening to her say, "Why didn't you just *decide* not to drink."

By late afternoon she could no longer stay settled in one place. Huddled on the chair in her room, she felt the restlessness swarming through her. She would get up, pace, go to the bathroom, pick up her book, try to read, put it down, get up. . . . An unquenchable dryness parched her body. The itch like crawling insects came and went on her body, arms, thighs, head. She frantically rubbed and scratched herself through her clothes. To get at the itching inside her nose, she massaged its tip with her palm.

She could hear radio music from another room and the noise of laughter. How could anybody be happy here! Furious, she went to the small lounge and sat by herself, eyes frightened as she rubbed her arms and ankles. Suddenly Abby was conscious of a stocky figure in a checked shirt standing in front of her. Startled, she looked up, brushing the hair back from her forehead. His face was large and square. A broad forehead extended up into an aisle of baldness across the top of his head. His cheeks were pink with a lacework of red veins. At his thick neck, where the shirt was unbuttoned, brown hair curled. Abby was amazed by the kindness in the blue eyes. He said, "When I came in here, I looked just like you do now." He pulled over a chair and sat down, bending toward her, forearms on his knees, large hands clasped. "I'm Larry McGruder. I don't want to be a pest, but there's something that helped me a lot. Whenever I thought I was going crazy, I'd count something. Anything. The lines in the ceiling. The squares on my bedspread. It kind of settled me."

Tears exploded into Abby's eyes, streaming down her face, her chest pumping out the sobs. She wiped the wetness with the back of her thin hand. A part of her mind, detached, watching, was dumbfounded. She *never* cried when she was sober. It was not permitted. Embarrassed, she covered her face with her hands, and felt one of Larry's hands on her knee and heard his voice saying, "Don't be scared. You'll be okay." He was silent, and then Abby heard him stand up and walk away. Still hiding her face, she wondered how she could endure all the stares. Maybe people would be laughing at her. They'd seen the mess inside her leaking out, so maybe now they wouldn't like her. Finally, ready to run, she lowered her hands. Nobody was paying any attention to her. Angry, she left the room.

That night, lying in bed, sweating, itching, breathing

rapidly, knees aching — Abby thought, "My God, what have I done to myself." She wondered if the alcohol had permanently damaged her muscles — or perhaps she had a crippling disease. She listed the possibilities in her head and settled on multiple sclerosis. A dull ache in the center of her chest was now building to a sharp pain and then receding and building again. Abby changed her mind. She was having, at last, her heart attack. She had to get a nurse. But she could not move. "If you get up, you'll run out of this place," said one of her voices.

The next day, Monday, Abby felt better. Her stomach was less queasy, and the itching and restlessness had subsided. Her leg muscles still jerked occasionally. At breakfast, drinking a cup of coffee, she looked longingly outdoors at the sun on the grass. Then, impulsively, she went through the reception lobby and out the front door, breaking the rule that patients could not leave the Center by themselves. "Absurd," she thought. "Two by two like Noah's ark."

Around a corner of the building she found a sunny nook and sat leaning against the bricks. She wondered how things were going at home — how Frederick was doing without her. He was too young to know what it meant, having a mother in a drunk tank. Judy was so interior. She'd be mulling it over — and probably happy to have Martin to heself. Evan would be triumphant. He had never screwed up like this! Would the children be embarrassed at school? Would they tell people the truth? What was Martin saying? If parents knew she was in a drunk tank, would they let their children play with Frederick? When she wasn't at Judy's Parent's Day, what would Judy say? Abby told herself, "Well, I just might be there."

The time had come to make her decision. She could not possibly survive through four weeks in this place, this *hospital*, where every thing, every person, was so alien. What would they *ever* know about her. It was all a terrible mistake. Of course, she had to do *something* about her life. But if she could get home and have just one drink to clear her head, she could figure out what to do. She always thought better after a drink.

Now, how should she go? Call a cab and walk out with her suitcase, bold as brass? Past the nurses' station? But then there would have to be explanations, arguments. Okay, she'd leave her bag behind, all packed in her room, and whip down the fire stairs and out the front door. She could call a cab from a pay phone and go to some hotel and wait for Martin to pick her up. Let him get the bag later. Serve him right. Okay. Everything was decided.

She stood up and went indoors, a sense of relief filling her like a tonic. On the third floor she looked around and laughed inside. These people couldn't lay a glove on her now. And at parties she was going to have some great stories about all this. In the lounge, she dug into the pocket of her slacks for her cigarettes. The pack was empty. She must have another in her room. Hurrying down the hall, she could feel the anxiety vibrating in her body. Frantically, she searched through her purse, the bureau drawers, other pockets, the wastebasket. No cigarettes. Even worse, no change for the cigarette machine. How could she have let this happen! The anxiety erupted. "Oh, *shit!*" This was absolutely the last straw. Now she really was going to leave this dump.

Abby jerked the partly packed suitcase down from the top shelf of the closet and opened it on the bed. With hectic, fretful movements she threw into it the few things in the room. She was going to do what was *really* important — get home and start putting the family back together. Suddenly, Abby froze. She'd forgotten. She had no money for a taxi. How stupid. Okay, she'd call Annie O'Reilly, who would come right away. And better yet, they'd go directly to a bar and celebrate. Just a glass of wine. The Ritz. She'd always wanted to go there.

Abby finished packing and shut the suitcase. She looked around the sterile chamber. Nothing left. No mark, no residue. She'd come and gone like a ghost. Abby looked at her watch. Annie wouldn't be home for an hour. This room was no place to wait and it was time for the orientation meeting. She might as well go. Maybe she'd learn something about this disease they said she had. And there'd be cigarettes there.

In a small corridor lounge on the third floor, smoking a cigarette begged from another patient, Abby sat with ten other newcomers in a rough circle of chairs around the walls of the room. Next to her was a small, pale, thin-faced girl, twentyish, whose hands shook and mouth visibly trembled. The speaker introduced himself as chemically dependent. He began his talk, explaining that alcoholism was a disease, and it had affected them mentally, spiritually, and physically. Abby sat nodding her head, elaborately riveted on his words. They'd see what a superlative patient she could be and how unaffected she was by her drinking. From time to time her legs twitched.

The speaker went on to say, "Hard as it sounds, you must not worry about your husbands, wives, lovers, partners, friends, children. They will survive, and this treatment is your chance to work on *you*." The girl beside Abby began to cry, sitting up straight, her face wet.

The speaker was now explaining that each patient would be assigned to a therapy group. The manual just distributed would explain group therapy interaction, and each patient was expected to spend time with his or her group members — eat with them, sit with them at lectures and in the lounges. The course of treatment was approximately four weeks, but it was the therapy group counselor who decided when a patient was ready to be released.

"Oh, my God," Abby thought. "Would they keep her any longer than that?"

The girl's face was still running with tears, which made Abby nervous — like a man when a woman cries. But at the same time there was a feeling almost forgotten. How long it had been, she wondered, since somebody else's troubles had moved her. Almost awkwardly, she rubbed the girl's quivering back.

The counselor was saying, ". . . and do not compare yourself to other patients. Whether you use drugs or pills or alcohol, you are all chemically dependent." Abby, wrinkling her forehead, leaned over and whispered, "Are you okay?" The girl nodded slightly. When the talk ended, Abby fetched a box of Kleenex from a far window sill, placed it on the girl's lap, and sat down, half sideways. "My name is Abby," she said, smiling. "Everybody tells me things will get better."

Making a quick gesture toward the name tag, the girl said, "I'm Kerry." Abby asked her where she came from. Kerry, wiping her eyes, blowing her nose, said she lived in Georgia, but was originally from Wisconsin. She had a husband and two small children. "I'm so lonely for my kids," she said. "My mother-in-law is taking care of them, but she's never liked me and I just don't know if they're going to be okay."

Abby said, "My youngest is ten. He's only fifty miles away, but he might as well be on a different continent. I don't know if I can ever make him understand about this."

"When they's so little . . ." said Kerry. "I've been saying the Lord's Prayer over and over, asking God to please help me and watch over my family and please help us out of this mess I've gotten us into. But I suppose it's selfish to ask Him for help."

"Why selfish?" Abby asked.

Kerry picked at a small hole in her jeans. "I guess I think God's got no reason to help me. I've been just *begging* Him." She was silent for a moment and then, talking through more tears, she went on. "I don't know whether I belong here. I don't know whether I belong any place. They've got my records. They've seen what a zero I am. Are they going to bring all that out in front of people?"

Abby did not know what to tell Kerry. She heard herself saying, "This place has worked for other people. It will work for us." Then she thought, "What an amazing thing for me to say. Do I believe that?"

The lunch bell rang — time for the third floor to eat. The second floor, Kerry's, ate in twenty minutes. The two walked together to the nurses' station, Kerry withdrawn now, as though embarrassed by her loss of control. When they parted, Abby touched her on the shoulder and said, "I hope you're okay."

Kerry shrugged.

Watching her disappear down the stairwell beside the elevator bank, Abby felt both sad and proud. It was awful to see somebody so swamped by fear. Kerry needed help, needed to be here. But it had been terrific to be able to comfort Kerry. It was nice, Abby thought, being sober, feeling better, being her real self. It had been years since she had had anything to give another person. At the same time, she was vaguely aware of a nagging anxiety, a nervousness. Was she *really* any different from Kerry? Abby shut off that thought and went to phone Annie to come get her.

In the booth she lifted the receiver, and then paused, planning what to say. But into her mind came, not words, but memories of the drama of her announcement to Annie and Jan — "This is your lucky day, folks . . ." Suddenly, she was sweating from a hot flash. How humiliating it was going to be, admitting to Annie that she was whipped after only three days. Maybe she should bite the bullet and call Martin. But he would try to argue her into staying. She might have to plead. When he picked her up, there would be his contempt and his superiority. He would say, "I knew you couldn't do it." And he would refuse to come immediately, driving an hour each way this late in the day. So she'd call him tomorrow. There was actually no hurry. Maybe she'd wait till the money arrived.

Abby felt the first stirrings of appetite and decided, since dinner was so convenient, to try a little food before she left. She stood in line with a medium-height man in his thirties who had been at the orientation lecture. He wore a blue jacket, nipped in at the waist, and tan pants belled at the bottom over black loafers. His long sideburns extended down toward the corners of his mouth, and, Abby thought, seemed ill at ease on his slightly pudgy face. His eyes were guarded and restless. The name tag, Garrett Owen, was pinned to a fitted blue shirt that molded two rolls of a beginning paunch.

In the line and then sitting together, they talked fitfully about the orientation meeting, and Garrett remarked that he was only there because of an intervention.

Abby asked what that was.

He explained that it was a way to get a drunk into treatment before the person hit bottom and asked for help. In his case, he said, he'd been called by his wife to come upstairs from his basement rec room. With a beer in his hand and irritated at the interruption of a TV basketball game, he had walked into the living room and found his brother from Buffalo, New York, his sister from Norfolk, Virginia, the minister of his church, and his boss from the hardware chain where he was a warehouse superintendent. "They went around the room," Garrett said, "and told me I was a drunk and a very bitter, angry person, and they wanted me to come to Riverside."

Abby laughed. "That violates every American's inalienable right to drink."

Garrett grinned sheepishly. "Well, they had a point. If somebody turned on the dishwasher at the wrong time, I'd get mad and leave and not come back for two days."

"Where'd you go?" Abby asked.

"I'd buy a bottle and check into a motel."

Abby thought, "Just like my father."

After dinner, Garrett suggested they attend the evening lecture and try to get a handle on this place. Her anxiety about cigarettes was a vague hum in her body — almost like the need for a drink. But Abby agreed. She'd like to hear at least one lecture before she left. Inside the hall on the second floor, sections of chairs were reserved for each therapy group, so they headed for the last row. Abby tried to look purposeful, but felt like the new girl at school.

The lecturer was a tallish, thin, red-haired man with a long, droll face. He said, "My name is Mike and I'm an alcoholic." Abby thought, "Boy, he's got guts to admit that in front of everybody." The entire audience called out, "Hi, Mike."

On the blackboard he drew four adjoining squares, like the panes of a window, and explained that they represented the four components of the self. "The first window," he said, "is everybody's open area — the safe information about ourselves we allow others to know — how many children we have, where we're from, whether we like eggs boiled or fried. Number two is the secret area — the dangerous self-knowledge we *never* share with anybody — the terrible things we did when we drank, the fact that we are scared and hurt and lonely. Window number three is our blind spots — the things we don't see in our behavior, but everybody else knows from their insights and intuitions. Number four is the subconscious that neither we nor our group can read."

Abby was impressed. They knew a lot here. This could be interesting.

"In your group," the lecturer was explaining, "when other members give you feedback, they are telling you what they see in window three — filling in our blind spots. When I was in treatment, I sincerely believed that I understood all about myself. When the group gave me feedback, I *knew* those guys were wrong — and told them so. Nothing happened for me until I learned to sit there and listen and hear."

"Ah," thought Abby. "I mustn't argue back in group. The counselor will think I'm not getting well. *If* I go to group."

After the lecture, she went back to her room. Chewing on her lower lip, she stood looking at the suitcase on her bed. The time was eight o'clock, and she was dreading the call to summon Martin, dreading his anger and disappoint-

71

ment. If Judy and Evan were off somewhere, he'd need a baby-sitter for Frederick. She'd have to hear about that, and all the work he'd been doing — cleaning up the chaos she had left behind. He'd say, "Don't you ever think about anybody but yourself?" She decided to stay there one more night and see what the morning brought. She would be assigned to a group tomorrow. She might even stick around and see what that was like. She mustn't be rash and silly about her decision. She could leave anytime. And Kerry needed her. Abby again hid the suitcase in the closet. Maybe tomorrow Martin's check would come.

She went to the large lounge for a coffee, bummed a cigarette, and sat wondering who her counselor might be — if she stayed. Seeing counselors in the corridors, hearing patients talk, Abby knew she did not want Fern Adams of the purposeful walk. "You can't con her," people said. "She can read you like a book." But inside Abby a voice was asking, "What if you *don't* get her? What if you get a counselor you can con? The treatment won't work."

Then her attention shifted to the room in front of her — the kids playing pool, flourishing their cues like lances. God, what energy! This room was becoming less scary. Individuals were emerging. A tall man, an urban frontiersman, wearing Levis, motorcycle boots, and a long beard. A kewpie doll of a woman wearing a quilted skirt to her ankles. An elderly black man wearing a blue suit and senatorial dignity. But everybody in the room — the ones who drew their chairs into chatty circles around the sofas — or the ones who sat remote, faces sealed, bored — everybody seemed to Abby to be subtly imprinted with defeat. It was a kind of hollowness, as though they were all, somehow, flotsam, uprooted in some central way, quietly desperate. "Do I have that look?" Abby asked herself. The sad eyes. Was she *really* one of them?

The next day, Tuesday, Abby was assigned to Fern Adams's group. "I knew it," she thought with a mixture of apprehension and relief. After lunch she went to her room to get ready, finally settling on a bluish cotton blouse and a skirt with horizontal stripes of pale red and blue. She pulled her hair back behind her ears and rolled it into a stodgy bun — befitting, she thought, a puritan Abigail. She rubbed blush over her pallor, and heightened her eyes with liner and mascara. In the mirror she tried out her wide smile, letting it flood her face, half closing her hazel eyes in the way that aunts thought adorable. That was what she wanted to be: sweet, pretty, clean. Maybe Fern would say, "Oh, you can't be an alcoholic. Your husband must have brainwashed you into Riverside. Let's take a look at *his* behavior."

The bell rang for group. In Fern's office, Abby sat on one of the plastic chairs that ringed the walls. The desk was in one corner, and above it was a bulletin board thick with name tags and notes from past patients. On the wall facing Abby a poster said, "The sign of God is that we are led where we did not mean to go."

On another wall hung a chart of the Twelve Steps of Alcoholics Anonymous. These, Abby vaguely knew, were written by the two men who founded AA and described the steps they took to become sober and stay sober. Idly she read the First Step — "We admitted we were powerless over alcohol — that our lives had become unmanageable." The sentence startled her. "Powerless." "Unmanageable." Terrifying words.

The other members were assembling. Abby already knew that Garrett Owen would be in the group, and he sat down beside her, today in brown leather jacket and designer jeans. "A real sharpie," Abby thought. Larry McGruder came in, and they smiled at each other across the room. There was something poignant, Abby decided, about a man so burly who futilely combed his hair sideways across his bare scalp. She was glad he was there. He, at least, wouldn't attack her. Fern entered and sat in her black chair with its roller wheels. She was a shortish, solid woman in her early sixties with gray hair worn in a bun on top of her head. Her face was benign — a broad, intelligent forehead, rounded cheeks, and smile lines like parentheses framing the mouth. Abby wondered what all the fuss was about. Then she looked into the shrewd blue eyes. "This woman can see right through me," she thought.

The group opened their little red books titled *A Day at a Time.* Abby had already glanced at hers, wondering, "Am I mixed up with Jesus freaks?" One of the men, in a startlingly deep, rich voice, read the reflection for that day. "In the late stages of our addiction, the will to resist has fled. Yet when we admit complete defeat, and when we become entirely ready to try the principles of the Program, our obsession leaves us and we enter a new dimension — freedom under God as we understand Him."

Then the reader said, "My name is Denton and I'm an alcoholic." Around the circle it went: "My name is Paula and I'm an alcoholic and chemically dependent."

Abby thought, " 'Chemically dependent.' That must mean drugs."

". . . My name is Doreen and I'm an alcoholic and chemically dependent." "My name is Marie and I'm an alcoholic and a nurse on the floor"; "I'm Fern Adams, counselor for the group"; "My name is Larry and I'm . . ." In her turn, assuming an air of utter naturalness and ease, Abby said, "My name is Abby and I'm an alcoholic." She was surprised. It came so easily, as though it didn't mean a thing.

The ritual introductions continued around the room, and then Fern said, "Okay, folks. It's your group. Who would like to work?"

There was a pause until Larry McGruder said, "Late last night I got in touch with some things I'd like to share." He went on to say that his wife was a TV addict, and he would actually be jealous of the machine and feel lonely and mad — so he would go outside and smoke pot till the feelings went away. "If it's late at night," he continued, "and I'm in bed and I approach her for romance, and she rejects me, I will lie there and wait for her to fall asleep so I can sneak out into the garage and smoke a joint." His voice became thick as he said, "But it's almost like I *want* her to reject me, so I can have that joint."

"What's going on inside you right now, Larry?" Fern asked.

He rubbed the tops of his thighs with his big hands. "I'm not sure. It's like I should be feeling more than I do. Nervous, I guess. Scared. I've never heard myself say what I just said."

"Can you talk about the fear?" Fern asked.

Larry said, "Maybe I'm scared I'll come unglued."

The man who had done the reading asked, "Larry, what's the worst thing that could happen to you if you came unglued?"

Larry leaned forward, hands gripping each other in his lap. "My last big drunk was about eight years ago at the end of two years of heavy, heavy drinking. I was never sober." He was managing a restaurant, he said, and late one night after a poker game he was alone there to count the day's receipts. "It was like I had separated into two people and I was watching me take a fire ax off the wall and destroy the inside of this restaurant. I smashed every chair and table and wrecked the cigarette machine, the jukebox, the bar. Broke every bottle of booze in the bar. After that I realized I was insane."

Abby was thinking, "That sweet, nice man. An ax! Now *he's* an alcoholic! *I* didn't do anything like that."

"Larry," Fern said, *"you* put that label on yourself. Think of it this way: When I drink, I'm capable of all that and much more. When I'm sober, I'd never do those things. I am a sane person."

Larry flexed his hands. "I've never been able to express anything," he said, "except when I'm drunk — and then it's always anger."

Fern explained, "The anger is a secondary emotion. There are *so* many feelings under that. Guilt. Remorse. Hurt. Loneliness. Low self-esteem. You come across like you're all put together, but I think in your heart of hearts you don't see yourself that way. I suspect there's a lot of anxiety, a lot of energy being expended to keep the lid on. So what are your feelings under that anger?"

"I don't know," Larry answered. Nervously he passed his hand over the top of his head, disarranging the hair covering his bald scalp.

"Think back. Your parents were alcoholic. Remember that you learned at a young age how to adapt to a very destructive situation."

Abby thought, "I never did adapt. I didn't want to adapt."

"We lived above this bar," Larry said, still leaning forward. "My parents used to come home about two or three in the morning. I used to wait up for them." Again he seemed near tears. "I was six or seven. I could hear their footsteps coming up the stairs, and I would be so high with relief and so glad . . ." Sobs choked off his words. Tears were running down his face.

Fern, leaning forward, asked, "What was missing for you, Larry? What did you need from them that you didn't get?"

Abby was angry at Fern — and Larry. Couldn't she see how much he was hurting? Why didn't Larry tell her to lay off?

"I don't know," Larry answered, wiping his face on his sleeve. "I just . . . I never understood how I could feel so good about something and then . . ." His voice choked off, and he put his face in his hands. The room was quiet. After a long moment, he dropped his hands and continued, "My dad used to yell at me, and sometimes he'd beat me and I'd hate him — and I could never get a handle on why he did it. My dad was my best friend. He always talked to me." Larry banged his palm down on his knee. "God, I hate this disease. I do!" Another man skidded a box of Kleenex across the floor to Larry, who wiped his eyes and blew his nose. Calmer now, he said, "I swore I'd *never* be like him. But the *only* reason I quit drinking liquor was because I wrecked that restaurant."

Abby was embarrassed. She had no such dramatic stories to tell.

"And what did you substitute for alcohol?" Fern asked.

"I guess I just switched drugs. Pot left me sort of laid back and accepting."

Marie, the nurse — a small woman with a pert face and frizzy hair — spoke. "I think all of us around this room have the same fear you do. My emotions were shut off for such a long time when I was drinking. I thought if I ever felt anything again, I would go to pieces and nobody would *ever* be able to put me back together. But you've got to give yourself permission to feel. If you do come apart, there are people here who can help. Trust us. Otherwise you'll crawl the walls backwards."

Larry said, "I made a contract with myself that if I didn't share today, I would leave."

"I'm glad you're staying," somebody said. Abby sincerely joined in the chorus of voices — "I'm glad." "I'm glad, too." But she herself wanted to leap from her chair and run out the door and out of Riverside. Did Fern go right around the room? Maybe all this was fine for Larry — but how would public exposure help *her?* She already knew her faults.

The room was silent, and Fern looked quizzically at the circle of faces. Then Abby's terror came true. The piercing blue eyes focused on her, and Fern said, "We have two new members in group today." Fern leaned back in her chair and continued, "Abby, would you like to tell us a little about yourself?"

Nausea rose in Abby's stomach. She *must* not seem nervous, *must* not disgrace herself. She must please Fern, give the right answers and show how eager and healthy she was. Shifting in her chair, uncrossing her legs, folding her hands demurely in her lap, she said, "My name is Abby Andrews and I'm from Worcester. I have a husband who is a stockbroker and three terrific children, a boy ten, a girl fifteen, and a boy seventeen — and I'm very glad to be here."

With a fleeting smile, Fern said, "Welcome to the group. You introduced yourself as an alcoholic. What tells you that you're an alcoholic?"

Abby was feeling giddy again. Her mouth was dry. She filled her voice with sincerity. "I really want to stop drinking and I don't know how. I don't even know whether I'm an alcoholic or not. My husband says I am."

"What made you come to Riverside?"

Abby licked her lips. "I chose it because some acquaintances came here, and I know it's the *best* and that's what I need." Abby looked out at the expressionless faces surrounding her and felt out of sync and alone. She gripped the sides of the chair seat. Staring at the floor, she said, "I guess I felt like the world had come down on my head. Nothing was going right, and I wanted to find out what was wrong. I *should* be happy. I've got a lot. But I'm really sick of feeling lousy all the time."

Fern's face was solemn. "Well, I certainly hope you mean what you say."

Fern turned her attention to Garrett Owen, and Abby switched off, feeling utterly drained. Soon the session ended, and the entire group formed a circle. Holding hands, they recited the Serenity Prayer — "God grant me the serenity to accept the things I cannot change, the courage to change the things I can, and the wisdom to know the difference." Abby cupped her hands slightly so nobody would feel the sweat pouring from her palms.

At dinner Abby was ravenously hungry and added two extra desserts to her tray. Dutifully, she was sitting with three group members. Larry was one, and she noted again the kindness in the blue eyes. But that ax! Another was Denton Rowe, who had done the reading. Abby guessed he was in his forties, and was amazed again at the voice — like an actor's — coming from his narrow, thin-lipped face, with his curly brown hair combed straight back. She discovered he was an Episcopal minister, which, she decided, explained why his nose seemed wrinkled in a permanent sniff — probably from smelling out so much sin. The third was Doreen Sulla, a rounded, blonde nineteen-year-old with a slight upturn at the end of her nose, a full mouth, and large, innocent brown eyes — a sexy milkmaid, Abby thought, in tight jeans and a man's blue shirt. Doreen's habitual tee shirts, Abby heard later, had been banned by Fern.

They were cordial, and Larry asked if she'd been scared in group this afternoon, and Abby answered, "God, yes. I had this picture of myself just *flailing,* pinned on the bulletin board with my hands and feet going in all directions."

"Underneath, Fern's a pussycat," Larry told her.

Abby wondered how he could act so regular and unembarrassed after this morning. "I hope I have the courage to do what you did when my time comes," she answered.

"You won't have much choice," Larry said.

After dinner she cadged a cigarette to smoke and another to hoard. She sat on a sill in the large lounge, one foot up beside her, an arm braced on the bent knee. Her face, pale despite the makeup, looked east across the river. She felt abnormal, like a cripple, like an inmate. She thought about her suitcase ready in the closet. In five minutes she could be out the front door and be normal again. Then she thought about group today, about Larry. Something important had happened to him.

She stayed on the window sill, but dropped the leg and turned back toward the crowded room. She thought what a pea soup of humanity this was. Fascinating. The human dramas! What an experience! Like watching live soap opera. She'd stick around a while longer. "I wouldn't want to miss the next installment," she thought, smiling to herself. And maybe they *would* tell her how to straighten out her life. Maybe she could learn how to drink like other people. And she could borrow cigarette money from Larry.

She left the sill and went down to the relative calm of her small corridor lounge, where she got a cigarette from Doreen Sulla, who was talking to another young woman. Repeatedly glancing at Abby, Doreen raised her voice slightly as she said, "I knew if I waited long enough on a certain corner, this pimp would come by with seven fourteens for me. I've always liked druggies better than drunks. But I like men, period." Doreen shot a quick glance at Abby, and went on, "It's only when I get into a relationship with a man that it doesn't work out. I remember I was living with this guy and I was mixing Equanil and Tylenol fours . . ."

Abby rose and left the room, feeling Doreen's eyes on her. "Why would Doreen want to shock me," Abby wondered. Like some sort of hazing. In her room she sat on the chair by the table and looked around at the barren walls. "If you're going to stay here a while," she thought, "you'll have to perk this place up." Idly she opened one of the required reading books on the desk and started the first paragraph: "Alcoholism is a fatal disease, one hundred percent fatal. Nobody survives alcoholism if it remains unchecked. We would estimate that ten percent of the drinkers in America will become alcoholic, and that . . ." Abby thought, "Holy God," and closed the book.

She lay down on top of the bed and sneaked her hoarded cigarette, knocking the ashes into a half-filled glass of water. Exhausted, she undressed and got into bed. But, once again, almost sick with fatigue and frustration, she could not fall asleep. If only she could have her Valium — now — when the awful thoughts were out of control — fears dancing like devils through her head. What would happen, she wondered, when Fern tried to open her up? Those blue eyes would blow all her circuits. Her brain would stop. She would not understand anything and she'd have no answers and would cry and completely fall apart — and everybody would see that she was an absolute nothing.

But even if they could fix her here, it would be useless. Her children would still hate her. They would say, "It's all been too awful and you're too late." She could not blame them. She'd let everybody down. She didn't deserve to have children. So many promises to Judy broken: the universal promise from birth that a daughter would be mothered. The daily promises: that she'd be picked up at three to go shopping, that the sleeves of the shirt would be shortened, that her parents would get home in time for dinner — like Mother's Day when Judy was twelve.

Judy's present that day was to cook the dinner. Martin and Abby went out for cocktails at a client's house, and Martin, drinking, having a good time, agreed to stay on for dinner. Abby, drunk by now, told herself again and again, "Go to the phone and call Judy." But picturing Judy as usual by the window, watching and waiting, Abby was in a paroxysm of guilt. She could not bring herself to recite the worn-out, lame excuses. Instead of phoning, she drank even more.

They came home at 1 A.M. The dining room table was lovingly set for Judy's dinner — the gold-rimmed china, the formal silverware, the specially ironed linen napkins. The food was neatly covered — spareribs, baked potatoes, salad, a small dessert. At the center of the table was a potted plant. Tucked among its stems and leaves were red hearts cut from a magazine. Leaning against the pot was a handmade Mother's Day card, which said that mothers were always there when needed, that they always understood and shared, always loved. Abby thought, "Jesus Christ, what have I done?" If she had had a gun, she might have shot herself.

Martin, also drunk, paid off the baby-sitter and went upstairs to bed. Abby went to Judy's room. In the darkness Judy's voice, pleading and accusing, cried out, "Mom, where *were* you?" Reeking of alcohol, Abby sat on the edge of the bed and began her empty litany of reasons — how they had gotten tied up, how their host had been using the phone. Judy was silent, hands clutching the covers close around her throat, as though to protect herself. Desperate for some response, Abby tried to hug her, and felt the tears on Judy's cheek. Then Judy turned her head away, a gesture that became permanent.

In her bed at Riverside, Abby wept as she scourged her-

81

CHAPTER

4

THE REST of that week — Wednesday through Friday —
Abby gradually settled into the treatment life. On Wednesday Martin's check for twenty dollars arrived and she immediately cashed it at the business office. She went directly
to the crowded lounge and opened a new pack of cigarettes,
tearing the top just to the stamp, making a little trapdoor
so nothing could fall out. Blissfully she drew the first drag
into her lungs. Leaning back in the chair, exhaling a long
breath of smoke, dressed in her twill pants and turtleneck
sweater — she was the handsome suburban wife and mother
who should have looked out of place. But in that melting
pot of drunks, the telltale marks were there at the corners
of the mobile mouth, beside the full-lidded eyes, webbed
across the forehead — the fine and inerasable lines printed
by alcohol and anguish.

After lecture that morning, she unpacked her suitcase and
stuck photographs of the children into the mirror frame above
the bureau. At the tiny gift shop on the first floor, she bought
a stenographer's notebook and mechanical pencil, and looked
through the cards and bought one that said, "It takes courage to grow up and be who we really are." In her room,
admiring herself as an enlightened, conscientious student,
she added it to the gallery in the mirror. But then, survey-
ing the rest of the room with its institutional smoothness of
plaster and plastic, its every angle exact, its indestructible

tidiness, she felt anonymous again. This place would always be a motel.

Later, in group, she sat like a frightened animal, stock-still, hoping to be invisible, terrified that she would say something dumb, use the wrong words, be found out. She told herself not to give them any way to grip her — no handholds, no corners. Look cool and competent. Show compassion and interest. Be very healthy — hair brushed, face scrubbed, clothes fresh, eyes intelligent. Be Fern's prize pupil. Get straight A's. Show her love of the English language by reading the Reflection of the Day — show her perfect inflection, her skill at emphasizing the crucial words. The day she did read, listening to herself, Abby thought, "I know how good I am, and the group knows, and *Fern* knows." And then she wondered why Fern's face stayed expressionless.

On Wednesday in group, Fern gave her and Garrett Owen a work sheet for doing their First Step by writing out their drinking history. Abby glanced up at the Twelve Step poster and reread the First Step: "We admitted we were powerless over alcohol — that our lives had become unmanageable." Abby's stomach contracted. Fern, explaining the value of the First Step, was saying, "What *will* mean something is when you start confronting *yourselves* and getting the garbage out on the floor and sorting through it. You will know if you're in touch with how it really was, because it will hurt. So I wish you a lot of pain, because then something is happening to you."

Abby looked at the circle of solemn faces. Why would this be painful for her? she wondered. She already knew what she'd done. Abby ran her eyes quickly down the page of fifteen questions: " 'Kinds, amounts, and frequency of use' — Well, scotch and rum, but she *can't* expect me to remember how much. 'Insane behavior' — Oh, yeah, that's the time I poured sangria on that guy. But that was *funny*. 'Effect on spirituality' — that doesn't apply because I didn't have any. 'Work' — that doesn't apply. 'Effect on health' — I'm in perfect health. 'Finances' — doesn't apply. I managed on what Martin gave me. 'Effect on sexuality and sex life' — hell, a drink made it all possible." She folded up the paper, thinking, "It'll be a snap."

Increasingly, Abby began sitting in her corridor lounge with members of her group. They gossiped about each other and swapped drinking experiences — their "war stories." Often in the telling, the agony was forgotten, and they could feel again the high, the euphoria. Drawn by his gentleness, Abby often sat with Larry. Once after a lunch, admiring the fresh spring day, he said, "If I wasn't in here, I would have gotten stoned and gone riding on my bicycle."

Abby agreed. "I would have been thinking, 'What a nice day. What could make it better?' "

In the lounge, she enjoyed griping about the number of books they were supposed to read and grumbling about Fern. "I'd be happy to work in group," Abby would announce. "But Fern ignores me. She just rolls her eyes and says, 'It's your group, folks.' If only she'd get on with it. If nothing happens soon, I'm going to see if I can get transferred to another group."

Abby complained constantly that Judy's Parent's Day was only two weeks away and that nobody cared. She told group members, "I've done enough to that girl. I just *can't* let her down now that I'm sober." As nurses padded down the green-walled hallway, their rubber-soled shoes squeaking on the waxed linoleum, Abby would come suddenly out of her room and ask about getting a leave of absence. Her head bent forward, eyes wide and earnest, she would say, "I'm very concerned about my daughter and it's really *important* that I be there." The nurses would say, "That's a long way down the road, Abby. This is still today. Stay in the now."

At first such talk was meaningless. "They should hand out a mumbo jumbo dictionary," Abby thought. But she wanted to understand the treatment process, find the key so she could make it work for her. Soon the lingo — words like sobriety, blaming, self-pity — began to feel good in her own mouth. She enjoyed a little rush of triumph when she spotted symptoms in other patients. When somebody was talking too fast, turning every minute into a nonstop crisis, she could say, "Wow, are you speedy! Slow down. Take it easy."

By Thursday, Abby's third day with Fern Adams, she was feeling perceptive in group, able to judge other patients' honesty. When a woman wept, she thought, "Stop turning on the waterworks to get sympathy." When a man cried, she was moved and impressed. She began approaching Fern after group to ask thoughtful questions. But Fern, answering distractedly, would suddenly tidy her desk and pack her briefcase. Friday morning, after group, Abby spoke to Fern about the Parent's Day emergency, saying "It's a *crucial* day."

Fern, busy at her desk, said absently, "I think Judy knows you're here to get well, and you'll discover that the world runs quite well without you there to organize it."

Abby, furious, thought, "But you don't understand!"

Also on Friday, Abby began venturing into the fearful waters of feedback — but clinging to the safety of treatment phrases, saying, "You're really angry, aren't you." Or, "You looked like you wanted to cry."

That afternoon, Garrett, nervously rubbing his big mustache, his shiny black loafers crossed under the chair, was explaining why he drank out of control. "The reasons are inside me," he said. "I put myself down. I have a low self-image, a lack of confidence."

Blandly, Larry asked, "If you changed all those things, would you be able to drink without a problem?"

"It's very possible," answered Garrett.

Abby thought, "Boy is he kidding himself." She could feel the group's derision and tell that Fern was poised to pounce. Abby, her eyes deep with concern, cut in with the perfect treatment cliché — "Garrett, that makes me really scared for you."

Fern looked across at her and said, "Abby, what's going on with you?"

A pulse began beating in Abby's temple. She felt herself turn inward, huddling deep down within herself. She said, "I don't know. Nothing, I guess."

Fern's voice was kind but firm. "It is impossible to sit here and listen and not have reactions, whether they make sense to you or not. You had better start getting in touch with your feelings." Fern swung back to Garrett. Abby sat perspiring with confusion and fright and defiance. What did Fern mean? It sounded like a threat. Fern must know that she was conning, that she was a phony creep. But so what! They couldn't get at her!

That night, lying in bed, staring upward into the darkness and the silence, Abby heard the same small, insistent voice saying the same words. "Conning." "Phony." She'd conned everybody — her friends, her parents, maybe even Martin. Not just about the drinking. They were always telling her, "You're very smart. You could do anything you wanted." But now, here, people were going to find out the truth she'd always known — that she was actually stupid. And Fern would decide she wasn't worth saving. What if the group told her, "Sorry, this is just a waste of our time. We're tired of you" — and everything piddled away into nothing and she had to face . . .

And Martin and the children were coming to visit tomorrow afternoon. She had avoided talking to them on the telephone, but now they would be there in person, bringing with them, like mud on their shoes, all the old awfulness. She could hardly deal with treatment. She couldn't possibly deal with *them*. "I want to scream," she thought, and imagined SCREAM printed on the darkness.

After lunch on Saturday, Abby paced the large lounge, sitting, standing, getting coffee, looking out the windows at the front sidewalk, moving to another chair. Then the elevator doors opened, and Martin and the children were there. As Frederick ran to her, she kneeled and received him, the bony arms hard as pipes around her neck, his cheek soft against hers. Abby's chest ached as if he had collided with her heart.

Holding on to one of his hands, she stood up to greet the other three. Martin kissed her cheek, carefully, as though afraid she might break apart. Evan said, "Hi, Mom," but he was looking past her into the lounge, and Abby thought she could read his mind: "That's a bunch of drunks in there, and my mother's one of them." Stabbed by guilt, she thought, "He's got some nerve; he's using drugs himself." Judy's face — a smooth echo of Abby's — was smiling, but her eyes were studying her mother, searching, Abby thought, for signs of change. "You look great, Mom," said Judy.

Abby wondered, "Does she mean it?" Guiding them into the lounge, Abby made an expansive sweep with her arm. "Well, folks," she said, "here it is. On a clear day you can see heaven — with side trips to the frozen tundra." As though eager to escape, Evan dragged Judy to the empty Ping-Pong table. That was Frederick's chance. He pulled his mother to a couch, leaving Martin standing awkwardly alone.

"Why are you here?" he demanded, his body tense. "I don't understand why you can't come home. Dad says you're sick. What's the matter with you? You look swell."

Abby took one of his hands. Her eyes were sad. "I have a disease called alcoholism," she said. "I drink too much and it's ruining my life. I'm trying to learn to live without it."

"I don't understand how something that you drink can make you have a disease."

Abby had no answer. She pulled him to her, and felt his body reluctantly go supple and fit itself to hers. She said, "Frizzer, when I get out, I'll have much more time for you and we'll play games and I'll take you to movies on Friday night and we'll go back to Martha's Vineyard. You've got all that to look forward to." She added, almost to herself, "I'll be the mother you thought you had."

She looked past Frederick at Martin. Standing there, the plumpish face ill at ease, the light hair drifting onto his high forehead, he did not appear so very dangerous. Without the bookkeeper look of his half-glasses, he seemed, in fact, almost vulnerable. But she could feel the fright inside her. She knew he could confuse her sense of what was real and what was imagined — convince her that she had no intelligence or abilities — until she would be finally and forever lost. Simultaneously, she felt a kind of joy in being at Riverside, on her turf, not his turf — free of his program for controlling her life, free of his everlasting martyrdom.

Abby rose. Hand in hand with Frederick she walked toward Martin, thinking that he was probably jealous of her with Frederick. Launching into small talk, she gave Martin no openings for intimacy. She thanked him for the money and apologized for not telephoning. There had been something scheduled every minute. She asked how the baby-sitter was working out. Who had offered casseroles. Where Frederick would sleep on Martin's Rotary night. Martin told her, "We're managing. It's going just fine. Don't worry. Judy is a godsend."

Now the family group headed down the corridor to see Abby's room. Abby put an arm around Judy and felt the elastic plumpness of the shoulder. "I'm really glad you came," Abby said, sensing the person inside that skin, barely blooming, still connected but tilting away toward independent life. She wondered what Judy would be like then, and noticed that her daughter had grown almost as tall as she was.

At the same time, ashamed of her offenses against this child — queasy, nervous — she wondered how to make an overture and begin to wipe the slate. She continued, "Don't let those men dump a lot of chores on you. Women aren't the only experts with a mop."

Judy answered, "Don't worry about anything, Mom. We're okay. You concentrate on getting well."

Abby felt rebuffed. Judy had refused to admit their female solidarity. Abby pushed on, saying, "They're trying to teach us here to forgive ourselves for the things we've done.

We wouldn't have done those things if we'd been sober."

"Mom, I know," Judy said. But her head was down, eyes on the floor. Abby, full of self-disgust, feeling unlovable, asked herself, "Why won't she talk to me?"

They entered her room, and Abby was embarrassed by its hospital barrenness. She did not want them to feel sorry for her. The family distributed themselves — Frederick up on the window sill, Martin on the small desk table, Judy on the bed, Abby leaning against the wall. Evan stood in the middle of the floor. "Going through this, Mom, will be terrific for you," he said. "Everything will be much better." Abby recognized the stance: narrow shoulders back, head cocked, the usually supple body stiffened and held slightly sideways — "The body language," she thought, "only a mother can know and hate. He's riding high — with his spurs on."

Evan was saying, "I knew how much you were drinking and I was really worried and I wanted to say something, but I knew you'd deny it and we'd have a fight."

Abby was thinking, "I get it. You're puffing away on grass, but you're not bad enough to land in a rehabilitation center." She almost fought back, saying, "Yeah, yeah, Evan. Let's have two words about me and one about yourself." But she mustn't appear angry at her son's honesty and concern. That would prove she was defensive and unreasonable. That would make them *right*. She said sweetly, "Thank you, Evan. I'm glad you support my decision."

To fill the vacancy between them, Abby began telling about treatment — about the lectures and the group and the other members and Fern. Looking at the four blank faces, she knew that her words about feedback and disease and the Twelve Steps meant nothing. She felt herself on a path that had taken her far away. She longed to have her words make sense, to have her family see that the angry reflexes could stop, that they could learn to lay down their weapons. But the faces remained unreadable. Abby's talk of self-image and powerlessness trailed off.

She said her good-byes to the family at the elevator. As the doors closed she waved, refusing to cry, her jaw rigid as cement. They were reentering the real world, leaving her floating far above in her green capsule. But when she turned back toward the lounge, she felt suddenly that this place was her reality. Her own home was shadowy and foreign. Looking around the large room at the motley crowd of alcoholics and drug addicts, Abby realized something else. She belonged here. She was deeply comfortable in this family of strangers, sharing the same guilts and crazy behaviors. In this rock-bottom world, anything could be said. Nobody was judged. Nothing was surprising. For the first time in her life, she did not have to work for acceptance. Abby decided that tonight she would unpack the suitcase stashed in her closet. She was sick of hauling it out every time she got dressed.

She walked to the window to watch the family leave. Evan and Frederick were already on the lawn, running. Somehow the race of impressions in Abby's head threw the scene below into slow motion — Evan gradually throwing the ball, a leap that hung in the air, arm back, long hair slowly bouncing — Frederick out ahead, looking back, laughing. They seemed so young and healthy and free, so untouched by pain and tawdriness. Through Abby's muscles surged the memory of schoolgirl field hockey, the feel of running — flying really — flat out to her limit and then finding a sudden burst of extra speed, of new strength — energy unlimited, life unfettered. And she could remember her certainty that everything in life turns out well.

She felt a rush of mother love. They were *hers*. They deserved better than she had given, deserved a good mother, not a mess. "If only I can be an example to my kids," she thought. "Maybe if I don't drink . . . maybe if Martin and I can . . ." Her eyes filled with tears. "I've got to make it." Then to Abby's own amazement, there came a wholly unexpected thought. "God's got to help me because *I'm* getting nowhere."

Abby left the large lounge, went to her room, tried to read, went to the small lounge. Doreen was there. Her rounded face with its upturned nose was flushed as she sounded off to Larry and the world at large: "Will somebody please tell me what they want in this place? Nothing makes any goddamn sense." Abby was immediately irritated. She knew that feeling of confusion all too well, but recoiled from anything in common with that girl.

Returning to her room, Abby decided to start work on her First Step. "The sooner I get going," she told herself, "the sooner I'll get it over with." At the little formica-topped table, she began reading the sheet of questions and her eyes stopped at the line: "Effects on character — list thirty values important to you and give examples of how you have compromised them as a result of your usage."

Suddenly Abby's mind was swirling with indictments — "ignoring — lying — people's feelings — the law — kids' needs — taking advantage . . ." Now the whirlpool was sucking her down toward unbearable horrors. She flipped the sheet of paper over and slapped her hand down on top of it. In a moment her head calmed and she thought, "I'll do it later."

Looking for fellow patients who could make her feel sensible and sane, Abby wandered into the big lounge. Kerry was with an older woman wearing rimless glasses and a teacherish air. Abby joined them. Kerry made the introductions: "Klair, this is Abby." Klair was saying, "It's so awful to be a woman and an alcoholic — the hiding you have to do, the denying — it really grinds your insides."

"Yes," Abby said. "That used to make me so mad."

"What made *me* mad was the unfairness," Klair continued. "It was okay for the men to be at the bar having fun. I was stuck at home. My husband and I had equal status till we got married, and then all of a sudden, plop!"

Abby said, "I got sick of being the bad guy in everybody's book. If I hadn't been drinking, I wonder who they would have blamed?"

Kerry frowned, her narrow forehead wrinkling. "My father used to always tell me, 'Be a lady. Nice girls don't do this; nice girls don't do that.' But when I started to drink, I began to steal, so I felt like I was . . ." Her voice trailed off.

Abby lit a cigarette, inhaling deeply, releasing the smoke with a small sigh. "My mother was always telling me, 'There is a proper, ladylike way to drink.' " Abby laughed ruefully. "But I wanted to drink like a man so I could be with the men."

"When I stole," Kerry said, "I had to be high. I couldn't do it sober."

Abby went on, "My mother said I was terribly weak if I couldn't stop drinking. She said if I had some willpower, I could get a grip on myself. But, of course, she didn't understand that to keep on drinking no matter *what,* takes *real* willpower."

On Monday, May tenth, Abby began her second week in Riverside and her first full week in Fern's group. In morning group that day, a beautiful young girl, Paula Christy, a fashion model, gave her First Step. As Paula read it aloud, her long fingers holding up the spiral notebook, Abby studied the unlined face. This girl couldn't be much over twenty. And that silver-gray hair. People who looked like that weren't supposed to have problems. From time to time a particular line would surge into Abby's consciousness — Paula saying, ". . . and at seventeen I was out every night and had three to six vodkas." Then in Abby's head would play her private home box office of film strips starring Abby Andrews: Abby at sixteen, helplessly drunk and sick, crawling up the front stairs; her mother shouting down at her, "What have you been doing, young lady? You're a disgrace!" Sitting there in Fern's group, Abby wondered, "Was I an alcoholic *then?* No. Not so early. But I couldn't remember anything afterwards. Was that a blackout?"

Paula was continuing, "To buy marijuana for me and my

boyfriend, I took two hundred dollars from his father's bureau." Now the film showed Abby in a boutique changing booth, stuffing a pair of slacks into her bag and saying to herself, "I buy a lot of clothes here. They'll never miss these."

Paula was talking about large modeling fees and cocaine at the age of nineteen, and parties, and giving away clothes and jewelry and cocaine to make people accept her. She described her bookings going down and down, and everything blamed except drugs and alcohol.

From her seat down the line from Paula, Abby looked at the astonishing hair, pulled down like curtains across the pearly cheeks and fastened behind the long neck. "My God," Abby thought. "Nothing shows!"

Soon Paula was talking about loss of moral values. She had fallen in love with a top fashion photographer named Phil and moved in with him. "I was just someone he could have and use," she said, "and I drank even more when he went away on assignments because I knew he'd be with another model. I lied to him practically every day. We fought every time we used alcohol and I have a foul mouth when I'm drunk and it cuts like a knife. And when Phil would say, 'Forget it,' and start to walk off, I'd throw something and he would grab me to stop me."

"Sounds like Martin," Abby thought. "Hurray for Paula." In her head she was watching her film of Martin shutting her off — his closed expression, the shrugged shoulders, the maddening slow turn of his body that left her marooned, trembling with unexploded tirades, with helplessness, with fear.

Paula was saying, ". . . and then we'd kick and fight, and I'd wake up with bruises all over my arms and legs, and he'd have scratches on his face. I'd have to cancel all my bookings for two weeks and heal myself."

Abby remembered the night Martin had locked himself in the bedroom and she had attacked the door with a carving knife. She could see herself again collapsed on the floor, weeping; and see the rage and terror and exhaustion in Martin's face as he stood in the open doorway, looking down. She had been overcome with terror. Would he hit her? Would he hurt her? But simultaneously, her constant guilt was saying almost soothingly, "Maybe now you'll get the punishment you deserve." And another voice was saying triumphantly, "Yippee, you finally got a reaction." The next morning she had covered the slash marks on the door with Christmas cards — "Joyeux Noël."

"We'd always say," continued Paula, " 'It's the booze, and we'll never do it again.' But I still didn't feel wanted. I still didn't feel loved. And that came out in violence. In three weeks it would happen again — a continual thing, almost planned — and we'd wake up the next morning holding each other, like two little lost kids, crying."

When Paula finished, there was silence. Abby's face, as it had throughout, showed only mild curiosity and surprise. The silence continued and suddenly Abby heard herself break her usual studied control and blurt out her own vital question: "When Phil hurt you, why didn't you leave him?"

Paula turned toward her, the illusive arrogance of her face odd beside her words. "I never seemed to have the courage. I wanted to go work in Europe. But then I'd be alone and have to take responsibility and work harder — sell myself. I was scared. I told myself I really loved Phil."

Abby asked another important question. "Have a lot of people told you that you're irresponsible?"

"Yes."

Fern said, "I bet you've got a lot of company in this room."

Abby could hear her mother: "All you care about is doing what you want to do. Abby, why can't you cooperate? If you would only cooperate."

There was more feedback from around the circle: "There will always be another Phil." "You're treating chemicals as a fad." "Get out of modeling." Paula rebutted: "Believe me, I'm frightened. I know I'm powerless against alcohol. I *know* it! But I'll join a therapy group in New York. I'll take some courses and get a high school diploma. I'll keep very busy. I love my career too much to quit. I feel like the balloon is going up and if I don't grab it, I'll miss something."

For a moment nobody spoke. Then Fern said, "Group, I'd like each one of you to write down in your notebooks one adjective that describes Paula for you." After a minute, one by one, the group members spoke their words — "unrealistic," "dishonest," "stubborn," "unhappy," "foolish." Fern, the last, said, "I agree with all of you. And I've cheated. I've put down two words. 'Immature.' 'Superficial.' " Facing Paula, she continued, "I'm very concerned whether you're going to make it or not. You say the right words. You say what you think we want to hear."

Abby's right moccasin began slowly circling in the air.

"But from where I sit," Fern continued, "I see you as a young woman completely unaware of how sick she is. You talk about alcohol, but you don't talk much about cocaine. You say, 'I really know.' But in modeling you're playing in big league dope circles. It's a way of life. If you don't use, you'll be out of step, and I'm not sure you can handle that. Women drug addicts get used and abused. I worry about you getting beat up again. I worry about the day you lose your looks. Ask yourself, what will you have then — except your addiction."

Intensely aware of the skin on her own face, Abby saw her face superimposed on Paula's, the two of them aging as she watched. She saw herself become what she had dreaded most — messy, blowzy, an object of disgust and boredom, a has-been broad.

Fern said, "Paula, here's the bottom line: To what lengths are you willing to go to stay straight?"

Paula licked her perfect lips. "I don't know," she answered.

When the group let out, Abby, upset, hurried down the crowded hall. In the past she would have been rushing for a drink. But now she did not know what to do about these disturbing emotions she could not identify. At the nurses' station a man in a sweat suit was saying, "We don't need this treatment, we need volleyball lessons." Abby grinned to herself, but was suddenly frantic to escape all this, even for a few minutes. The chapel. There was time before lunch. She took the elevator to the second floor and pushed through the two wide doors.

It was like wading into a warm lake of silence. In front of her, silhouetted against a plain brick wall, was the white altar, a gigantic block of marble. To its left, suspended from the wall, a single candle burned in a red glass cylinder. The side walls were entirely stained glass, and the setting sun flooded in from the right, casting a long, iridescent mosaic across the floor and rows of chairs. Abby sank down in the first seat of the second row and let the peace wash over her head.

It brought memories of the peace she had felt in the apple tree she had climbed as a child, the long branch that dipped like a saddle, a horn in front, a rise behind, two stirrup branches below for her feet. She called that spot, high and secure among the branches, "my comfortable place" and thought of it as a horse — white, of course — that transported her into dreams — long hair glittering with diamonds, beautiful dresses that sparkled. And there was another dream: to have parents who liked each other.

Now, in the chapel, old anxieties splintered the calm. She remembered the tension, electric in the air, when her mother and father had exchanged their glares and clenched their lips. She remembered the tension along her spine and the blackness of her terror — the sense of dangling by a thread above a void. If her parents were divorced and she lost her father forever, the thread would snap, plunging her downward into even greater loneliness. She always ran to her tree, to her comfortable place, and threw herself forward, hugging the limb and talking to her tree, telling it her terrible fears until she felt the relief and the quiet that always came. Sitting

97

in the chapel, Abby wondered whether she would ever again find that soul's ease.

Abby's thoughts moved to her father. She could hear again the five o'clock whistle that meant he would be home in fifteen minutes. She could remember his happy look when he saw her, when he watched her ride her bike and asked about school and wanted to be with *her*. She was never afraid of him. But there was another memory: her father old and a little senile, abusing her mother. Abby could hear her own scolding voice afterward, out in the driveway, calling him a stubborn old fool. Two months later he was dead. In the chapel, her eyes were wet. She murmured aloud, "I'm so *sorry*." But she was also angry. Why did he have to leave her all alone?

At lunch she sat with Larry. Paula joined them. Abby was immediately tense. Should she say something about group this morning? But what? Fern had been so tough — and was right to be. Feeling a little like a mother speaking to a formidable child, Abby asked her, "Do you ever get just blotto from facts? Yesterday, I think I filled my floppy disk. How long have you been here?"

"Five weeks."

Abby's heart sank. "Why so long?"

Paula looked quickly at Abby. "I thought *everybody* knew. I used coke in my second week and they let me start over again."

"Oh," said Abby feebly, embarrassed. To her relief, it was time for lecture. In the auditorium, she sat with a new member of Fern's group — Julia Waugh — a tall, middle-aged, round-shouldered woman with graying hair and a small potbelly that pushed out her denim skirt. When Abby asked the ritual questions, Julia's eyes slid away, avoiding. She was from Scarsdale, New York, was married to a lawyer, and had a son in college. Noticing the alcoholic puffiness of her face, and feeling like an old-timer in treatment, Abby smiled radiantly and said, "Welcome to the club."

The lecturer began: "In the real world we were never taught

to identify our feelings — glad, sad, mad, hurt, lonely. But even if our heads didn't know we were having an emotion, our bodies were feeling a whole lot of things."

Abby shook her head, thinking, "I've always known how I felt. Right now I'm feeling really antsy-pantsy."

Walking down the hall to afternoon group, Abby fell in step with Garrett Owen, today in a pink, formfitting shirt under a Levi jacket. She smiled and said, "The hot seat awaits us." He laughed grimly. In the room Abby took her accustomed chair, diagonally distant from Fern. The reflection for the day was read by Frank Ruyter, a nice-looking man in his forties with short brown hair, black horn-rimmed glasses, and an air of diffidence. Holding the book, his hands trembled slightly. "As the doubter tries the process of prayer, he would do well to add up the results. If he persists, he'll almost surely find more serenity, more tolerance, less fear, and less anger."

After the ritual introductions around the circle — "My name is Abby and I'm . . ." — there was the usual anxious silence. Doreen plunged in, speaking rapidly, breathlessly. "I would like to talk before I have time to cop out. I've conned a lot of people. I mean I feel like I've been cheating on the group." She paused and looked around the circle of friendly eyes. Taking a deep breath, she continued, "After I promised you I'd stop telephoning the guy I was living with, I was kind of available and I gave somebody on the second floor the impression I wanted a relationship." She stopped again, looking at Fern, who said nothing.

Abby had been examining Doreen — the long blonde hair, the sultry mouth turned down at the corners, the huge brown eyes. Abby's gaze shifted to the rounded body. "Men must adore a build like that," she thought. "I was so skinny and geeky. But in ten years she'll be absolutely over the top."

Doreen, after shifting in her chair, went on, still speaking fast. "I talked a lot with Larry last night 'cause I didn't like the feelings I was having about it. I felt so low about myself — even though the guy and I didn't do anything. Larry said I should tell the group and I'd feel better."

Now Fern spoke, her voice quiet. "What are you feeling right now, Doreen?"

"I feel like I really want to sink right through the floor."

Fern said, "Doreen, that isn't a feeling. Anybody want to help her out?"

Doreen shot back, "Well, *that's* the way I *feel.*"

Denton Rowe, his nose in its perpetual sniff, said, "Any sentence with a 'that' or a 'like' in it doesn't give a true feeling. Feelings are mad, glad, sad . . ."

There was a long pause. "Well," Doreen said, her voice still belligerent, "I feel really lousy. Is that a feeling?"

"Okay," Fern said. "Keep going."

Mollified, Doreen said, "I guess I feel guilty. Talking to Larry I figured out this is the first time I didn't have booze or pills to blame it on. That's really scary."

"You're being straight with us today," Fern said, "and I want to give you a lot of support for that."

Doreen continued. "I thought at first I did want to have a relationship. But I think now I only wanted what my boyfriend doesn't give me." She stopped again and looked at the floor, breathing rapidly.

Denton Rowe's ministerial voice broke the silence in the room. "Doreen, what did you want?" he asked.

She looked up toward Denton, her full lower lip quivering, her large eyes glistening. "I wanted to be held and to be wanted and comforted — to feel like somebody didn't need to screw me to care about me. The only affection I've ever gotten has been from guys who went to bed with me."

Abby's heart ached. She could feel her own desolation when she reached out to Martin for tenderness that did not come. She could feel the defeat and violation after empty sex — lying there in the dark wondering if it would ever be beautiful again, wondering why the drinks had not helped her to lose herself.

Garrett Owen was saying, "Seems like you needed that guy just like you've needed a drink."

"Yeah," Doreen answered, "I figured out when I don't have something I want, I put something else — like drugs — in its place."

"Okay," Fern said. "If you've learned something from this, it's worth the pain. Maybe you've learned that you set yourself up to be hurt and to be used — and then turn to chemicals because you feel so lousy and ashamed. But this time you've handled your problem differently. That's called growth."

Abby was envious. If only she could figure out things about herself — and say them — and be complimented by Fern.

Fern continued with Doreen, saying, "After this I would like you to be aware that you reinforce your low self-worth with your behavior, even here in treatment." Fern smiled. "But I think that's enough for today. You've done good work, and I hope you'll think about the things you've said today. I believe that everything that happens in this treatment center is just a microcosm of how you handle things outside. Not just you. Everybody. If you can learn from what you do or don't do in here, if you can begin doing something different, that's altering the old behavior that set you up for the use of chemicals. Now, Doreen, will you make a contract with me? Will you choose one person from this group who you will talk to the next time you are lonely."

"Okay."

"Who would you like to pick?"

"Abby Andrews."

"Good," said Fern, glancing at Abby with a half smile.

After group ended, after the holding hands and the final prayer — "God grant me the serenity to accept the things I cannot change . . ." — Abby moved quickly out of the room ahead of Doreen, and catching up with Paula Christy, started an animated conversation about modeling. While

Paula told her that she was a runway model who did high fashion, Abby glanced furtively back to check that Doreen was far behind. At the elevators Abby headed for the kitchen and coffee, after noting that Doreen was going to the small lounge. Abby felt shy and awkward, astonished, elated. Doreen had chosen *her*. Doreen must consider her stable and reassuring even here in treatment. Doreen trusted her. Nobody had done that for a long time.

Abby was buoyant the rest of the day. At dinner she was "just meeting and greeting and glad-pattying around," as she called it. At the evening lecture she felt like a truant schoolgirl as she passed a note to Paula Christy — "Why don't they talk about the mice in our heads?"

Only one fragment of the lecture made an impression — the speaker saying, "I am addicted to changing my mood. I am even addicted to chemicals I have never tried, and ultimately it doesn't make any difference to me whether I drink or snort or shoot my drug of choice. I just want to alter my mood, change the way I feel."

After the lecture Abby went to the small lounge and sat in her favorite spot: the motel-modern sofa against the inside wall, facing the row of windows and the billowing treetops against the open sky. She put her head back and let the top of the sponge-rubber cushion press against the tension in her neck. She lifted her legs onto the blond wood coffee table and lit a cigarette — the delicious first pull into the lungs, the releasing sigh.

Larry came into the room and Abby smiled at him and brushed invisible crumbs from the place beside her. She wondered, as he sat down, whether the sun or alcohol caused the red web of capillaries in his cheeks. She asked about the business problems that she knew had worried him. After a while he suggested a game of backgammon, and Abby, sucking in her cheeks with girlish concentration, threw double sixes twice and won and laughed at Larry's mock outrage.

Then, suddenly, she felt utterly depleted. A nameless depression was moving in on her. She excused herself. "I'd

better go do my homework like a good little freshperson."
In her room she considered starting her First Step. She was
too tired. She'd do it tomorrow. Abby lay on the bed, looking up at the ceiling, smoking, the half glass of water perched
precariously on the coverlet. Things were happening for the
others. They seemed hooked into something. She was getting nowhere in treatment, spinning her wheels in mud.
Why? She was being what people always said they wanted —
polite, mature, dignified — a well person. But they didn't
seem to want that here. "Damned if you do, damned if you
don't," she thought.

There must be a key that would make everything fall into
place. So why didn't Fern explain it to her? Could the group
help? No. They were too different from her. They could never
really understand her. Why was she being allowed to sit there
wasting time and money? What was going to happen that
would keep her from drinking again? She was like Kerry.
She didn't belong anywhere. If she went home, she could
not survive Martin without the help of alcohol. If she did
not go home, how would she live? If she stayed, nothing
would happen but more of this limbo of no action. She tried
to pray, but could not find the words. Everything sounded
stupid in her mind.

The next morning, Tuesday, the routine delivered Abby
into Fern's room. On that day the public-address system
suddenly announced, "Abby Andrews, report to the nurses'
station. Abby Andrews . . ." She rose, her stomach muscles clenching — "What's wrong?" — and left the room.

At the nurses' station, in his white smock, stood Dr.
Richardson. He smiled, but Abby saw no cheer in the eyes
behind the glasses. They went to her room, and Dr. Richardson took the chair. Abby sat on the side of the high hospital bed, clutching her notebook in her lap. Her dangling
feet did not reach the floor. She felt lilliputian, like a very
small child facing a frightening teacher. Dr. Richardson
crossed his legs, rested his clipboard on his knees and stud-

103

ied Abby. He said conversationally, "Well, how's it been going?"

Abby could feel the tension across her shoulders, the burning in her stomach, sharp as hunger. She thought, "This is it. The long arm of the law." She answered aloud, "Well, fine, I guess. But nothing much is happening."

"What should be happening?"

"I don't really know," Abby said. "But *something*. I feel ignored. I know Fern is supposed to be a terrific counselor, but she just sits there and gives me these funny little looks."

"Can she make treatment happen for you?" The doctor's voice was flat, his round face inscrutable.

Abby thought, "He's telling me I have to do it myself." She felt a surge of panic, which she tried to mask, saying, "I'm just worried I'll pass through treatment and nothing will change and it won't work." The inside of her right elbow began flexing nervously.

"What will happen if it doesn't work?"

Abby thought, "Jesus, he's relentless." She said, "I'll go back home and Martin will start in on me and I'll drink again."

"I see. That's interesting. Tell me about Martin. How do you feel when you're with him?"

"I feel really uncomfortable a lot of the time."

"Why do you feel uncomfortable?"

Thinking, "I don't feel too comfy right now," Abby answered, "He is constantly judging me, constantly wanting me to be different from what I am. So I'm constantly changing my behavior to suit him." Abby felt a surge of relief. It felt good speaking honestly about Martin — after days of being dishonest about herself. She added, "I'm damned if I'm going to be some little badminton birdy going whiz whiz at the whim of Martin Andrews."

There was no sympathetic smile from the doctor. "Then why do you keep changing your behavior for him?" he asked.

"Because I'm afraid of him. I'm afraid if I don't conform

to whatever mold he wants to put me in, then he'll be sarcastic and cut me down and load all the dice against me."

"Does that remind you of anybody else, Abby?"

"No. It doesn't."

"Can you think of anybody else who does the same thing?"

"Yes, my mother. All my life I have been trying to make things come out right with her, make three go into two, customize myself — but it was never enough because it was never her way."

"Well, how do you feel, Abby, when Martin and your mother don't do what *you* want? Do you try to change them? Do you try to prove to them that they are actually wrong and you are right — and if only they would do things your way . . . ?"

As this line of questioning continued, targeting on a devastating truth, Abby, unable to squirm away, became furious. She hated this man. She wanted to run. Her voice was louder as she told the doctor, "He doesn't have to treat me like a shrine and fall at my feet. I just want a mutual peace."

"On whose terms?"

Abby rode through the question. "I just want to be listened to and understood and accepted the way I am."

"Abby, do you ever deliberately act in a way that will push Martin away and cut off communication?"

"That's ridiculous, I . . ." She stopped. This was a new idea. For just a second, she glimpsed the immensity of her problems, of the damage, of the changes that must take place. Pain flooded through Abby and her head swam and again she wanted to run.

"What are you afraid of with Martin?" Dr. Richardson asked.

"I don't trust him."

"Why don't you trust him?"

"Because, when I open up to him, he treats me like a child." She could not explain to this man about punishing

Martin by withholding her feelings — and how it was when sometimes she broke her resolve and confided deep feelings. Then Martin ridiculed her and she was furious with herself for betraying herself. Later when Martin looked at her, she would think, "Now he knows my secrets. Now he's judging me."

"Isn't there somebody else you don't trust?" Dr. Richardson asked.

"My mother." Abby's face was clenched and her throat ached from the effort of holding back the tears. She must not cry, she must not humble herself by being weak, by showing how much she hurt.

"Why don't you trust her?"

"She's always trying to catch me off base so she can tag me."

"Is there anybody else you don't trust?"

"No."

"I think there's still somebody else," said Dr. Richardson, almost casually.

"I don't know," Abby said frantically. Dr. Richardson was silent. She could feel a pressure building inside her, something she could not identify, but too large to contain. The tears sprang loose and streamed down her face. "Fern!" she exclaimed. "That's it. Fern. I don't trust her either." But the pressure was still growing inside.

"I agree," Dr. Richardson said. "You probably have not trusted Fern — or the group." So far his manner had been almost placid. Now he leaned forward. His voice was urgent. "But, Abby, who is it you *really* don't trust? What are you *really* afraid of?"

Then she understood. "*ME!*"

Dr. Richardson leaned back. "And what are you going to do about it?"

Out of control, shaking with sobs, Abby stood up. She slammed her notebook onto the desk. She shouted, "All right, I'll deal with it! Right now!" She charged out the door and down the hall. She flung open Fern's door and saw a flash of startled faces. Saying, "Excuse me," she grabbed a chair, dragged it bumping across the floor, and sat down facing Fern.

Bending forward, arms on her knees, hair swinging out around her hot cheeks, Abby blurted out in one long breath, "I have just come from Dr. Richardson. And I want you to know that I've been saying that you weren't helping me — that you didn't care about my recovery. I've been blaming you and everybody else — and actually it's been *me!* I have never shared anything about me because I have never trusted you. And the reason I haven't trusted you is because I haven't trusted anybody in my whole life — and the reason for that is I don't trust *myself.*" Days — years — of hidden feelings had been swelling in her throat and they now released themselves into more tears. She covered her offending eyes while shouting inside, "Stop it! Stop it! You're out of control again." But the other voice was saying, "At last. Let it come."

Fern's face had become softer, almost tender. "I know," she said. "I know that. I've been very concerned about you." She smiled. "But this is a beginning."

CHAPTER

5

AFTER GROUP, Abby returned to her room and sat on the bed, arms crossed as though hugging herself. Something extraordinarily important had happened and she wanted to savor the moment. She had spoken a dangerous truth and nobody had recoiled, nobody had put her down. In fact, people had drawn closer. After the session, group members came to her and patted her on the back and said, "Congratulations" and "Thank God" and "We thought it would never happen." Larry put his arms around her and said, "Welcome to the group." It was such a paradox. What had seemed so hard, and promised only pain and problems, had made everything easier.

Enjoying her unfamiliar feeling of lightness and freedom, Abby decided that the worst might be over. Maybe treatment would be smoother sailing now. Maybe her life would change and Martin and she could work things out. But then the scene in Fern's group came back, the tears, the self-exposure. Had she made a fool of herself again? Abby pushed away that thought. No, she had done what she was supposed to do — and was going to let herself be glad.

She breezed through that day in high spirits, only mildly interested and even less comprehending when the evening lecturer discussed the four stages of recovery. "The first," he said, "is the admission that you are an alcoholic. In our definition here, an alcoholic is somebody whose personal, social, or business life is being damaged by alcohol, and who will not or cannot do anything about it. The second stage of recovery is compliance, passively going along with treatment, while inwardly defying and denying. The third is acceptance, the realization that alcoholism is not a failure of moral fiber, but a chronic, fatal disease. The fourth is surrender, the visceral certainty that you are powerless against alcohol and cannot control your addiction by yourself, without help."

That evening in the lounge, leaning back in the sofa, her moccasins up on the coffee table among the mugs, Abby sat with Julia Waugh. Abby liked this tall, angular woman with the nicotine-stained fingers and small potbelly. Julia was smart. And once you got behind the air of sadness, and got used to the eyes that slid away from contact, she could be fun. Tonight they were swapping drinking experiences and laughing at the insanity of it all — Abby giggling about the night she drove into a tree by a friend's driveway. ". . . and I went right up to the dinner table and announced, 'Damn it, Grace, you had your driveway relandscaped and you didn't tell your friends.' And everybody thought I was kidding."

They laughed, too, about hiding places for bottles, Julia saying, ". . . but my hands always shook so badly, the bottle would hit the tin air duct and sound like thunder, and I'd be sure my husband could hear it." Gleefully they remembered tormenting their keeper husbands. "I'd fill a scotch bottle with tea and then pour out a drink," Abby said, "and watch Martin go out of his mind."

The next day, Wednesday, May twelfth, the euphoria had gone. Walking down the sterile hall to group, her spiral notebook clasped to her chest, Abby could feel the anxiety humming along her nerves. What other, even more horrible truths were they going to wring out of her? Sitting in her chair, feeling vulnerable, longing for a cigarette, Abby thought, "What can I possibly do for an encore?"

In the room was a former patient from Fern's group, Stanley Morris, back for a refresher week after three months of sobriety. He was a man in his fifties with a large, sweeping forehead but narrow jaw. She thought of him as Turnip Head, and scolded herself for unkindness. She had disliked him from the first day he appeared in the small lounge, talking about his recovery — so smug, she thought, like an old grad giving the received gospel to the freshmen. Halfway through this group session, he was giving feedback to a new young member, Jerold Steele, a tall, shy young man in his early twenties, with a long jaw and acne on hollow cheeks. Stanley was saying, "Nothing happened for me until I understood that booze was my problem, not the answer to my problem. To get out of prison you have to realize you're in prison."

Rage vibrated in Abby's head. She had had enough of this self-important, pontificating know-it-all. They wanted her to be honest? Okay, she'd *be* honest! She spoke out, "Stan, I don't like your coming back here after only three months and acting like you've got it all together and are so smart and are going to cure us all."

"Hold it!" Fern exclaimed, swiveling toward Abby. "What's going on with you?"

"I'm just fed up with him being so self-righteous." She could feel her hands trembling.

Paula chimed in. "I agree with Abby. I've felt Stan has been trying to control me, and I don't like that."

"Maybe so," Fern said. "But what's that anger *really* about, Abby?"

Silent, fighting for composure, Abby looked down. Then she said resentfully, "He's just like my husband."

"Okay," Fern said conversationally, "tell me about your husband."

Suddenly, Abby felt warm and confident. At last they were going to see how terrible it had been for her. Now they would understand why she drank. "Martin's not interested in anything I say or anything about me," she said. "In his eyes,

I'm a mess. I am obviously a very selfish person. Whatever I do, I could have done it better. He tells me to get all the arrangements to go somewhere and coordinate this and do that — and then he says, 'Why did you do it that way?' If I get mad, he says, 'You wipe out all the positives. You can't hear the good things.' "

"If he was nice to you," Larry asked from across the room, "would you still drink?"

Feeling the ground shifting from under her, Abby said, "I would drink, but not as much."

Larry kept pressing. "How does he make you drink more?"

Abby slid her hands under her thighs. "Well, I get so mad . . .. maybe there's some revenge mixed in there."

"I just heard something honest," Fern said, "and I congratulate you." Abby's wide mouth parted in a tentative smile. Fern continued, "So what was your reward for getting mad?"

Instantly, Abby's mind swam. Her head began to ache. Her mouth was dry. With both feet on the floor, she pressed herself back against the chair. "I don't know. Maybe I was getting something out of my system."

After a long pause of awful silence, Fern spoke again, quietly, matter-of-factly. "There was a great big reward, and I'm not sure you want to give it up."

Abby could feel the circle of eyes watching her. Finally she said, tentatively, "Maybe part of the reward was an excuse to drink more."

"Part?" asked Fern, cocking an eyebrow.

"A lot," Abby said.

"*All!*" Larry said.

"Do you see," Fern said, "that your anger has been one of the dynamics of your alcoholism?"

There was another long pause. Abby felt a fear she could not explain. She said, "But sometimes I drank because I was so happy."

Larry asked, "What would make you happy so you'd take a drink?"

Abby laughed. "Not taking a drink."

Fern was unsmiling. "I don't know whether you do that in your relationships, but humor is a way of getting off the hook and stopping communication. The way I saw it, Larry was trying to help and you made a joke. Then he's down and you're up. Take a look at that, Abby." Fern paused and then turned away, saying, "Anybody like to give some feedback?"

Paula said, "Listening to you talk in the lounge and at meals — you don't say much in group — I hear you skating away from your addiction as often as possible, either looking for outside things to blame or making it into a big laugh."

Abby's heart contracted.

The pretty nurse with the frizzy hair, Marie, who sat regularly in group, smiled and said, "I used to think I couldn't do anything about my drinking until everybody else started doing things right. Then *I* could feel good and wouldn't have to drink."

Fern spoke. "I urge you to accept what has been said, Abby. I've been very concerned about you. In group you've been what I call a woodwork wormie, sinking right into the woodwork and not participating and expecting everybody else to come and dig you out. I don't see you making any progress toward accepting the disease concept and the fact that you are powerless over alcohol — which tells me that you are not working on your First Step. You will not get into treatment until you begin focusing on *you,* your addiction, and how it has affected you."

Fern was silent. Then, abruptly, she asked, "Where are you, Abby, in your motivation to stay sober?" Before Abby could answer, Fern spun away, and began explaining to Jerold Steele about the First Step.

Abby's skin burned with anger and humiliation. She wanted to disappear. She despised being stared at — a specimen impaled on a pin. And what did Fern *mean?* Abby thought she had been doing well in group — being so attentive, giving such intelligent feedback. What about her breakthrough? Didn't that prove she was serious about treatment? And she had so admired Fern. Now she hated her.

After group, Abby hurried away to an isolated chair in the lounge. She wanted a cigarette before lunch. She wanted to think. She replayed the fiasco in group — Fern's voice zapping her for that joke. Again she felt marooned in a hot funk of embarrassment, like a little girl caught red-handed.

Denton Rowe's rich voice broke into her trance. "Abby, don't look so down. It happens to the best of us."

Looking up, she smiled ruefully and answered, "A day without Fern is a day without sunshine." Denton patted her shoulder and left her alone.

Now Abby felt a flush like a prickly rash spreading up her throat and across her face. She had just done it again, made a joke to shut off Denton.

The lunch bell rang and Abby went downstairs. Still choosing to be alone, she sat with patients she did not know and listened idly to the two men across from her. One asked the other, "What did they say was the matter?"

"My liver," was the answer.

"Is that true, or are you lying?"

"No," said the second man, "there's liver damage."

"Is that enough to scare you into not drinking?"

"I don't know."

Abby poked disconsolately at the cardboard hamburger. Alcoholics really were crazy. This man had a bad liver and still might drink. "What possesses us?" she wondered. "Why do I have to be different from normal people? Why am I missing a cog?"

By lecture time, Abby's depression had deepened. Seated in the rear, far from her group, she felt a black weight pressing downward on her mind. She hated these ups and downs of mood — this roller coaster — thinking you had something to hold on to, then plunging down into even deeper confusion. Were you *supposed* to lurch about in your head — like a drunk? This afternoon's group would be a nightmare. She definitely could not con Fern. She would *have* to be honest. Did she still know how to be honest?

During the lecture, one set of sentences penetrated Abby's anxiety. "In treatment," the lecturer said, "a fellow told me he had come in here feeling optimistic that things were going to be okay. But now he was feeling rotten and lonely and scared, and he thought he was getting sicker. I said to him, 'You're getting well. For a guy in your situation to feel optimistic — that's sick.' "

When the bell rang, she could hardly force herself into Fern's room. Then she was afraid to stay there. And afraid to run. So she sat in her chair saying, "My name is Abby and I'm an alcoholic" — and telling herself, "You have *got* to talk."

That afternoon, Julia, slouching round-shouldered in her chair, told about her drinking patterns, and Abby recognized them all. "There was no way," Julia said, "that I could go to a dentist or a doctor without drinking first. So I never went. Finally I got a strep throat that was so bad that . . ."

Listening, Abby pictured her own parent-teacher conferences, arriving fortified with vodka, sitting in the tiny desks, feeling confined and trapped — the way she did now. She had always felt so ashamed. Other mothers did not have to get drunk to show up at their children's school. Now, as Fern asked for feedback to Julia, Abby pushed that memory away. It was too close to the bone, too much of a window to her self-disgust. Instead, speaking very rapidly, she said, "I really identify with what you said about dentists and doctors because when I *had* to go to the dentist, I'd drink vodka and then brush my teeth and gargle and eat a whole pack of mints on the way — and the dentist would be bending over me with his eyes watering and . . ."

Fern interrupted, her voice kind. "Abby, Abby, slow

down." Fern bent toward her, the blue eyes intense. "What are you feeling right now?"

Formless sensations were washing through Abby's head — fear, hurt, loneliness, guilt, sadness, melancholy — all flowing, bending, melting, spinning. She could not think. She closed her eyes and clenched her teeth. "I don't *know*," she wailed. "I'm so *confused*."

Fern's voice was calm. "Abby, I'd like to share something with you. I am not an alcoholic, but part of my training was to go through treatment at an alcoholism treatment center. When I was on patient status, I discovered I had been emotionally shut down for a long, long time. I couldn't have recognized a feeling if it had hit me in the face. And suddenly I started getting in touch with my feelings, and the energy was so tremendous, I thought I was crazy. All I could do was cry for two weeks. Finally I was able to talk about some of the pain that I didn't even know was there."

Abby sat nodding her head. Fern smiled, the parentheses at her mouth deepening. "I think it's time we did a little exercise with you. In the hope that they will be honest, would you be willing to ask the group how they see you today?"

"Okay," she said, half choking.

Denton Rowe spoke first, his preacher's voice mellifluous in his thin mouth. "I don't think I know who you are. I see a proper lady: how you sit, how you respond, so nicely and orderly and properly. But sometimes I'm intimidated because you're sort of smart and making jokes and covering up. And that comes across as not caring — first about yourself and then about us."

"Bull," Abby thought. Couldn't he see she was only being cheerful and helpful and positive — her real self for a change!

"For a long time," said Doreen Sulla, turning her rounded body toward Abby, "I couldn't figure out why you were here. You seemed so together. Your husband stuck by you. You've got a nice house, kids, a cleaning lady. You had *everything*."

That showed how little they understood her, Abby

thought. And if Doreen was jealous, why had she picked her as a confidante?

Garrett Owen tugged on a sideburn and then spoke. "I always feel that you're almost too clever, and you could turn sarcastic and cutting. I'm a little afraid of you."

Abby's stomach was getting queasy.

Paula Christy spoke, a frown appearing on her seamless brow. "I think behind that smile you are a very angry woman."

Abby began to sweat. Her skin felt tight. Tears stood in her eyes. It was finally happening. The moment she had dreaded. She was being exposed. But it was not Fern, as she had expected, who had found her out. The group was her enemy.

It was Larry McGruder's turn. "When I hear you talking about yourself, it's like your alcoholism is a problem that's just been sort of dropped in your lap, and why can't some-body come and take it out of your lap and throw it away."

Swiveling her head from person to person, she blurted out, "I'm not like that."

Fern's voice was quiet, "I don't want you to respond, Abby. Just think very hard about what your group is reflecting back to you."

Then Abby thought, "Screw them all!"

At dinner Abby was sitting alone, lingering over dessert and warming her spirits with a second cup of coffee. She had flipped the switch that turned off all emotions — "rest-ing the circuits," she called it. Kerry, the girl from the ori-entation meeting, arriving with the second shift, slid her tray in opposite her, and they smiled at each other. Kerry looked a little better, Abby thought. The narrow face was a touch fuller, the eyes more alive.

Abby, protecting her numbness, asked Kerry questions: how were her children, had she heard from her husband, did she like her counselor. When Abby asked how her group was going, Kerry shook her head and laughed. A man, poor guy, was having family week. Abby nodded, but she didn't want to think about that — the fact that week after next Martin and the children would be coming to Riverside for five days and having their own lectures and therapy group down on the first floor. She had seen the self-conscious families, with their blue name tags, eating in clusters in the dining hall. She had heard other patients talk about their terror of the "fishbowl"; the family facing the patient in the middle of the circle during afternoon group; the family telling exactly what it was like living with a drunk. But Abby had always been able to brush this vision away, thinking, "I'm not worried. I know everything I did."

Kerry was saying, "Before he knew it his kids were crying and his guts were lying all over the floor." Now Abby could see Frederick's brown eyes wide with hurt, red with crying. And Judy. Her rage. Abby stood up and lifted her tray. She smiled and said, "I've got to go oil my defense mechanisms."

After the evening lecture, Larry joined Abby on her favorite sofa. She felt pleasantly slender beside his boxlike body. They talked about everything but treatment — things they liked — food, movies, favorite vacations. A half hour later, Doreen pulled up a chair and launched on her favorite litany. Why the hell couldn't she get a handle on anything and why couldn't anybody help her? The more Doreen talked, her full mouth down at the corners, the more desolate Abby felt, as though Doreen's every breath sucked on Abby's spirit. The hollowness inside her spread and swelled into a huge hopelessness. She said quietly to Larry, "I feel really shaky." He looked quickly down at her. Then she added, "As a matter of fact, I'm going to cry." The tears exploded — teeth bared, deep gasps, almost like laughter. She bolted past Doreen's amazed face and out the door.

Larry caught up to her in the hall where she had stopped, face to the wall, blinded by tears. He put a bulky arm around her back. "Do you want company?" he asked.

Mute with sobs, she nodded her head. Finally she quieted

and then the two figures — the slim, suburban mother in jeans and fitted jacket, the balding, thick-necked workman in a checked shirt — walked side by side down the long, green-walled corridor. Larry asked, "Is there anything you want to talk about?"

"That's the trouble," answered Abby, looking at the floor. "I don't know what's the matter." She lifted her face up toward Larry, the deep hazel eyes still wet. With her palms she wiped her cheeks. "I'm sorry I'm such a cry baby. I feel like a big bag of tears."

"That's okay," Larry said, touching her lightly on the back with his hand. "Your pain is part of my recovery."

Abby said, "I don't understand."

"If you share your pain with me, I don't feel so alone in my own pain. And if you can share yours, that helps me to share mine and let go of it."

Abby reached out and squeezed his hand. "Thanks," she said, feeling a surge of determination — and defiance. The group thought she was a phony waiting for somebody to fix her. She would show them. She would get going on her First Step.

In her room, she sat at the little table and took out a big yellow pad and the outline sheet from Fern. Once again she read the First Step: "We admitted we were powerless over alcohol — that our lives had become unmanageable." Then she read the instructions: "It would be impossible to over-estimate the importance of the First Step, because treatment and recovery are impossible until the patient accepts the seriousness and totality of the illness. Each patient is expected to make a list of destructive behaviors caused by his or her (1) Powerlessness over alcohol, and (2) Unmanageable life. Areas in which powerlessness and unmanageability are demonstrated by the chemically dependent person are given below."

The first item was: *"Preoccupation with chemicals — thinking about using, looking forward to using, planning, hiding."* Under this were fourteen more questions, all overwhelming.

With her defenses rising again, she went to work. "What do they mean, *'Preoccupation'*?" she wondered. "I don't think I was preoccupied with alcohol. I had a lot more important stuff on my mind. When I wanted a drink, I just had it. So what kind of things shall I put down so they'll think I'm on the right track?"

Then she told herself, "Stop it, Abby. You can't con them. Get honest." She had heard other patients' First Steps rejected, heard the group say, "Knock off the little jokes; it's not funny"; heard Fern say, "Please stop the rationalization and the minimizing." That must not happen to her! She couldn't stand the embarrassment.

Abby read the question again, years of fear and denial still in her mind like sludge. *"Hiding."* Well, keeping a bottle of booze in a piano is not exactly normal. If she'd put a bottle of milk in there, Martin would have sent for the men in the white suits. Was that *"planning?"* Yes. She had even said to herself, as she put the vodka into her purse, "Plan Ahead."

"Thinking about using." Well, she was awfully relieved when Martin wasn't home to yell when she had a drink. And what about the fights she picked with Martin so she could storm off to a friend's house and complain and drink? "I guess I really was preoccupied," Abby thought, amazed. She began to write, "I always had a reserve supply of vodka stashed . . ."

The next question was: *"Attempts to control use of chemicals — including attempts at cutting down, quitting, switching, previous treatment, geographical moves."* Curious about what lay ahead, she skipped that one and read further. She looked for a long time at number six: *"Effects on sexuality and sex life."* She was thinking back to those early years with Martin — their bedtime ceremony of firelight and brandy. The drinks dissolved all self-consciousness and let her abandon herself to sensation. She could remember her happiness after making love, lying by Martin and holding hands. She had felt bathed in peace and warmth. Everything forgiven. No dangers threatening. Everything right in her womanly world.

But late in their first decade of marriage, sex began to sour. Abby told herself she was growing even more zestful and adventurous — while Martin was getting more conservative and stodgy. In the evenings he would go upstairs early, though she would beg him to hear another record or more stories about her father — and have another drink. Often, incredibly, he would leave behind a half-full glass. Two or three drinks later, when she was feeling mellow, she would ascend to the bedroom in a mood for making love. But Martin, lying in bed watching her undress, would make one of his remarks: "Do you realize that bottle of vodka was full this morning?"

Like a Fourth of July flare, Abby would erupt. "What's your idea in starting in on that? Why am I always the bad guy?" And she would tell Martin why she drank, tell him that he treated her like a retard, that he was only interested in himself and what he wanted, that she felt abandoned, that, in short, he was a son of a bitch.

Later, lying in bed, the drinks wearing off, facing tomorrow's hangover, she would start to punish herself. She would remember crumbs of the argument and glimpse how she must have looked and sounded. Sometimes she wept silently, thinking about their lost past, wondering if things would be this way forever, be so bad. And she would search her mind for reasons why it was happening to them.

Sometimes when there had been no explosion between them, she left off her nightgown and slid in behind Martin, fitting her body along his back. Often he would shrug slightly away from her, or would say, "God, Abby, I'm really whipped tonight," or once in a while, "Do you have any idea how you smell?" Moving back across the cold center of the bed, she would be consumed with anger, promising herself many drinks tomorrow. But for now, two Valium. Often, after she had taken the yellow pills, she slept in the guest room.

Sometimes, almost by luck, they would miss the booby traps and barriers and come together in bed — Abby hoping that this time it would be good again and they would reconnect with love. But the tender intimacy, the joy, would not be there, especially when she mismanaged the dosage of alcohol or took her bedtime Valium too soon and the mellowness turned to numbness. Afterward she would lie on her side of the bed, suffering a loneliness beyond tears, beyond help, beyond hope. If there had been pleasure, she felt betrayed by her body and her desolation was even deeper. Finally, she and Martin had given up and simply watched each other across a minefield of old rejections and rages.

Abby proceeded down the list of First Step questions, laboring over her yellow pad, but strangely detached — on the outside of her troubles, looking in. After an hour, with a pleasant glow of accomplishment, she turned the pad face down and put on a tape of Schubert. The voluptuous sound, the one vestige of her old life, returned her for a moment to the regular person she used to be — the nice woman who went to concerts and had a family and was trusted and drank normally. She picked up a copy of the *National Enquirer* brought from the lounge and relaxed into its bubble bath of gossip, resting again from self-scrutiny, relishing this waste of time.

Sleep came easily that night. Then at 3 A.M. she drifted into wakefulness, the cloud shapes of her dreams firming into random, fleeting thoughts. Did anybody at home miss her? Why didn't she want to talk to them? She was lucky Martin hadn't left her. Why hadn't he left her?

Then she thought, "I can never get high again. Never." Could she actually face the world, face her family without a drink? Could she function normally? Did she know any more what normal was? Did she have the strength to change so much? And would it be worth the effort? Would she like herself then? Would other people like her?

"I will never be high again," she repeated, and felt an aching grief. Now she would be losing her dearest friend, her lover, her solace. She had already alienated her family and most of her friends. "But if I drink, I'll die," she told herself, firmly. "I've *got* to give up the booze." Faintly, from some interior crevice, a tiny, second voice added, "But maybe I won't. Maybe I don't care if I die."

The next afternoon, Thursday, May thirteenth, Fern leaned back as usual and said, "Okay, folks, it's your group."

Doreen spoke up. "I never know where to start," she said. "I admit I'm an alcoholic and I *am* powerless — but I don't understand about surrender, and can anybody tell me how to do that? I try to listen to everything people say to me and I repeat the words over and over in my mind, but I just get more confused."

Watching Doreen, Abby felt she was peering into her self of the last two weeks. Suddenly her head felt radiantly clear, and her heart seemed ready to leap from her chest with excitement and fright. She was going to speak the truth. She said, "Doreen, I hear you every night saying in the same tone of voice that you don't understand what the group is talking about and don't know what Fern wants. I think you're conning us. I think you do know. I think you're using confusion and not knowing to get out of doing your work." Instantly, Abby wanted to cover her face with her hands, but willed them to stay in her lap. She thought, "Was that really me?"

Larry spoke. "I agree. You're always asking us to do your work for you."

Garrett, wearing his brown leather suit jacket, crossed his arms and said, "It's getting boring. If I thought I was really doing you some good, that would be different."

Abby felt better — until the session ended and Doreen stood glumly alone. Abby, feeling guilty, went to her and smiled and said, "I hope there are no hard feelings."

Fern spun around to Abby. "Don't Band-Aid her!" she said sharply. "You finally said something honest and don't apologize. If Doreen can't handle it, she has to learn."

In the lounge, restoring herself with coffee and a cigarette, Abby thought about her feedback. She hadn't been disagreeable. But, at last, she had not been trying to please.

She had expressed a strong feeling, instead of keeping it inside where it would chew her nerves. She had done what they wanted and she was proud. She went down to dinner, and there was Doreen in line, still morose. But Abby, feeling her stomach tighten, now more than ever wanted Doreen to like her, wanted to keep alive Doreen's contract to confide in her. Approaching Doreen with a wide smile, she said, "Here we go for ten thousand new calories."

Doreen said, "Hi," her voice flat, the full lips sullen.

Abby said, "I wonder if we're going to have mystery meat again."

Doreen was silent.

Caught up now in the fellowship of treatment, remembering Larry's words about shared pain, Abby said sympathetically, "I'm sorry you're having such a bad day."

Doreen turned half away and said, "I'm okay."

Abby flushed. She felt ambushed. The rejection was so intense, so unexpected, that she felt tears starting behind her eyes. She fought them back with rage, thinking, "Goddamn it, shit on you, Doreen."

Abby loaded her tray in silence and then, mechanically eating the beef stew and rice, retreated into her anger at Doreen — and at herself. She hadn't done what she was supposed to do. She hadn't looked behind her anger. She hadn't said right away what she was feeling, gotten rid of it. So now she was miserable. But what was she feeling? Her mind was a blank. She reviewed the list of feelings permanently written down one side of Fern's blackboard — sad, glad, lonely, scared, happy, guilty, unloved, hurt . . . That was it. Hurt. Okay, she should have taken the risk and told Doreen she felt hurt. But that was so scary, alone, outside group.

Abby sat through the evening lecture and heard the lecturer say, "Self-worth declines faster in the alcoholic woman because she tends not to have a job and therefore no ego verification." After the lecture, Abby went back up to the third floor and headed down the hall to the lounge. Glancing through the open door of Doreen's room, Abby saw her lying face down on the bed, dressed in shorts and tight tee shirt. Feeling the adrenaline rising, Abby stepped into the room and spoke to the figure on the bed. "Our contract has a clause saying I can ask you how you're feeling."

"Come on in," said Doreen without moving.

Abby sat on the edge of the twin bed. "If it's my feedback this morning," she said, "that was one of the hardest things I've ever done."

"No, you were right," Doreen said, her voice muffled by the pillow.

"Then why didn't you talk to me in line?" Abby asked. "That really bothered me."

Doreen rolled onto her side facing Abby. "I just didn't feel like talking to anybody about anything. I'm thinking about cutting out of here."

"You mean leave treatment?" Abby was astonished and frightened. Doreen made it sound so easy. Almost natural. "But why?" she asked.

"This place is a bunch of bullshit," Doreen answered, the full lips curling into a faint sneer. "I'm wasting my time. I'm not getting anywhere and I'm bored."

Abby sat for a moment, twisting the wedding ring on her finger. "Doreen," she said, "when I first came, I almost left. Nobody in their right mind wants to be in here. But we're not in our right minds. If you leave now, you'll use drugs again. I don't know about you, but I'm really, really terrified of going down the tube."

"I can handle myself."

Abby's voice was stiff. "If you can handle yourself so well, how come you ended up here?"

Doreen rolled onto her back. Abby looked at the voluptuous body in the tiny, tight clothes and thought, "How cheap and tacky." She wondered if this was a lost cause — and was immediately ashamed of herself. Bracing her forearms on her knees, she bent toward Doreen and asked, "What's really bugging you? What is it?"

Staring at the ceiling, arms at her sides, Doreen said, "I don't want to talk about it."

"But you made a contract."

"I don't care. You can't understand because it never happened to you."

"How can you be so sure if you don't tell me?"

Doreen, still not looking at Abby, said, "I've never told anybody. It's too horrible."

Abby felt her body tensing. Intuitively, she knew. "Were you raped?"

"Worse than that."

Abby said, "Something happened to me when I was about six. I was visiting my grandmother in Chicago." Doreen rolled toward Abby, who continued, "Behind my grandmother's house was an alleyway that ran the length of the block, and I was sitting on the back steps in the sun, and I remember it was early Sunday morning. There was a ragman who went up and down the alleys with a wagon collecting stuff, and I don't know if it was the ragman or who it was, but I remember suddenly there was this huge dark shape — a man — right over me. The next thing I remember, I'm upstairs in my mother's bedroom crying and screaming and frantic — and being told it was all my imagination."

Doreen's fingers were picking at the bedspread. Her voice was softer, sad. "With me it was my uncle. Every time it happened, I was so afraid I thought I'd die. I couldn't move. I was ashamed to tell anybody. I felt so dirty. I felt like shit." Doreen turned onto her back and frowned up at the ceiling. "I still do," she said, matter-of-factly.

Abby sat stunned, feeling her own shame kindling, pushing up through her. She thought she had resolved all this for herself. Nothing had been her fault. She was so young. Maybe it had been her imagination. Why, then, had she always kept it a secret? Because she, too, had been permanently ashamed. Abby sat up straight again and looked away from Doreen, and saw a brassiere hanging slackly from the bathroom doorknob. She looked back at Doreen, at the long blonde hair which fanned out over the light blue bedspread. "I'm like you," Abby said. "I always wanted to tell somebody, but who do you tell? A stranger on an airplane?"

Suddenly, holding on to the edge of the bed, her face naked, Abby began to cry. She was sick of crying. That was all she did here. She was a mess. Suddenly, Doreen was sitting beside her, shorter, like a wise old daughter. With an expression close to tenderness, Doreen took one hand. With her other hand, Abby covered her eyes, saying, "I'm sorry. I don't know what's the matter."

Doreen's face turned fierce. "I know. I wouldn't trust those shitheads as far as I could throw one."

Abby dragged up the edge of the coverlet and wiped her face. "Doreen," she said, "please forgive me for misjudging you. Sometimes I can't help myself. I thought I wasn't like you. I thought I was better than you, but we're all the same and I feel so close to you. Can you forgive me?"

"Cut it out," Doreen said with a smile. "We're up to our necks in turds together."

Just before leaving the room, Abby turned for a second and said, "Please don't leave. Give it some more time."

In the hall Abby folded her arms across her stomach, almost a clasp to hold herself together, and began walking, anywhere, everywhere, head down, swinging curls of hair forward in front of her shoulders. She was aware only of the eyes of the nurses each time she passed their central station. Finally she returned to her room and lay on the bed in the semidarkness, able now to think.

Had whatever happened in that alleyway affected her relationship with men? With Martin? She thought about the night of her high school junior prom, how pretty she felt in her blue strapless gown, how romantic it was parking with her date in the full moonlight, how much she wanted him to kiss her. But then his fingers moved off her shoulders to the top of her dress. She went berserk. Ripping off her corsage, she screamed, "Don't you touch me! Don't you *ever* touch me again!" — and she stabbed him with the long pin.

126

But eventually, alcohol had taken care of everything. Had she ever made love cold sober? She wasn't sure.

She thought about Doreen and men — what had come out in group, how she tantalized men. Had she herself been punishing Martin for being a man? Sometimes she did drink to hurt him. But they said it was only an excuse to drink. Everything was too complicated for her now. She was exhausted.

The next morning — Friday, May fourteenth — Abby felt at peace. She had decided what to do for Doreen and for herself, and until group, would simply ride with the routine.

The lecture after breakfast was titled, "Alcohol, the Disease." Abby listened with interest. "We have a lot of people in our society who drink too much, too long, but never manifest the symptoms of alcoholism. So we point to the possibility of an inherited capacity — a constitutional liability we call the X-factor. Studies all over the world clearly show that genetics — more than any other combination of social, environmental factors — determine whether or not you will be an alcoholic."

Abby thought, "I'm sure it's hereditary. Look at me."

The lecturer was saying, "In Sweden, an American psychiatrist named Dr. Robert Cloninger did a study based on all the children born out of wedlock in Stockholm between 1930 and 1949. He found 862 sons and 913 daughters of alcoholic parents who were placed at an early age with nonrelatives in stable adoptive homes. These children were found to be at three to four times greater risk of becoming alcoholics themselves.

"Most of the children, however, did not develop alcoholism unless their genetic susceptibility was combined with stress factors in the adoptive home. The most important stress factor in Sweden seemed to be low occupational status. These were blue-collar people who got out of work, went home, and got drunk as a form of recreation.

127

"The conclusion is that after six months, six years, sixteen years of misuse, those who have this inherited X-factor will cross the invisible line into loss of control. That does not mean that every time we take a drink, we will get drunk. Very rarely does an alcoholic drink that way. But an obsession, a compulsion, has been triggered in us, and, like the diabetic, we are ill with a chronic, incurable disease."

Abby shook her head. "I believe it in my head," she thought. "But it's hard." How could a liquid in a glass — something that's been your friend and gotten you through the worst days of your life — give some people a disease and not do it to other people?

"That leads us to the question," continued the lecturer, "What is this disease, this X-factor, this predisposition that can be inherited? Why is it that in a nation where eighty percent of the people drink alcohol, ten percent turn out to be chemically dependent? Why is it possible to addict any animal to these chemicals? There are not yet final answers. But there is intensive research, mainly with animals, and there are some extremely compelling theories. For example, there is the work of Dr. Robert Myers. According to his theory, when an alcoholic drinks, a complicated series of chemical reactions produces two compounds in the brain. One is THIQ, which is a precursor of morphine and highly addictive. The other is a group of chemicals called beta-carbolines, which attach to the anxiety receptors in the brain and increase anxiety. When the alcoholic drinks to medicate the anxiety, more THIQ and beta-carbolines are produced — which accounts for the vicious circle of alcoholism.

Dr. Kenneth Blume, whose work parallels Dr. Myers's research, has concentrated on the brain's neurotransmitters — the chemical messengers between two nerve cells. There is a group of neurotransmitters called endorphins, a sort of natural heroin, that affects how we feel, how we react, how we experience pain. Dr. Blume has found evidence that certain people are born with a deficiency of endorphins. So they search for another chemical, like alcohol, to make them feel good. But again, the alcohol creates THIQ in the brain and that lowers the level of endorphins. So the more somebody drinks, the less endorphins they have, and the more THIQ is produced in the brain — which depresses the endorphin levels even more. There is no evidence that once the change has taken place the levels ever increase. But whatever the predisposition may be that we alcoholics inherit, we obviously have no control or willpower over our brain chemistry. All we ever wanted was to be social drinkers. Because we're different, things changed. We got sick."

After the lecture, Abby stayed behind in her chair, smoking, thinking. Disease meant germs and doctors and medicines and tests that hurt. But she wanted to believe what she had just heard, desperately wanted to believe. And she did, sort of. It made sense. If she was actually different, *physically* different from other people, then she wasn't a walking character defect — spineless, morally deficient.

Her mind went to her father. Had he thought he was a degenerate? Those mysterious disappearances. A week or more. Then she would be hustled out of the house. Some excuse she didn't believe. When she came back, he was home. Behind a locked door. Abby felt again the confusion and hurt when she could not see him; and her fear of the weary, angry look on her mother's face. How did she finally learn the truth? Somehow. Her father had been holed up in a hotel room with a case of gin. Now, sitting alone in the ranks of metal and plastic chairs, Abby thought, "You really are your father's daughter. All your life you've tried to be like him, and how odd and ironic that it's taken this turn."

It was time for morning group. In Fern's room Abby took her accustomed chair, avoiding Doreen while acting studiedly natural. There was the round of introductions: "My name is . . ." There was the reading for the day: ". . . we find release from our troubles and worries through a new way of looking at things . . ." Then Fern sat waiting for somebody to speak.

Abby jumped into the silence. "There is something I have to do. If I don't, I will never forgive myself for standing by and not saying anything. I'm going to ask Doreen if she would be willing to share with group something that she's considering doing." Abby's chest was tight, but she felt good. She was being responsible.

Doreen moved uneasily in her chair and flashed Abby an unreadable look. "I told Abby I was going to quit treatment," Doreen said, looking at the floor.

Abby felt a communal tremor vibrate through the room. Julia asked, "Why do you want to leave?"

Doreen's voice was harsh. "I can't stand it here anymore. I'm told a dozen times a day that I don't listen, and it burns me up and hurts because I *do* listen. And I still don't know what you all want."

Denton, ministerial in dark blue sweater and pants, said, "Right now we want you to be scared that you'll use again. We're all like adolescents driving cars. We think we're immortal. We know alcohol and drugs kill, but we seem surprised when it happens. And we certainly don't think it's ever going to happen to *us*."

Abby said, "I know how you feel, and I really care how you feel, so . . ."

Doreen snapped her head up and said caustically, "How do you know anything about me, Miss Rich Bitch? You don't have a clue about my life and what I've been through."

Abby felt struck in the chest. She flushed hot red. In the silence, Fern's voice was soft. "Doreen," she said, "look around this circle. What do you see in the faces?"

Doreen's eyes made the circuit and then, biting her lower lip, she stared down at the floor.

Fern said, "They really do care, don't they?" There was another silence. Fern continued gently, "I see in you a lot of pain, a lot of confusion, a lot of roadblocks you don't mean. What's really happening with you?"

Doreen's voice was low and choked. "Two nights ago I had my dream." She stopped talking.

Fern waited and then said, "Would you be willing to tell us about it?"

Doreen answered, "I had to tell somebody, so I told Abby yesterday."

There was a very long silence and Fern waited quietly. Then Julia said, "Maybe it would help if you told all of us. We've got our nightmares too, Doreen."

Doreen, quivering, said, "I always dream that I'm in my grandmother's bed — I used to sleep there a lot — and I'm hearing voices and music downstairs like there's a party. Then somebody gets in bed with me, and it's not my grandmother. It's my uncle." She stopped. There was another silence.

Abby's breathing was shallow. She was back in the Chicago alley, the giant form looming over her, blocking out the sky. Fern, moving her chair across the room, took Doreen's hands, and Abby felt her own hands touched. Doreen began crying softly, and Abby's eyes brimmed.

Speaking gently, Fern asked Doreen, "What does your uncle do in the dream?"

"I don't remember," Doreen moaned.

"Try to remember. It's important that you do. I think you can."

Abby's back was rigid with strain. She was struggling to remember what had happened to her next in the alley. Why couldn't she? If she remembered, would that take away the shame that was choking her?

Doreen said, "He's playing with me and then he does it to me and afterward he gives me a quarter. I want to scream but I just lie there. Nobody would hear me and if they did, they'd come and bawl me out."

Fern squeezed Doreen's hands and said, tenderly, "Is this something that really happened to you?"

Doreen's voice was very small. "Yes. I don't know how many times. I used to wish he would die. He'd try to make me sit on his lap and my parents would say, 'Why aren't you nicer when Uncle Roger brings you presents?' I would be so ashamed."

Now Fern's voice was very definite. "I want you to hear me, Doreen. Occurrences such as this are common among women alcoholics. You have a lot of company. It is important that you understand that you did *not* cause this. You are *not* responsible. Can you believe that?"

"I guess so."

" 'Guess' isn't good enough. You've got to *believe*."

Abby wondered what she herself believed. Did she feel responsible? How could she? She was six and it was a chance encounter. Then why this knot forever inside her?

Fern was saying to Doreen, "Would you be willing to do something now?"

"Okay."

"Would you be willing to go around the circle and reach out to every person and ask, 'What do you see when you look at me?' "

"Right now?"

"Not next week."

"The staff, too?"

"You made a deal."

Abby, heart thudding, watched Doreen stand up and start around the room. The faces turning up toward her, one after another, were fervent with feeling. Garrett, seated next to her, held out his hands and Doreen took them. Instantly, tears streamed down Doreen's cheeks. "What do you see when you look at me?"

"I see somebody who can be gentle and soft and giving when she lets herself."

Julia Waugh lifted her gray head and sad eyes toward Doreen's plump, wet face. They clasped hands and Doreen asked the question. Julia answered, "I see a girl young enough to be my daughter who feels completely alone and abandoned."

A flash went off in Abby's head. That was the answer.

Abandoned. Sounding in her mind were her desperate screams and the cool voice of her mother saying, "It's just your imagination."

Now Doreen, still sobbing, was holding Larry's big hands, and he was saying, "I see a sensitive, caring person who's never been with people she can trust and who will listen to her." Denton Rowe, his thin mouth in a smile, told her, "I see a person who doesn't have to punish herself anymore." Paula Christy, tears on her own flawless skin, said, "My heart goes out to you. You've lived with such an awful feeling about your yourself for so long."

Then it was Abby's turn. Looking up into Doreen's eyes, which were almost sightless with tears, Abby gripped the feverish hands and felt a rush of sympathy so intense she dared not speak for fear of breaking down. Standing up, she put her arms around Doreen and hugged her close. A corner of Abby's mind felt the padded pliancy of this body against her, and knew she had never embraced a woman in this way. She heard Doreen whisper, "I'm sorry I said what I did." Abby gave her an extra squeeze. When Abby sat down, she felt light with a tremendous relief. Completing the circuit, Doreen sat down. Garrett put the Kleenex box in her lap, and she daubed at her face and blew her nose.

Fern asked, "What did you learn from that, Doreen?"

"That there's a lot of love in this room."

Fern smiled. "So nobody ran out the door screaming because you're such a bad person."

Doreen laughed ruefully. "No."

"Do you think you're worth all that caring?" Fern asked. "*I* do. Give yourself a big pat on the back. It took a lot of courage to do that."

The bell sounded, ending the session. Fern stood, holding out her hands and the group formed its circle and spoke in unison, "God grant me the serenity to accept the things I cannot change, courage to change the things I can . . ."

After group, Doreen went directly to her room, and Abby,

too, wanted special solitude. She walked to the chapel. Moving down the aisle toward her same seat in the second row, she was again aware of advancing into a pool of peace. Seated now, she felt purged, released. The mood of comfort in the room seemed like the touch of God she remembered in her girlhood. Perhaps He had not abandoned her. Perhaps He would still keep those promises she had felt in church and in her apple tree. Silently, tentatively, Abby said, "Please, God, help me." But the words felt empty, and, like an answer, Martin's words came back to her — "Religion is the opiate of the masses."

Her mind wandered back to this morning's group. Was it true that she could not understand Doreen's life? Maybe it was the other way around. Maybe Doreen did not have a clue about *her:* how it felt to be an alcoholic wife and mother, to be the keeper of the hearth and a drunk, to be an example to your children and a con artist. Abby pushed those thoughts away. She wanted to keep her sense of ease. They had told her to slow down and to meditate. They had said, "Let the thoughts float through your mind like leaves on a stream. Don't fight them." But suppose you hated certain thoughts. Why couldn't you reach out and sink them?

For the afternoon lecture, a slide projector was set up and Abby eyed it nervously. What treat did they have in store? The lights were turned off and the speaker pressed the button for the first slide. The screen blazed with white, blank light. "That's the brain after thirty years of alcoholic drinking," he announced, and went on to describe how alcohol operates. "It is water soluble and diffuses into all the cells of the body." Then, with horrifying slides, he described the effects of prolonged drinking. He talked about delerium tremens: "indiscriminate electrical impulses in the brain." Korsakoff's syndrome, called "wet brain," and "causing brain deterioration leading to memory loss and confusion." Cirrhosis of the liver: "scarred liver causing unexpected, sudden death from bleeding or 'liver coma.' " Dilated blood vessels in the throat causing "unstoppable hemorrhaging." Diseased pancreas — "enzymes digesting the pancreas." Cardiac arrhythmias that "cause heart failure and cardiac arrest." And on and on.

Abby sat terrified, her stomach like a fist. She was lucky to be alive! How could anybody risk those things! And yet, a rebellious voice was whispering inside, "Okay, but booze did everything for you that you ever asked."

After group that afternoon, filing out of Fern's room, Abby bent her chestnut head down toward Doreen's blonde head. "I don't know if I can handle many more days like this," Abby said, smiling.

"Yeah," said Doreen. "It's a bitch. Sometimes I think I'm going completely wacko."

They walked together in silence and then Abby said, "I've thought a lot about group this morning, and I want to ask you — what do *you* see when you look at me?"

Doreen stopped and somberly regarded Abby in her twill pants, brown moccasins, man-tailored white shirt; the wide, quickly smiling mouth, the high cheekbones and lucid eyes. "When I first saw you so all together, I figured you to be a bitch. Now I think you're okay. I guess I still envy you. I think you're going to make it."

"Why do you think I'll make it?"

"Because you're smart. I feel like I'm too dumb to understand anything."

"I don't think you're supposed to understand it in your head," Abby said. "It just sort of happens to you in little bits, and you gradually feel different. I think it's happening to me — except when I feel rotten again."

Doreen shrugged. Walking again, she said, "I remember once I got loaded and I was banging my head against the wall, and the guy I was with said, 'Doreen, what the hell are you doing? You're banging your head against the wall.' And I said, 'What do you expect?' "

By silent agreement, they went into Doreen's room. Looking at her bed, Doreen said, "I lie in here like I'm fifteen, thinking, 'What am I all about? What am I on earth for?' "

"We've been pickled for so long," Abby said, "we hardly know anything about ourselves, except the bad stuff we want to forget. Some days I think I can never go home and face the things I've done. How will anybody be able to love me?"

Doreen forced her hands into the pockets of her tight jeans and looked down. "That's a hard word for me. Love. I'm not the sort of person that people get close to — so if they can't get close to me, how can I love them?"

"But you're a really loving person."

Doreen smiled without humor. "When you tell me that a million times, I'll start believing it."

Abby grinned. "Okay, I'll start. You're a really loving person. You're a really . . ."

Doreen laughed, the turned-up nose crinkling. But in a moment her face turned bitter. "How in the world could anybody love *me?*"

Abby's heart ached. There was nothing to say that would not sound silly. She reached out toward Doreen, but when Abby's hands touched her shoulders, Doreen leaned away. Abby jerked her hands back as though singed. In a flash of hurt, Abby blurted, "I'm sorry."

Doreen sat down on the bed, her lips trembling with suppressed tears. "See? I can't do anything right. I can't even hug."

"That's all right," Abby said, her own eyes filling. "I understand. The shame is too raw. It's all-consuming. There are no edges to it. And it wells up inside and fills you, and you try to throw it up and it won't move. How are we ever going to get rid of it?" Their eyes met. The instant was more than Abby could bear. She turned and fled.

The next day was Saturday, May fifteenth. Abby had committed it to her First Step. She worked in twenty- and thirty-minute bursts till she could find an excuse to pause — a snack, a cup of coffee. Then she would end up in the lounge for a chat, before forcing herself back to stare again at the questions on the list. During one of her coffee breaks in the lounge, Abby heard the latest piece of gossip. The night before, some young male patients, forced into treatment by the courts, had been out in the parking lot, probably using drugs. Doreen had been there with them.

Abby was flabbergasted. Her mind was a jumble: "Impossible — so stupid — the poor girl — after all her tears — would I do that?" Numbly she listened to the talk around her, Larry saying, "Doreen's looking to get caught. She's telling the world, 'Wash your hands of me and throw me away.' "

Abby forced herself back to her room to work on her First Step. But she could not focus herself and sat fitfully tapping the pencil on the pad. Was Doreen going to be kicked out of treatment? Maybe none of it was true. Should she find Doreen and ask? Or would Doreen find *her?* How could Doreen be so dumb? Finally, Abby went in search of Doreen, checking the lounges, knocking on her door, pushing it open. Where could she be? Frustrated, anxious, mystified, Abby returned to her desk and her struggle to concentrate.

That evening the grapevine delivered another bulletin. Doreen was down in the entrance lobby with her suitcase. She was leaving treatment. There was a quick conference. Some of the group said, "Let her go. We've got our own treatments to worry about." But now Abby was terrified, frantic. Whatever happened to Doreen could happen to her. She had to have answers. She had to save Doreen — and save herself. She argued vehemently, "We owe it to ourselves and our treatments to be responsible. We *have* to try."

Garrett, Larry, and Julia agreed. They found Doreen in the deserted reception area to the right of the main front door, sitting on a sofa with a scuffed, plastic suitcase beside her feet. She was dressed in jeans, a sweater, and a brown cloth coat. Her face was expressionless, except for the eyes that said, "I dare you."

Part of Abby wanted to run to her and hug this waif and pull her back from the brink. But there was no flicker of recognition, no message that anything important had ever happened between them. So Abby listened to her other, angry voice that whispered, "How could she have done this to me?" Abby joined the others in a half circle of chairs in front of the sofa.

Larry said, "Doreen, we care a lot about you and we want you to stay. Whatever the matter is, we're here to do everything we can to help."

Doreen was silent, face unchanging. Abby asked, "Where will you go? What will you do?"

Doreen's voice was milder than her eyes. "My boyfriend's going to pick me up and he'll take care of me till I get a job. Don't worry."

Garrett said, "You can't stay straight all by yourself. You may never get back into treatment and you'll just go out and die."

Abby felt immensely sad. "You're a beautiful person inside," she said. "There's so much to you when you let it come out and the vulnerability comes through."

Speaking to Abby, Doreen answered, "Everybody wants me to be somebody I'm not. I feel so hemmed in. I can't be myself."

Abby was dumbfounded. What had happened to the yearning, caring Doreen? Abby bent forward. She put her hand on Doreen's knee and stared directly into the hard eyes, which wavered and looked away. Abby said, "I almost left here, and I thank God I stayed. A lot's been happening for both of us. We both have a second chance in life. Don't throw it away. Don't leave. We need you." Abby paused and then took the leap. "I need you."

Doreen moved her knee from under Abby's hand. She said, "I guess deep at heart, I'm chicken shit."

Abby leaned back, stowing the hurt deep, deep inside her. Julia asked, "Is your boyfriend using?"

"Yes."

"Then how can you hope to stay straight?"

Doreen said nothing.

Garrett spoke, his voice rough. "That guy's got to be a dirtbag, taking you out of here like this. You're too damn pretty and smart to throw everything away for somebody like that. He's just looking for another notch on his cock to prove how many scores he's made. It's just a matter of time before you and he will be using together."

Doreen flared, snapping her eyes from person to person around the half circle. "Nobody should *ever* tell somebody they won't make it. How can you make that judgment on me? Can you see into the future? How about your own futures? You're all so goddamned righteous. It makes me want to go right out and shoot up tonight."

The half circle looked daunted and uncomfortable, except Larry, who said, "Stay, Doreen. Stay until you feel good about yourself."

"Oh, screw this place," Doreen exploded, standing up. She grabbed the suitcase and hurried out through the glass doors. Abby sat for a moment, an emptiness taking possession of her. She stood up and looked out at the short figure in the cloth coat, beyond their reach now in the twilight of a street lamp. Abby wondered dispassionately if someday, somewhere, in some way, she would ever be that figure. She joined the group in front of the elevators. Garrett broke the heavy silence, saying, "Well, we tried." Nobody answered. In the elevator Abby felt tears rising up from the expanding hollowness at her center.

Larry put his arm around her. "You'll be all right," he said. "Doreen wasn't finished playing with dangerous things. She believed what she wanted to believe."

Exhausted, drained, Abby went to bed, but only to lie awake, reviewing that scene in the lobby. Had they done everything possible? Yes. How strange that a girl like Doreen, so foreign to her, had been the one to unlock so much of her. But why had Doreen changed so suddenly? What had possessed her? Abby thought about the line Fern kept repeating about alcoholism — "It's cunning. It's powerful. It's baffling. And it's *very* patient."

Abby, frightened, turned on her side toward the darkness away from the window. She was like Doreen. She herself had almost walked out that door. And now she might still go through treatment and fail and drink again, the way she had always failed at everything important. Then she reminded herself of the Serenity Prayer — "God grant me the serenity to accept the things I cannot change." She reminded herself of Fern's words, that Riverside was a microcosm of what she would face outside. She reminded herself of the slogan — "It's a selfish program." She had to put herself and her recovery ahead of everything.

Abby's mind went back to Doreen. They should not judge her. Doreen had been right. She might still make it. Abby resolved to go to the service tomorrow in the chapel and say a prayer.

PART THREE

CHAPTER

6

ABBY SLEPT deeply and late. The next morning, moving into consciousness, her mind ordering itself, she thought about her commitment, made so easily the night before. It was Sunday, May sixteenth, and chapel now loomed unpleasantly. Solitary meditation was one thing. Clergy and ceremony were something else. For years she had been dodging priests, sneaking out side doors after services, too ashamed to pass close to one of God's agents. But keeping commitments was part of getting well. Okay. She'd go.

At nine-thirty Abby walked through the two chapel doors and found a rustling throng of people crowding out the silence and peace, filling up the chairs — *her* chair in the second row. She slipped into a seat in the last row and looked enviously at the devout, serene faces around her. Behind the small oak lectern the priest was reading the psalm, ". . . be not silent to me: lest, if Thou be silent to me, I become like them that go down into the pit."

Just as she had feared! Down in the pit — where she was — the sensation of sin was too great, as if it had grown up out of her soul and sent its creepers into her heart and brain and all her womanhood. To pray for Doreen or herself, even silently in her head, would be presumptuous. And somehow these smug people around her would overhear the prayers and show their contempt.

Unbearably restless, Abby slipped out of the chapel into

the safety of the hallway, leaving behind the voice of the priest: "Give to them according to their deeds, and according to the wickedness of their endeavors." She walked to the elevators, stood irresolute, then headed down the stairs to the entrance lobby from which Doreen had fled the night before. Abby continued through the first set of front doors and stood in the small vestibule with her hands on the horizontal bar that unlatched the second doors.

She looked out at the sidewalk and could see in her mind the angry, woeful figure of Doreen waiting for her boyfriend. The same mind's eye watched herself, now gripping that steel bar on the door, knuckles white — a forty-two-year-old wife and mother dependent on alcohol, shut up in a treatment center, years of her life wasted. Rage filled her — rage at herself — but Abby also felt a surge of strength. She would do whatever she had to do to change her life.

Coming toward her along the walk was an elderly black man carrying a large box. Abby held the door open for him, and he smiled and thanked her and said, "Good morning. Beautiful day." So friendly. She smiled back at him and said automatically, "Yes, it is." Looking out again, as though to check on this possibility, Abby was startled. For the first time she noticed the rows of marigolds bordering the walk, and they looked like a stream of gold. Abby thought, "The world isn't that bad. Maybe I *can* belong to it." She ordered herself back to the chapel service. She did not *have* to pray or go to communion. She could just be there.

Abby sat again in the back row, feeling tears gathering in her eyes as she listened to the Gospel. ". . . while he was still a long way off, his father caught sight of him and was deeply moved. He ran out to meet him and threw his arms around his neck and kissed him."

At the end of the service, while the other patients filed out, Abby sat immobilized, waiting for the priest, large in his black cassock, to leave the doorway. As the room emptied, she sensed his eyes on her, seeing deep inside her, judging her. Finally she had to leave; there was no side door, no escape. As Abby went by the priest, her head down, he reached out and touched her lightly on the shoulder.

Walking back upstairs, Abby was in a trance. She was incredulous. That priest had not condemned her. His touch had been a sort of blessing. Maybe there was hope for her. Thoughts of her father mingled in her mind — the warmth that had surrounded her when she sat in his lap. How should she build on this moment? What should she do now?

Passing along the third-floor hall toward her room, Abby stopped at the bank of telephone cubicles. Suffused with forgiveness, open to the old affections, she wanted to share her euphoria with Martin. Until now, she had cut herself off from the outside world, unwilling to risk Martin's tone of triumph, Frederick's stifled tears, her mother's recriminations — "Honestly, Abby, there was no need to cause a *public* scandal by going into a *hospital.*" But now, slipping a dime into the telephone, dialing her home number, which felt both familiar and strange, Abby was excited and eager for the sound of her family's voices.

Judy answered — "Hello?" — her voice bright and expectant.

"Hi, sweetie. It's Mom."

"Hi, Mom."

Abby could hear the surprise, and a stifled note of fear. She felt punctured, and fell back on humor. "We here at Stalag Seventeen wondered how things are going. So how are things going?"

"Fine, Mom." Silence.

"Did you get that paper written? Are you getting enough to eat? Are your clothes *all* under the bed by now? If you want, you can answer with just one all-purpose yes."

"Oh, *Mom,*" Judy said. "We're doing fine. We really are."

"Well, tell me *something* about yourself. I'll settle for a single news flash."

There was a pause. "I went to a dance at Alice's house on Friday night."

"Was it fun?" Abby asked. "Did you dance?"

"No, we just hung out and talked." Another pause. "Dad's playing golf. But Frederick's here. Do you want to talk to him?"

"Sure. Judy!"

"Yes?"

"I love you."

"Thanks, Mom."

Frederick's eager voice came on the phone. "Hi, Mother."

Abby's heart swelled. "Hi, Frizzer. What are you doing?"

He giggled. "I'm talking to you on the telephone."

"No, silly. Tell me about something that makes you feel all squishy good inside."

"Daddy bought me a puppy, and he's *so* cute with the biggest eyes and he licks me all the time and when he chews my hand his teeth are like sharp little rocks."

Abby, stunned, was instantly furious. "Dad bought you a dog without consulting me?"

"Honestly, Mom," Frederick pleaded. "You'll love him. His name is Bo. He follows me everywhere."

Despising the irritation in her voice, Abby answered, "Well, I know who'll end up taking care of him. *Me.*"

Frederick, very earnest, answered, "No, Mom. *I'm* taking care of him. Every day when I get home from school, I take him for a walk in the park and I think about when we walked on the beach and you talked to me about things."

The steam of Abby's anger chilled to damp guilt. How could she begrudge this child anything that gave comfort and pleasure — even a dog — especially when she was here and he was there, deserving a real mother hitched to the stove making chocolate chip cookies. "Frizzer," she said, "I've got to go now. But I'm getting well, and pretty soon I'll be home and hugging you till maybe I crack some ribs. I love you, sweetie."

"I love you, too."

Abby hung up close to tears. She felt let down, cheated, helpless against the old patterns. She had so wanted to show off this new person that she felt beginning inside her, so wanted a pat on the back. She had planned to tell them, "I'm glad I'm here."

She turned away and went to the kitchen. Leaning one hip against the stainless steel counter, she watched the stream of coffee from the large urn rise inside her mug, and felt anger rising up into her head. She knew why Martin had bought that puppy! He was trying to take Frederick away from her while she was safely locked up. That son of a bitch. He was always trying to buy the children's love. She poured milk into the mug, added two teaspoons of sugar, and took the first delicious sip, sensuously hot on the tongue, consolingly warm in the throat and stomach. She remembered long ago when Martin would bring her a cup of coffee and take a little drink from it first. Then, with mock outrage, she would protest that he was stealing the first sip, the *best* sip — and they would both laugh.

Calm again, Abby went back down the corridor, analyzing that burst of anger, trying to use what she had been learning. She asked herself what had been behind the anger. Maybe fear — her terror of going home. Maybe loneliness — her longing for the tenderness that used to be there. "Would it ever come back?" And would good and bad always be battling like this inside her, keeping her on this roller coaster? It was too exhausting.

Abby continued past her room to the small lounge. Garrett was there. Looking at the bushy mustache, the leather suit jacket only half covering his small paunch, Abby wondered if he had delusions of machismo. She challenged him to a game of backgammon. He was a beginner. Teasing him about his pondering pauses, Abby kept calling him Bobby Fischer. He laughed and called her Don Rickles. Abby said she hoped she had a better figure than *that*. After the game, Garrett left and she leaned back on the couch, hands clasped against the dark hair behind her neck, hazel eyes focused on nothingness. She was thinking about her exhilaration after chapel. That kind of high used to come with booze. And, amazingly, she didn't miss alcohol anymore. That was good. It was progress. But change — having new reactions — was the *real* goal.

Back in her room Abby turned over the yellow lined pad on her desk, unfolded the list of questions for her First Step, bit her bottom lip, and read the next topic. *"Effects on social life and friends."* She told herself again to be honest. She wanted to get well, didn't she? Abby could remember her pride that she was always there in the crunch for her friends — rock solid — when the sober, straight-arrow people were nowhere to be found. But then she had begun forgetting engagements, was not where she had promised to be, did not do what she had promised to do — and couldn't even remember promising. And what about the lunches with friends — choosing the eligibles, only drinkers, only the ones who did not watch her.

Suddenly, Abby stood up. No, goddamn it. She was being brainwashed! Those had been great, laughing lunches. She could have called *anybody!* She had not drunk *that* much. But the other voice was still saying, "Be honest." What about those lunches alone at sleazy bars, wearing sunglasses, having a beer and a hamburger, talking to strangers — desperate to have somebody next to her doing what she was doing. And when Martin asked where she'd been, there were the lies about friends and nice restaurants. Abby forced herself back to the table and, with bone-melting boredom, began to write, "There were women I could not speak to without embarrassment, and I . . ."

The next morning — Monday, May seventeenth — Abby joined the streams of patients heading toward lecture. She felt like a schoolgirl sentenced to a first period class, though today's topic was "Why Feelings?," which sounded interesting. Seated between Julia and Larry, she made notes. "If you take a balloon away from a small child," the lecturer said, "the chances are that the child will start to cry, which is our body's natural way of releasing sadness and grief. Usually some adult will try to turn off the crying, will comfort the child, get another balloon, or shame the child for crying — do something so that the feelings of sadness are not released. That can go on, one way or another, for years, until we adults are carrying around an enormous load of unresolved grief."

Abby shook her head. You *had* to comfort your children, if you loved them.

"When that balloon was taken," the lecturer continued, "the child probably did some angry talking and made fitful body movements, which are signs of the body releasing anger."

Abby was thrilled. Those scenes with Martin had been healthy. "But," continued the lecturer, "I'd like to stress here that *violence* — throwing a plate on the floor, hitting, being abusive — may *feel* satisfying, but does not release anger, any more than running away releases fear."

Abby, deflated, nervously fiddled with her wedding ring.

"All our lives people around us have been scared by anger, so we are taught to stuff it. As adults we have huge stockpiles of accumulated anger that we act out by being violent or sarcastic, or by giving the silent treatment — a hundred ways."

Well, Abby told herself, it was *Martin* who got sarcastic. But the small voice was telling her, "This is what they mean when they say that you are an angry person."

"If that balloon was taken away by a bigger child," the lecturer said, "there might have been fear involved. Quivering, cold sweats, shaking are the signs that the body is letting go of fear. But it is scary to really *feel* fears and release them. So we have the flight or fight response — either run away, or get angry. Anything but feel the fear."

Here was anger again, Abby noticed. As Fern had said, anger covering up emotions.

"I think sadness, anger, and fear are the big feelings, and we can lump them under one word — distress. It is distress that pushes us into all kinds of rigid behaviors — being crabby, mistrustful, cynical, violent, passive, bossy — the

149

list is endless. We accumulate this distress because we never expressed our feelings fully enough. We were struggling for survival in a society that did not want to hear about feelings. When we got older, many of us used alcohol and drugs to block feelings. But at the same time, we were numbing all ability to feel any joy or zest for living."

"He's crazy," Abby thought. "Drinking was the only way I *could* feel any joy."

But all that morning, the lecture kept filtering back into Abby's mind; during the last, hurried cigarette to get her through group; during the session at odd moments; during lunch with Larry and Garrett. What was the truth about her, she wondered. She had always considered herself a feeling person — sensitive, responsive, caring, full of zest. What could she remember in the past five years? Loneliness. Boredom. Guilt. Anxiety. Lots of anger. "Stockpiles of anger" — that's what he'd said. Yes. The Quaker Oats box. "Pull string at perforation." And the string always broke a quarter of the way around. She'd fish for the end of the string, fighting the rising rage, giving in to fury, clamping the box under her feet like a log, wildly sawing at it with a carving knife. And ever afterward, when she opened the cupboard, there was the box with its ragged top, a silent reproof.

In afternoon group, her skin crawling as she thought, "That's me!" — Abby read the prayer for the day. "If we felt guilty, degraded or ashamed of either our addiction itself or the things we did while 'under the influence,' that served to magnify our feelings of being outcasts. On occasion, we secretly feared or actually believed that we *deserved* every painful feeling . . ."

It was the start of Larry's family week. Side by side in the circle of patients were his wife, Sally, a thirtyish woman with an oval face, plucked eyebrows above anxious eyes, long brown hair pushed behind ears with small, gold hoop earrings in the pierced lobes, an eager-to-please smile; the teenage daughter, plump and pale; the younger boy, wiry, with bright brown eyes. They were going to be there, Abby knew, every afternoon through Thursday.

After Fern welcomed the McGruder family into the group, she had them move their chairs out into the middle of the circle. In front of them sat Larry — square face expression-less, muscular arms folded across his barrel chest, the bare scalp glistening through the veil of hair. Abby rammed her hands under her legs so nobody would see them shake. *She* would be in that chair next week. She felt her loyalty go out to Larry, to the gentleness behind the burliness, to the sym-pathy that had never failed her.

"I want to encourage you to speak fully and openly," Fern said. "We have asked you to prepare a written list of the times that Larry was high or drunk, what happened, and especially, how you felt. I hope you have those lists with you. Your information is very important, not just to the pa-tient, but to the group, which uses it to force the patient to face the reality of his or her addiction."

Encouraged by Fern, Sally McGruder described her life with Larry. Abby listened with curiosity and embarrass-ment, a little guilty about eavesdropping on such fearful in-timacy. As the picture of Larry's drinking rages took shape, Sally's tone rose with the strength of pent-up anger. There was the afternoon he found Sally in the kitchen serving cof-fee to the father of their son's best friend. After the man left, Larry, screaming accusations, went looking for his gun. Sally hid under a bed, shivering with terror. When he found her, Larry lay on the floor, cursing and throwing lighted matches at her as she cowered in that narrow, dusty space, weeping. And then there was the Sunday when Larry, watching pro football at his bar, lost all his bets. That night at a party, he stood over Sally, screaming at her and pound-ing the table while she sat silent with closed eyes and clenched fists. Then he hauled the tablecloth, dishes, food — every-thing — onto the floor.

Sally paused in her recital, and Fern said, "Go on, you're doing fine. He needs to hear these things. He may not remember any of them."

Sally wiped tears from her eyes with a balled-up Kleenex, slightly smudging her eye shadow. "When you cheated on me," she continued, looking straight into Larry's sealed face, "that hurt so bad, I couldn't ever trust you again. My ego is pretty much down the drain. It's like I'm a zero. You never talk to me, only to your friends sitting at a bar. You don't like to come home. You've told us that. And when you do — if there's no cheese in the refrigerator — your stupid Kraft cheese — or no cigarettes and beer — you get mad and start yelling. I try to pretend like everything's all right. But I'm scared and lonely. There's a great big emptiness where you ought to be."

Abby studied Larry, stolid in the chair. The vision of that powerful body out of control was terrifying. They couldn't be talking about Larry, so strong, so vulnerable, always there, no matter how bad the day, so comforting, making things better. But she knew the stories were true, and she shivered inside at the terrible power of alcohol. She wondered how she felt about Larry, now that she knew the truth. Disappointed? Angry? He had deceived them all. But was she any different?

Then Abby's control shattered. Larry's thirteen-year-old daughter said just two sentences. "I'm upset that you lied to me. You always told us *never* to lie." These words split Abby's heart. Watching the crumpled, weeping girl, Abby was swamped with guilt. Tears gathered under her lids. But ruthlessly she pushed away the grief. It was not Frederick in that chair. He was untouched.

Reviving herself in the lounge with a cigarette, the deep draft into the lungs, her mind went yet again to the morning lecture — to the sadness and anger and fear in her life — especially to the anger. She had felt so futile, so hopeless against her mother's power, against Martin's power. Compliance had not freed her. Defiance had not freed her. School had not freed her. Marriage had not freed her. She had *thought* that booze freed her.

Then, gears shifting beyond her control, she wondered if she would ever be whole. On an impulse Abby turned to Julia and said, "I'm sorry, but may I ask a question?"

Answering with a pleasant smile, Julia said, "Certainly." But the eyes did not meet Abby's.

"You've been in treatment before, haven't you?"

"Yes. Twice. In New Jersey."

"Can you tell me why it didn't work?"

Julia's eyes never left the cigarette held between two mustard-colored fingers. "I don't know," she said. "That's why I'm here, I guess. To find out. And to see if there's any of me still worth saving."

Abby persisted. "How long were you sober after treatment?"

"The first time, one month. The second, six beautiful months." Julia's voice lifted. "I've never been so happy. I had a wonderful feeling of steadiness and strength. I'd get a cup of coffee and a chocolate bar and think how strong I was and how I didn't need a drink — and *certainly* couldn't have one."

"Why did you drink again?" Abby asked, her heart tight in her chest.

"I could go crazy trying to analyze that," Julia answered, still speaking away from Abby. Julia described a dinner at a restaurant with a friend who ordered a glass of scotch, good scotch, with a single ice cube. Julia sat looking at the drink, thinking, "That's what I used to love." Then, six weeks later, still very happy, she and her family drove to her parents' rambling old farmhouse in Vermont for Thanksgiving. On Thanksgiving night she lay beside her sleeping husband, reflecting on the excellence of her life. She said to herself, "I think I'll go downstairs and have a little drink because everything is so nice. I can handle just one." She could see in her mind that single ice cube floating in the delicious brown fluid.

Telling this story, Julia's voice had become animated. She was, Abby realized, enjoying herself. And Abby, too, felt her heart pumping. She could almost savor that drink in her mouth.

Now Julia described in detail how she gingerly climbed from the bed, how she quietly opened the bedroom door, gently closed it, tiptoed past her parents' room and down the back stairs — staying close to the wall so the old boards would not squeak — and finally arrived in the big farm kitchen. Abby could feel a rising exhilaration inside her, as though she herself was moving stealthily toward a drink. Maybe someday she really could have one more glass of that wonderful stuff — just one.

Julia was describing the liquor bottles, gallons, on the floor in a corner of the kitchen, so close together she could hardly lift the scotch bottle without clinking it against the others. She poured the scotch into a glass, took time to add ice, and carried it victoriously into the parlor. There she sat down in a rocker, crossed her legs, leaned back, and took a sip.

Abby, bending toward Julia, wanted to know every detail. "What were you thinking?" she asked.

Julia laughed ruefully. "Well, I told myself, 'Isn't it wonderful that we're having such a nice time up here this Thanksgiving. And doesn't this taste good! And see? It doesn't hurt me, and it will help me to sleep tonight, and nobody will ever know. I won't have to do this when I get home because I'm in Vermont. I wonder if I'll have to call this my last drink, or can I have my first anniversary in AA and pretend I haven't had a drink since last June?' " Julia paused and then added, "It worked so well, I did it again the next night. I kissed my husband good night, and lay beside him, trembling with anticipation, waiting for him to go to sleep."

Oh, how Abby knew that feeling! That glorious suspense. The masochistic pleasure from impatience soon to be satisfied. But, reliving that excitement, she also felt a tightness in her chest and pain in her throat as the old horror swept through her. The results of drinking again would be too horrendous, too harrowing. She asked her original question. "But why? What happened to everything you'd learned in treatment? Where was it?"

"I don't know," Julia answered again, looking down at her hands clasped in front of her distended stomach.

Abby knew that symptom. It was all around her at Riverside. An enlarged liver. And yet Julia had kept drinking.

Julia continued, "I wasn't thinking at all. I was in a sort of trance. Maybe it was self-hypnosis. I really thought I was one of those who would *never* drink again. I told myself I wouldn't even think of Christmas or birthdays because I couldn't drink again. It wasn't until the moment was upon me that . . ."

"What happened when you got home?" Abby asked.

Julia's voice was flat again. "The old story: walking on egg shells. I'd tell myself, 'No, you cannot have a drink,' and then I'd be in a grocery store and I'd think, 'Well, maybe just a little vanilla extract,' which preserved my dignity because I wasn't touching a whiskey bottle. But pretty soon, when I'd finished the vanilla, I was able to convince myself that one shot out of a bottle wouldn't hurt. So I pussyfooted along, very crafty, knowing there would be some horrible penalty if I got caught. Miserable! Still sick every morning — but from guilt. And from breath mints!" Julia laughed, sadly.

"Have you learned anything new in here?" Abby asked.

"They've told me because I drank again, I had never properly done the First Step. I thought I had."

Abby stood up and touched Julia on the knee, saying, "Thank you for sharing that. I've got a lot to think about."

Out in the hall, the long green tunnel, Abby felt forlorn.

She was fed up with treatment, this constant tugging and hauling on her insides. She was a piece of meat being thumped and smashed into digestibility. She wanted to step out of herself, be somebody else, somebody lovely and talented and serene. She went to the kitchen for an ice cream bar and carried it to her bedroom. She ate it staring out her window at the rooftops and backs of buildings. Riverside was such a dumb name. All these names: Chit Chat Lodge, Silver Hill. So cutesy. So deceitful. They should be more imaginative. Garden Path Cottage. Mother's Milk Acres. Or be more honest. Perdition Fields. Bad Manor. Lost Horizon.

She smiled grimly and lay down on the bed, hoping to doze. Loneliness settled into an ache at the top of her stomach. Staring upward at the pristine ceiling, she longed for the cracks in her ceiling at home, her rivers. She wanted to go home and get started on being a good mother, get going on making it all up to the children. She pictured the children right now. Frederick drawing superheroes on a shirt cardboard (Does he miss me?). Judy getting dinner (I've robbed her of her childhood). Evan watching TV with his guitar on his knees (He calls it an ax. Ugly!). Parenthood was impossible. Groping along on impulse and instinct. Making a million off-the-cuff decisions. Ending up with teenagers you hardly knew — who don't want to know you. She couldn't even claim to have done her best. She had done her worst.

The dinner bell rang, and, still in her rummaging mood, Abby headed downstairs. She sat at a table near two families just arrived at Riverside for family week. They seemed such outlanders — dressed in their best clothes, glancing curiously, nervously, at the patients. They were talking about their day, and she gathered that their routine was much like hers — a morning lecture for spouses and children, followed by their own group sessions with a family counselor. She tried, but failed, to imagine Martin and the children sitting there. Family week! One week from today. When

Martin and the children faced her in the center of the group, what would they say? Could they hurt her? Was there *anything* she had not punished herself for, a thousand times over? She pushed away from the table and left the dining room to look for distraction in the lounge. But the fear hung on, smoldering in the back of her mind.

During the evening lecture, the speaker asked, "If we remove chemicals from our lives, what are we going to replace them with? We suggest that you replace them with people. I always knew how much alcohol to use to medicate myself when I felt guilty or hurt or lonely. But I found out that if I shared those feelings with another person, I felt different. I felt better."

"That's peachy keen in here," Abby thought. But what would happen if she talked feelings with Martin? He'd tell her to stop being so self-centered, "always me, me, me."

Back in her room, she sat down at her desk, the wooden chair hard against her spine. "Mortifying the flesh," she thought. Dutifully, she tried to read an assigned book on alcoholism. But her mind drifted back to family week. Next Monday! Would she be able to admit the terrible things she had done? What would happen if she couldn't? Could she stand hearing Judy's and Evan's pain, perhaps seeing them cry? But she needed that. Family week was her last chance. She wasn't getting anywhere. Other people were progressing. She was so dammed up. And the days were slipping away, and she didn't understand anything.

The next morning, Tuesday, May eighteenth, as the group assembled in Fern's office, Abby sat in her chair, legs crossed, right foot moving slowly up and down in the air. The night before, she had lain awake for hours, her mind whirling through the past — failures, the roads not taken, the if-onlys, the sins and decisions and grievances. The introductions proceeded around the circle, Abby saying the ritual, ". . . and I'm an alcoholic."

Paula did the daily reading, the inspirational words strange coming from that dramatic, slightly haughty face. Then the usual expectant silence hung in the air. Abby leaped into it. "There's something I've been doing a lot of drinking over for a lot of years," she said, "and I'd like to share it with the group." Abby paused and breathed deeply, trying to relax herself. Her heart thumped like a fist inside her chest. She could feel cold beads of perspiration running down her sides. She dried her palms on her twill pants. "I've never told anybody how I really felt about this," she continued. "I tried to tell Martin, but he said I was being ridiculous and overdramatic again."

Momentarily disorganized, she stopped. Then, with feet dug in beneath her chair, hands pushed under her thighs, she started up again. "Two weeks before my last baby was due, the placenta came out and the baby wasn't getting any oxygen. I was rushed to the hospital for a caesarean, and while I was lying on one of those carts . . . I should say here that earlier I'd told my doctor that with three children, I didn't figure on having any more kids and was thinking of having my tubes tied. But I sure hadn't made a decision. Anyway, I was on the cart just before the operation, and the doctor said that while he had me opened, he should do a hysterectomy. He said it would reduce the risk of cancer later on. I was already in shock and terrified for the baby — and I trusted him. Martin was there saying I should do it. I signed the permission form. The whole thing took about one minute."

Abby stopped again, conscious of the circle of interested eyes. She went on. "My baby boy was alive and he was *healthy*, and at first I was thrilled. But after I'd been home awhile, I felt like one minute ago I was twelve years old and looking forward to growing up and getting married and having children. It was all going to beautiful. Then, one minute later, I am washed up — cut off from what women are programmed to believe life is all about. I began feeling barren and stale and stripped out — incomplete — and I'd cry for no reason. That was when I started drinking really a lot."

The group was silent and Abby sat with downcast eyes, twisting and twisting her wedding ring.

The rich voice of Denton Rowe sounded. "Abby, are you telling us that you drink because of your hysterectomy?"

Abby's head snapped up. "No, I'm not!" What nerve he had! But a man couldn't know what she'd been through. One of Fern's eyebrows lifted, and Abby hurried on. "I'm just saying it was some kind of a turning point. Martin was so patronizing, bucking me up, saying, 'Hundreds of women have had hysterectomies. You'll be fine.' I'd get mad and then go make a drink. I felt like that doctor, with his cheerleader pep talk, was one more male person in control of me, taking away one more thing from me, taking away my choice of whether or not to have another child. Hysterectomies are easy for doctors, just go in and lop here and lop there and lop you someplace else, and then charge you a thousand dollars."

"What's behind that anger?" asked Fern, quietly.

Abby looked at Fern. The ache in her throat was as big as a baseball. Would she be able to speak? This was the fatal moment. Now people were going to laugh and cringe away from her. Feeling as though she was stepping off a precipice, Abby plunged ahead. "This fantasy I have. It's off the wall, I know. But ever since the operation, I've felt like there's a box right here." Abby pulled one hand out from under a leg and placed it just above her stomach. "And if you open its door," she continued, "there is a layer of bright pink skin and on it is stamped DEFECTIVE. Great big letters. Stamped like a box of merchandise — defective — twenty-five percent off. I have truly believed that it had to do with that hysterectomy. It was like the doctor had gotten in there and seen what I was really like and stamped me defective. It's such a crazy idea. But I've always kept that door closed. As long as nobody ever looked in there, nobody would ever know — except the doctor."

Abby glanced anxiously around at the faces. Nobody was smiling. Nobody even looked amazed. Julia was staring at the floor. In Paula's eyes there was sympathy. Fern seemed impressed. Abby suddenly felt light. This secret she had carried so long was out. She had not known it was so heavy. She folded her hands in her lap and brought her feet out from under the chair.

Larry, his voice conversational, said, "Abby, what's the *real* reason you feel defective?"

"Everybody thinks I am," she answered, relaxed now, almost light-headed. She had confessed her central flaw. Now she could go on and tell how it had been for her. "My mother has said it to me all my life. Martin thinks I can never do anything right. I've always felt on the edge of things. I never felt like I belonged in my family. Once, at a family reunion, when they wanted me to pose with everybody for a picture, I ran off and hid on the other side of the house, and my father came and found me where I was behind a bush and took a picture of me — and I hated him for that." The words were pouring out of Abby now. "I only felt I was a person when I was being bad behind people's backs. I thought if I got along like normal people, I would lose myself. I wouldn't have *me*."

Paula unfolded her arms and said, "My mom and my older sister always got along real well, and I would just shrivel at things my mom would say to me, and bury them deep inside me. I can still feel my heart falling down."

Washing through Abby now was the old childhood loneliness, and the fear that she was still that person set apart. She answered Paula, "I'd reject people before they rejected me. But I could always make them laugh. That made me feel bright."

Paula said, "I stole money from my parents to buy kids candy."

Now Fern spoke. "Abby, I'd like to follow through on Larry's question. What does defective mean to you? Put Abby in a chair and describe her — how you view yourself in the outside world. I'll write it down on the blackboard." Fern rose, like a round, gray-haired teacher, and stood expectantly by the board, arm lifted, chalk in hand. "You are . . . ?"

"Scared shitless," said Abby, laughing nervously.

Fern did not smile. Repeating the words aloud, she wrote, "Scared shitless."

Abby felt a strange mix of anticipation and dread. She was going to find out things about herself that maybe she could fix. But it was going to hurt. Tension swelled again in her throat. "Stupid, ugly," she said, and then stalled.

After a moment, Fern said, "What else?"

The tension was now choking Abby's brain. Finally she said, "Liar, cheat, sneak."

"What else?"

After a long pause, "Unlovable, irresponsible, bad mother."

"What else?"

"Isn't that rotten enough?" Abby answered, laughing to cover her terror. She felt totally, hopelessly exposed, naked, open to every hurt.

"Okay." Fern sat down and waited, silent.

Larry shook his balding head. "It just blows me away how much you hate yourself."

The tears poured from Abby's eyes so suddenly, she was more shocked than upset. Covering her face with her hands, she noticed how unpleasantly the wetness smeared against her palms. Then the full horror hit. She had admitted everything. She had opened the little box, and they could see the stamp. DEFECTIVE. Now everybody knew for sure that she was basically a bad person, that she did not know right from wrong, that she was pathological and could not be cured. Now they were going to tell her to get out of the group.

Through her grief, Abby heard the voice of Frank Ruyter — so defenseless himself with his pale face and trembling hands. But his words penetrated like bullets. "Stop the self-pity," he said. "You're hiding behind your tears."

Abby's anger, surging as instantly as the tears, dried her eyes. Jerking her hands down, she glared at Frank and said,

"When everybody's on my case, you don't have to worry about *you,* do you?"

Fern stepped in. "Abby, I see you deflecting now. I know this is painful, but it's supposed to hurt." She glanced up at the blackboard. "You say you are a liar. What tells you that you are a liar?"

"I say so. I mean, I *am.* I look my husband right in the eye and tell him I haven't had a drink all day, when I've just slugged vodka out of a bottle — eight ounces straight — and it's still burning in my throat and stomach. And then I tell my kids, 'Don't *ever* lie to me. You'll never be punished for what you did, as much as you'll be punished for lying about it.' I'm such a hypocrite!"

Fern asked, "Before you drank, did you lie?"

"Yes, I did. When somebody asked my opinion, I'd tell them what they wanted to hear."

"Have you always done that?"

"No." Abby laughed without mirth, her cheeks crinkling. "I was a late bloomer."

Fern checked the blackboard. "What tells you that you're a bad mother?"

"I was never there for my children. When my husband was away on business trips, I'd encourage them to sleep over with friends, so I could be alone and drink. Even when I was home, I wasn't really there for them. I'd be reading my youngest a bedtime story, and rushing through it so I could get a drink."

Fern asked, "What sort of mother were you before you started drinking?"

Abby's voice was almost defiant. "I was a good, good mother, and I did it out of love, not because I had to. I wanted my kids to have the childhood I didn't have. I taught them to ride bikes, and we'd ride to the park for picnics. I made them Halloween costumes, but I don't know if I did it for them or for me." Her wide mouth opened suddenly into a laugh. "I could have been Mother of the Year."

Fern asked, "What tells you that you're irresponsible?"

"Driving the kids around when I'm tight."

"*Drunk!*" Fern said.

"Drunk."

"What tells you that you're unlovable?"

"Like I said. Never part of the group. Ugly inside."

"Did booze help that problem?"

Abby's feet were back under the chair. "Yes, it did. It made me forget about myself. I could come off the sidelines and feel interesting. I was the life of the party — always invited."

Larry spoke. "So booze was the solution to everything."

Abby jammed her hands under her thighs. Her voice was low. "After a while drinking made things worse. I'd get drunk and I wasn't interesting. Just repeating myself. The next morning I'd be the ugly person I'd always been, except worse. Everybody was mad at me and I felt bloated and sweaty and dirty — and ashamed — and angry — and sick."

"Do you see the pattern?" Fern asked.

"Yes," Abby said, hunched forward, feeling helpless and lonely and terrified.

"What is it?"

"My pattern is that I have always found a way to screw up."

Fern sat regarding her quietly. "Anybody got anything to say?"

Garrett stretched out his legs in their tan bell-bottom pants. "I think your hysterectomy has been a nice ticket to drink."

Then Julia Waugh spoke, her voice throaty with emotion. "Abby, everything you said about yourself — I'm all those things — and more."

Turning toward Julia, Abby was comforted and heartened, and deeply touched. In this moment, finally, Julia was looking straight at her with pale, sad eyes.

Larry asked, "Do you think Julia is a bad woman?"

"No," Abby said. "I've never thought that about Julia."

"Is she shallow and phony?"

"No. No." A small uncertainty, perhaps one candle-power, began to burn within Abby. Maybe she was missing something crucial, something good.

Julia smiled. "Thank you."

Fern spoke. "Abby, what brought you into Riverside?"

There was a long pause. Abby's throat was jammed by a thickness she could neither spit up nor swallow. "Drinking," she murmured, at last.

"Okay," Fern said, almost grandmotherly. But under the gray hair, her sharp blue eyes held Abby's. Fern continued, "What you need to come to, Abby, is the understanding that 'When I drink, I am capable of all those terrible things and much more. When I don't drink, I am these things: a good mother, honest, efficient, a giving person.' Can you see that?"

Abby, gripping the edge of the chair, frowned and said, "It can't be the alcohol. That's too simple. I'm defective. My life is too complicated for something so simple to cause it all."

Fern's tone was still kind, but firm. "The overwhelming feeling I have of you is shame. That tells me a couple of things. You are still not connecting with how powerless you are against alcohol. And you have not accepted the fact that you have a very serious disease. Unless you begin to do that, you will not get well, and the odds are that you will go out of here and drink, and if you do not get back into treatment, you will eventually die. It gives me no pleasure to tell you that. But if I don't tell you the truth, that's called 'killing you softly.' "

The thickness in Abby's throat exploded. She felt collapsed, as though her breath had been sucked out of her. Her stomach seemed to fall out. Her joints felt weak. Through her mind, sharp in every detail, flashed pictures of herself in a satin-lined casket, dead, dressed in her black ball gown, face gray, lips blue; then the faces of her children screaming; then somebody screwing down the top of the coffin, dirt falling on the coffin, stygian darkness. Clutching her chair, Abby was swept by panic.

Fern's voice continued inexorably. "How angry are you at being an alcoholic?"

Abby, her head down, body heaving with dry sobs, could not speak. When she dared unclamp her mouth, her voice was a wailing cry. "I'm so *ashamed!*"

"Would you be ashamed," Fern asked matter-of-factly, "if you had cancer? Or diabetes? They're just as fatal." Abby sat silent again, chest still heaving, hands still gripping the edge of the chair. Suddenly Fern moved her own chair across the room and faced Abby, knee to knee. Bending forward, she drew Abby's hands from the chair into hers. "Are you a bad woman?" she asked.

"Yes," said Abby softly, face glistening wet.

"Are you a bad woman?" The voice was penetrating, insistent.

"Yes. Only a rotten person would . . ."

"Are you a bad person?"

"Yes." But though her mouth still quivered, Abby was beginning to feel ridiculous — showboat Abby being overdramatic again. All those things she had said about herself: liar, cheat, bad mother, irresponsible. Was she *really* like that, when she despised those traits?

"Are you a bad woman?"

Abby felt a sudden rush of warmth, almost like alcohol in her veins. If she hated those traits, then her basic values must be good. But that was too easy. Yet once again she felt a flooding sense of release, a light blooming inside her. "No," she answered Fern, "I'm not a bad woman."

Instantly, Abby was pounded again by tears, convulsing, inhaling her sobs in long gasps. Blinded, she bent down her head, and felt her hands squeezed again as Fern said tenderly, "Abby, you're *okay*." Abby lifted her head and through her tears saw the concern suffusing Fern's face, the softness filling those blue eyes. The inexorable voice had become soothing, nurturing. "Abby, it's all right to feel the hurts. Allow yourself to feel the pain so you won't *ever* want to go back to that again. I hope you leave everything here — that freight train of garbage. You have punished yourself far more than I, the group, your family could *ever* punish you. And now you need a large dose of self-forgiveness. You are a fine, strong woman who, through no fault of her own, has a disease called alcoholism." Releasing Abby's hands, Fern smiled and pulled her chair back to her desk. While the group work proceeded, Abby sat crying gently, unable to stop, unwilling to stop, overcome with relief.

After group, after the Serenity Prayer — ". . . the wisdom to know the difference." — Abby moved toward the door. Larry, a smile on his square face, put a heavy arm across her shoulders and said, "I was rooting for you." Abby, who had always disliked such touching, leaned against him and giggled. Paula, tall and willowy, came up saying, "You really did it. I'm envious." Garrett winked at her, his wide mustache twitching upward. And even Frank Ruyter, so sealed off behind his black-rimmed glasses, touched her on the arm as he passed. Abby was euphoric. They had seen how truly pathetic she was, and they still cared about her. Basking in their acceptance, she felt wonderful — ready for a celebration.

She went directly to the kitchen, which was jammed with patients getting coffee, digging in the refrigerator. Wedging through the crowd, she called out, "Here comes the sweet tooth. Make way for the sweet tooth." At the freezer chest, she searched out her favorite ice cream bar, maple walnut covered with a crust of nuts. Immediately, standing over the freezer, she took the first bite, the nut crust crackling under her teeth and mingling with the buttery softness inside. She cradled the sweetness between the taste buds of her tongue and the roof of her mouth; then let the chill cream slide smoothly over her tonsils. Then she took another bite, cheerful that it was so richly deserved.

That night, heading down the hallway to bed, Abby still felt a high that seemed to her above any alcohol high. Even the smooth green walls seemed fresh and sparkling. She had never had such lightness in her body, such clarity in her head. Her heart felt warm and soft and glowing, not like a stone hanging in an empty space. She wondered whether this would last. Was it real? She lay on the bed wondering why she felt so good. If she could analyze it, break it down, she could bring it on again. And she knew now, without even discussing it with herself, that alcohol had been the problem — not Martin, not the children, not the jitters. It seemed so obvious. What a dummy she had been! Why hadn't she seen that! She got off the bed and went to the small table. She tore the cardboard back off her yellow pad. Using a magic marker, she wrote in large, block letters, I'M TERRIFIC — and taped it above the desk.

CHAPTER

7

THE NEXT day was Wednesday, May nineteenth — the second half of Abby's treatment and five days before her family week. Lying in bed for a last, lingering, luxurious moment, she gazed with satisfaction at her new sign above the desk. She got up, and in the bathroom grinned at herself in the mirror. As though her face was a specimen to be studied, she bent close to her reflection, watching her nose balloon larger, the wide mouth expand into a frieze of teeth. She winked one of the giant hazel eyes, and said aloud, "My God, kid. You're gorgeous."

She strode along the halls to breakfast, then hurried to morning lecture. The subject of the lecture was the difference between men and women alcoholics. Enjoying this nice, academic subject, free of landmines and bombshells, Abby sat at ease.

"It's kind of accepted and tolerated that men get this illness," the lecturer said. "It's still not okay for an intelligent, active woman to become an alcoholic or chemically dependent. She is still a disgrace to her family and her church and anybody else she comes in contact with. If a woman wants to ask for help in this society, she is terrified that her husband is going to leave her, that her friends will abandon her, that her kids will reject her, that her employer will fire her, that her doctor won't know how to treat her — and very often this is true. The doctor gives her a prescription drug to take care of the anxiety, and tells her to go easy on the drinks.

"Amen," thought Abby.

"The AA population is one woman to every three men, but that may not be a true ratio. Women seem better able to hide their illness. Eighty-eight percent of the women tell us they did most of their using at home, where they could not be seen. More women than men use prescription drugs along with alcohol. If you use pills on the sly and only drink a little in public, you don't seem to be using much alcohol. Also a woman is protected a bit more than a man. When a policeman stops her for driving erratically, he is probably going to say, 'You look like a nice lady. Why don't you go home and behave yourself.'

"If the woman has a husband, he doesn't want to take her out and be embarrassed by her behavior. So he will buy her a nice bottle of wine to keep her happy while he goes off to his business meeting or whatever. The children protect their mother and take over her responsibilities because they are ashamed and because they see her as an ill person. They are also protecting themselves, because if Dad comes home and all the little chores aren't done, he'll be angry — but not at Mom, who is in her room feeling sick. The anger will come out sideways at the kids."

Abby felt a little hurt. Hadn't the children been doing some of that out of love?

In group that morning, Julia, eyes fixed on the middle of the floor, talked about her sense of detachment. "I arrived here numb," Julia said, "and I still am. I'm having a hard time finding emotions. I know I'm desperate, but my feelings aren't that deep. I'm not frightened. I'm not lonely. I just know there's a job to be done." Abby had known that deadness at the core. Now she could help Julia see the light, help her toward revelation and liberation. Abby said, "Julia, I went through that phase and know how you feel. But when you are able to let go in group and be honest with yourself, it's like stars lighting up inside you, and everything comes so clear." Abby sensed a slight smile on Fern's mouth, but put away that thought.

After group, Abby went directly to a telephone. She wanted to tell Martin about her extraordinary leap forward into health, and, in a way, confirm it. She reached him at his office. He said, "Hi," his voice guarded. "How are you? You haven't called, so I figured you wanted to be left alone."

Abby thought, "Good excuse," but plunged immediately into her glad tidings — how happy she was to be at Riverside, how wonderfully the treatment was working. Martin said nothing while Abby bubbled on. Only vaguely did she notice Martin's continuing silence. When her torrent of optimism ended, she remarked, almost as an afterthought, "Incidentally, I'm out of cash. Would you send me twenty dollars?"

On the other end of the line Martin said tersely, "I don't have it."

Rage, hurt, disbelief stunned Abby — like a club across the head. "But I don't have any money," she exclaimed. "I'm almost out of cigarettes! Certainly you *must* have twenty dollars."

Martin answered, "When I haven't got it, I haven't got it. That place is costing me four thousand dollars."

Abby hung up. Her hand, releasing the phone, trembled. That roar of fury was in her head. Oh, how she wanted to get her hands on Martin. But she was trapped. A prisoner. Almost sobbing with frustration, she ran down the hall and into her room, slamming the door, throwing herself on the bed, lying there rigid and hot. That son of a bitch! *He* knew how much she needed her cigarettes. Oh, God, how she hated him. How could she ever go back home? Abby, lying on her back, began to cry. She was sure now that even if she got sober, nothing would change.

A knock sounded and Marie opened the door. "Are you all right?" she asked.

"Hell, no. I'm not all right. I'm mad. Leave me alone."

Marie sat down on the bed next to Abby. "Can I stay

with you for a few minutes?" she asked. Abby rolled away and lay on her side, knees up, body shaking. Marie put her hand on Abby's shoulder and said, "It's all right to be mad. But you'll feel better if you can talk about it."

Abby remained huddled on her side. Finally, she rolled onto her back and spoke upward at the ceiling. As she talked — "I was feeling so terrific about myself so I . . ." — the frustration overwhelmed her again and her eyes were pools of tears.

"You know," Marie said after Abby finished, "you've given that man an awful lot of power over you. All he has to do is refuse you twenty dollars and he's made you miserable and ruined your day. Is the world going to end because you can't buy cigarettes?"

"In this place, it might," Abby answered.

Marie continued. "Alcoholism in a family makes the other members feel powerless, so when they think they have some power, they want to use it. Another thing: your husband still has all the same feelings he had before you came into treatment. He's been very, very angry at you for a long time, angrier than even he knows. And just because you're feeling super doesn't mean *he's* feeling super. Maybe the house is a mess; maybe the kids aren't doing what they're supposed to do. Did you ask him how he was?"

Abby was not sure. "I don't think so."

"Okay. Maybe it sounds to him like you're only interested in yourself. Maybe he thinks the only reason you called was to ask for money."

Turning her head, Abby looked at Marie's electric hair, shooting out around her small face. Fleetingly, irrelevantly, Abby wondered, if Marie too had a terrible temper. Now Abby's voice was thoughtful. "He says he feels used and that he resents it."

"Well, when you were drinking, you *were* using him. On the phone you verified those feelings." Marie smiled. "It sounds like you've got something to think about besides the twenty dollars."

But Abby only glared at the ceiling. "That son of a bitch is always going to keep me under his thumb. He's got the money and he's going to hold that over my head, like I'm some kid."

"Is there anything you can change?"

Abby laughed grimly. "I can't change *him*."

"What can you change?"

"I'll go back to work. I'll get my own money."

"Were you always powerless in the family? What was it like before you were drinking alcoholically?"

"It was good."

Marie, resting her weight on one arm, bent toward Abby. "Your husband has only as much power as you give him," she said. "The irresponsibility part of your disease made you give up all your power, and the way to get it back is to change into a responsible person again. When you are making a contribution to the family and can feel your maturity, your share of the power and the family income should come back to you."

"That's a lot of crap," Abby answered, twisting her mouth. "I'll go home sober and everything will still be the same." While she spoke, another part of Abby's mind was worrying about cigarettes. Maybe she could borrow a dollar from Larry. That would cover candy, too.

The nurse answered, "Maybe nothing will change. That's a real possibility. But this time, if you are sober, you will have some choices about what you do. After family week, your options will be a lot clearer."

Abby was silent. The nurse laid a hand on Abby's thick hair, and said, "Don't be discouraged. It takes a long time to get sick and a long time to get better. The healing is a lifetime process. But living can truly be marvelous again. I know." She paused. "I have to go. If you want to talk, I'll be around." She rose and left the room.

Abby stayed on the bed, drained and exhausted. Seeing her sign — I'M TERRIFIC — she smiled thinly and thought,

"Not yet." A lifetime, the nurse had said. How could she do it living with Martin? The nurse had said to wait for family week. Maybe that would help. Maybe Martin would realize she wasn't the only one who had to change. Wait till the group got going. They would expose him. Finally somebody else would see how controlling and unfeeling he was.

Abby rolled over onto her stomach, face buried in the pillow, hands bunched below her throat. The problems seemed so enormous! What she *really* needed was a smoke! Abby went to the bureau and opened the top drawer. At the right end, on top of her lisle knee socks, was her supply — two packs of Parliament 100's. She stared anxiously down at the two shiny boxes, her one defense against hysteria. Maybe she should call Martin back. No! She would have to make these last. But right now she owed herself a smoke. Abby opened the top pack, took out one cigarette, and returned the box to its hiding place.

At lunch, Abby was resolutely lighthearted. She and Larry laughed over the awfulness of Sundays for drunks: the horrendous hangovers, the eternity of time to be endured under the watchful eyes of families. Abby described the brunches she organized in order to drink legitimately, pretending to be superhostess, grilling hamburgers and sipping mimosas. What is a mimosa? Larry wanted to know. She told him, champagne and orange juice with a daisy blossom floating on top.

Larry talked about the wait till noon when his favorite bar opened and the fraternity gathered, each man with his stool assigned by unspoken consent — the ritual minimum of drinks: the "walk-in," the "giveaway," the "roader." What is a roader? Abby wanted to know. A drink in a plastic glass for the drive home, Larry told her. Then Abby asked how he got out of the house in the first place. "I always ran out of cigarettes," Larry said, grinning, and added, "One time on a Sunday my wife sent me to get walnuts for banana bread, and I didn't come home for two days."

Smiling, Abby thought how strange and nice it was to be so comfortable with this bullnecked bar drinker, who wanted nothing from her except understanding and friendship. Then, as she carried her tray toward the dumping window, there was Larry's family at one of the tables. Four days from now, that would be Martin and the kids. Looking at Sally Mc-Gruder, the plucked eyebrows, the gold hoop earrings — her struggle to be good-looking, to hold together at the center of tragedy — Abby's heart clenched. How could she feel sorry for this woman, see gallantry in her, and yet be so angry at Martin? It was crazy. And the plump daughter and sinewy son, scrubbed and normal, with such pain in their eyes. There it was — what they talked about here — alcoholism, the family disease. And she and Larry were the causes. How could they have laughed? God would surely strike them. But if you didn't laugh, you might kill yourself.

Abby hurried back to her room and the bureau drawer. The smoke after a meal was the best of all. She could not be expected to miss that one. She'd skip her bedtime cigarette.

At group that afternoon the family week tableau once again assembled — Larry facing his family in the center of the room. Today was Larry's turn to speak, and he talked about his own guilt and anguish and asked for their forgiveness. Fern said, "What would you like to do, Larry?"

"Hug them," Larry answered.

"Go ahead."

Abby, with tears in her own eyes, watched the wife and two children rise up through the weight of their pain — joining Larry — the four of them holding on to each other, arms reaching and clasping, wet faces lifted and bent, and Larry kissing them one by one.

Fern sent them away to be alone together, and, while Abby wiped her eyes, Denton asked for the group's time. He was completing treatment at the end of the week and was terrified of going back to his parish, his old drinking environ-

174

ment. Abby looked at him curiously, the thin body and face, the curly hair combed fussily back. All at odds with the fluent voice and wiser-than-thou manner. "You sanctimonious son of a bitch," Abby thought. It was priests like him who had stood up in front of God and the world and condemned her sin and made her feel like shit.

Denton was describing his session with one of the spiritual counselors, a Roman Catholic priest, also an alcoholic. Denton said, "He kept reiterating, 'God created you first a human being.' He meant that it's *okay* to have all the human frailties, and I shouldn't wrap myself in my priesthood and pretend I'm immune from making mistakes. When I told him I understood, he said, 'Welcome to the human race.' "

Abby felt twinges of sympathy for Denton. It must be such a struggle in the soul, that double life as man of God and fallible human. And he'd had enormous pressures — dealing with parish problems and keeping up that know-it-all front. No wonder he drank. And probably he got lots of gifts of wine and brandy. But still it was unfair. He could drink behind his priestly cloak of righteousness, while she had been exposed to the world.

Denton continued, "I think I finally understand about surrender, and truly turning my life and will over to God. Surrender has always been associated in my mind with giving up and defeat. So I used to tell God that I surrendered everything to him — and then I'd pick up everything again and walk out of the room, still trying to be in control."

"If you're not in control," Abby wondered, "how can you keep from drinking?"

The rest of that day, on and off, Abby kept thinking about Denton. Something about him had shaken her. She wanted to feel better about him, but she could not shake her sense of triumph. The high and mighty clergy who judged her had been brought low, to her level. She was a sinner before God, and so was Denton. But at the same time she wanted him to be better than that, to be a *priest,* incorruptible.

But these thoughts were not crisp in her mind. They were fuzzy impressions, part of larger confusions simmering in her head. Occasionally an idea broke the surface like a steam bubble, but then collapsed back into the general muddle. Bewildered, confused, overwhelmed, she felt she was drowning in this cereal of psychology and religion. The word "surrender" kept churning in her mind. What was it? What did it feel like? Could she ever do it? Especially if she didn't know what it was? Would the patron saint of drunks (Who would that be?) touch her on the forehead? Or probably on the lips?

With these thoughts stewing inside her, Abby sat on her favorite sofa in the lounge, looking out into the sky, where a seagull would occasionally hang and then wheel and soar free. At the other end of Abby's couch was the tall, round-shouldered figure of Julia, smoking a cigarette, her eyes cast downward.

Abby wondered what she was thinking. Was she thrashing inside with the same fears and confusions? It was called obsessing, Abby knew, and was a trait of alcoholics. They should be living one day at a time, and turning the future over to God. That was the Third Step. But how did you turn your life and will over to God? Become superreligious? A Jesus freak? What would happen if she surrendered the reins of her life to God? How did that work? Would her life change drastically? Would she lose Martin and the children? Probably God would want to punish her. Could she dare take that risk? If Denton was having trouble turning over *his* life to God, how could *she* do it? They said in the Twelve Steps, ". . . God as we understood Him." Suppose you didn't understand Him. Or maybe even believe in Him. Denton lived with God every day, worked for Him, had a relationship with Him. She could not imagine what that was like and envied Denton, and was resentful.

Feeling the jitters coming on, Abby hurried to her cache of cigarettes. She *had* to have one. Returning to the small lounge, she lit the precious cylinder and took the first, deep, therapeutic drag. Now she could relax. And maybe she could get up a bridge game. She looked around the lounge. Not with Garrett, his legs stretched out in designer jeans, hands clasped over his small paunch, lounging, Abby thought, like a girl-watcher on a park bench. But the others would. Paula, smoking, staring out the window, head turned on the long neck, her slender arm graceful along the back of the couch. So would Julia, her thin gray hair bent over a book, her stomach round under a denim skirt. And maybe that short man over there. Must be a stranger from another corridor.

Abby collected them around the square table at the near end of the lounge. The game felt good to Abby, doing this thing from her healthy past, plotting strategy, counting points, remembering tricks — her mind clear and precise again. It seemed far more real than alcoholism, as though she could, in fact, put the disease aside.

After the game, enjoying her sense of normality, Abby started back to her room to wash for dinner. Suddenly, down the long tube of the hall, in the brighter lights of the nurses' station, there was Annie O'Reilly — elegantly groomed, probably perfumed, carrying a shopping bag with flowers poking out the top. Abby spun on her heel and hurried back through the lounge and down the fire stairs. Between floors she stopped, irresolute, paralyzed by a kind of stage fright, as though ordered to do a performance, but given no lines. What could she and Annie have in common now? They were separated by an infinity of new experiences. How could she possibly describe herself to Annie? How could Annie possibly understand about surrender and powerlessness and family week — and Larry's heartbroken daughter?

Abby continued down the back stairs and skulked along the first floor hall to the dinner line. She sat that evening with Paula and studied her across the foreground of their brown plastic trays. Abby wondered about the illusive air of arrogance, a haughtiness Paula clearly did not feel. Was it the slight tilt of her curved chin? Or a face too smooth, too unlined to be readable. Or was it a model's cultivated look of challenge?

So the conversation drifted, as it usually did in Riverside, to their common bond — their addiction. Abby asked how Paula could possibly have used during treatment there at Riverside. Paula's eyes gleamed. Her mouth smiled. Her voice rose, almost excited. She said, "This guy came in and said he had some coke in his room. In a split second I was into a high like I'd already used it. I told him, *'Go get it!'* While I waited, I had all the sensations in my body — my blood rushing, my pulse fast, my stomach juiced up. I knew exactly how I would feel when I snorted it. But he didn't come back, and I was depressed, like I had come down from coke. I got mad and I followed him around till he finally came to my room and laid two lines. I snorted them and got the relief." Paula's voice dropped. "But after he was gone, I was left with this total anger, because when you snort cocaine, you want much more than two lines."

Abby listened, mesmerized, wondering what she herself would do if she found a glass of vodka back in her room. She did not know. She asked Paula, "Didn't the treatment you'd had do you *any* good?"

Paula looked embarrassed. "I thought I would learn the Program and get my tools — learn about myself, my low self-worth, what makes me use drugs — so then I could have my drugs, but know when to stop."

Paula excused herself and Abby sat alone over her coffee, able now to consider the day's experiences. She thought about that disastrous phone call to Martin. Maybe she hadn't been fair to him. No "How are you?" No anything, really. And he was home taking care of everybody when he'd rather be out playing golf. And he'd heard a million times that everything was going to be different and better. How could she expect any enthusiasm from him? Or belief?

But, damn it, why couldn't she expect twenty dollars? It was so little! He spent that on golf balls without a second thought. Oh, God, she was so sick of scrounging and scrounging — always dependent on handouts — like some bum. But she'd been a bum. She deserved whatever lumps she got. Marie was right. She must change, or this would go on and on and on.

She thought about her recent happiness. They talked about treatment highs. Well, whatever it was, she wanted it back — that sense of progress. She ached to get better, to leave all the horrors behind her, to be safe, to be herself again and have her life back. Well, she had to lay herself open again in group. She had to finish her First Step and give it. She thought about the poster on Fern's wall — "The Truth Will Set You Free. But First It Will Make You Miserable." So be it.

Resolutely, Abby returned to her room. On the long, low bureau was a pot of red begonias. A note was propped among the stalks. It read, "Abby, dear, I am so sorry not to see you and hug you in person. Anyway, this is to remind you that a lot of people love you and are rooting for you. That's a pun, honey. Affectionately, Annie."

"Nice," Abby thought. Annie was a good friend. It had been a mistake, running away. The new Abby wouldn't have done that. But it was going to be good, having something alive to care for. Maybe if she could keep a plant alive, she could keep herself alive. Abby checked the soil with her finger. It was dry. She fed it a glass of water and felt pleasurably domestic. Then she went to work on her First Step.

Three hours later, just before she went to bed, Abby sneaked a cigarette in her room. She had earned this one, too. The job was finished, and she had done it well.

The next morning was Thursday, May twentieth. Abby moved with the flow of patients down the hallway to their various groups. Fern's door was closed, and the group backed up and eddied and spread out again, waiting. Dressed with studied casualness, in a skirt, checked gingham shirt, sneakers, Abby paced up and down the hall, clutching her yellow legal pad. Her heart thumped. Her throat hurt. On the backs of her hands were blotchy patches that itched. Julia was leaning on the railing along the wall. Abby joined her, saying, "If only I didn't have to *read* my First Step. If only I could just answer questions. Then the focus wouldn't be *all* on me."

Julia put her hand on Abby's narrow shoulder. "It'll be okay."

Fern opened the door, and the group funneled in. Abby chose a seat directly across from Fern and felt virtuous and brave. With her pad in her lap she sat on her hands, watching the group, her executioners, fill the anonymous plastic chairs. Her glance took in the three pots of African violets on the window sill — a homey touch of normalcy — and over Fern's desk the bulletin board covered with name tags. Like the crutches, Abby thought, hung in Bernadette's grotto at Lourdes. She reread the posters: ". . . but first it will make you miserable." ". . . lead you where you did not intend to go." She thought about the anguish these walls had absorbed, truly sponged up, she decided, because the feeling of the room was benign. That was hopeful. Maybe what they said was true. That if you could speak your most terrifying secrets, you could leave the burden here forever.

Nevertheless, nervousness hummed in her body. She pulled her hands from under her legs and scratched the red patches. She crossed her legs, then stretched out her legs; then hooked them back under the chair and began picking at her fingernails — until she jammed her hands back under her thighs. She was sure the group could hear her heart pounding. She wondered if anybody had ever died of a heart attack giving a First Step. Maybe she would be the first. She could feel Fern watching her.

After the reading for the day — "Alcoholism is called the 'lonely disease' " — Fern said, smiling, "I sense that Abby is eager to have the floor." Abby felt flattened against her chair by the circle of eyes watching her expectantly. She opened her mouth, but that lump, huge and hurting in her throat, blocked her words.

Fern smiled encouragingly. "Try a deep breath."

Abby inhaled and began to read. "The First Step says, 'We admitted we were powerless over alcohol — that our lives had become unmanageable." Nervously Abby joked, "But of course my life has been unmanageble since *birth*." Nobody smiled. She read on. "My early stage of drinking was from age seventeen to thirty-two. The middle stage was from thirty-two until about thirty-seven, and the late stage was the past five years." Abby kept her eyes fixed on the yellow paper, shutting out everybody in the room. "*Preoccupation with chemicals*. In the first stage I looked forward to the Friday and Saturday night parties at college. After I was married, I looked forward all day to my husband coming home so we could have our cocktails. I was always happy to go out to dinner because I knew it would be all right to drink."

Abby could hear her voice trembling with tension. She pressed on. "In the second stage I began making lunch dates with women who I knew liked to drink. My husband was frequently late getting home and I would start cocktails without him, using the excuse of a rough day with the kids. We were involved in a lot of business entertaining and I would always have one or two drinks while I got dressed. In the third stage, most of my day was planned around drinking. I would set up a lunch date so I could drink early in the day and then sober up enough to look normal when my husband came home. Sometimes I would drink olive oil to coat my stomach so I could drink more without showing it. Sometimes, when I was by myself, I'd make a drink and telephone a friend — so I could tell myself I wasn't drinking alone.

"When we entertained I never served dinner until about eleven because I didn't want to stop drinking. It got to be a joke, guests saying they were going to call the Biafra Rescue League. I'd plan dishes with wine in them so I could drink the rest of the bottle. When my husband began checking up on the bar bottles, I kept my own supply hidden in the house. I would never go anywhere without vodka in my purse for insurance. Each morning I would check my bottle and if I needed more, I would make sure I went to a different liquor store so nobody would know how much I was drinking. I usually had the bottle gift wrapped. To pay for my vodka, I padded my food budget and bought a lot of hamburger."

Hearing her own voice describing herself, summing up her compulsion, Abby was astounded. Why hadn't she *seen* how far it had gone? How could she have told herself she didn't have a problem? At the same time her mind was flowing with memories: that feeling when she had two full bottles hidden in the house, the warm security.

Now her consciousness turned wholly inward. The tension was gone and the words rose off the page at the slightest touch of her eyes. She read on, reliving her attempts to control her drinking: cutting down at parties or drinking dry vermouth, which she hated, and then in the third stage switching to wine or trying to make one bottle last the whole weekend. She described the effects on her physical health — the hangovers, the exhaustion, the nerves, the nausea.

She reached the entry *Effects on Sexuality,* and felt in her stomach the old knots of resentment. Her voice hardened slightly, its edges rough. She read, "Sometimes drinking hurt my sex life because of arguments. Eventually, I was so afraid of being rejected and hurt, I never made any overtures and neither did he. I don't think he is sexually interested in me anymore, and I basically do not care about him. I have thought there is something physically wrong with me. Maybe after my hysterectomy I'm having an early menopause."

But these written words were inadequate for the anger rising inside Abby. She looked up from the yellow pad. Her high-boned cheeks were stiff, her eyes fierce. She searched the circle for understanding. "I was so *lonely.* I *wanted* to be close. I *wanted* love. But he wanted to go to sleep because he was tired. And he'd always have his little sarcastic remarks that made me feel like everything was *my* fault."

182

Fleetingly, Abby noticed some people looking away, others shifting uncomfortably in their chairs.

Abby immersed herself again in the yellow pad, reciting the effects on emotional and feeling life: ". . . Sometimes I was like a vacuum with no feelings at all, unable to relate to anybody, not even myself . . ." Next came effects on social life: ". . . I noticed people making excuses to get away from me at parties because I was repetitive and boring . . ." Then effects on spiritual life: "I have always believed in God as my higher power. I don't think alcohol changed that. But when I was drinking, I was embarrassed to ask God for anything, and when I forced myself to go to church, I couldn't wait to get home for Bloody Marys."

She read the effects on work, on finances, on character; the violation of her closely held values — honesty, responsibility, patience, forgiveness, humility, trust, pride, loyalty, optimism, sensitivity. She recited her insane behavior: ". . . I had forgotten to defrost the Thanksgiving turkey, so I put it in the clothes dryer. But then I couldn't remember what I had done with the turkey, until I heard this terrible thumping in the basement . . ." She recounted her blackouts: ". . . In the morning my personal phone book would be open next to the phone, and I would die because I didn't know who I'd called or where, and every month I dreaded finding out when the phone bill came . . ."

She described her destructive behavior: ". . . One evening, my husband came home from work and said, 'Don't tell me you're just now washing the breakfast dishes.' I threw a pan through the kitchen window." She described the accidents caused by drinking: ". . . I couldn't get out of bed, I was so hung over. The kids were little, and they decided to cheer up their mom by baking me cookies. A towel caught fire and they dragged it across the floor and caught the carpet on fire. Their little act of love almost burned the house down, because I was so paralyzed by alcohol."

Now Abby had reached the final category — how family members had suffered from her chemical dependency. Her voice was matter-of-fact as she read, "I have seen my husband change from a man who was kind, loving, honest, and open — to a man who is hostile, devious, bitter, and thoroughly frustrated because of my drinking. We started out with a beautiful relationship and now he drives me crazy and I drive him crazy." Abby looked appraisingly around the group, checking her audience. "Nothing is more important to my husband than his work. At a testimonial dinner during a silence between speeches, I said to him in a loud voice, 'How can you stand all these horses' asses?' Another time, at a dance, my husband said I was drunk and he wouldn't dance with me, so I lay down on the floor and refused to move until he danced with me."

Next on the yellow pad Abby had written, "How I hurt my children." As she came to this heading, her hand holding the pad began to shake slightly. The lump was there in her throat again, and she could feel a pulse beating painfully over her right eye. She read, "I never physically abused my daughter, Judy, but I abused her verbally and emotionally. When I was drinking, I criticized everything she did. She is a good, bright, funny kid, but I never saw that. I saw a slob who did not clean up her room, who did not do what she was told. Even though I knew it hurt her teenage vanity, I would hassle her about bad taste in clothes and tacky friends and her weight. When she told me about problems, I would dismiss them with such phrases as, 'You'll outgrow that childish behavior,' or, 'You should choose your friends more carefully.' "

Her face wet now, Abby spoke directly to Fern. "Sometimes in the night I would wake up in the darkness and I would know what I was doing and think what a horrible bitch I was." Abby choked and put her head down and covered her eyes with her blotchy hand. She could hear Fern's voice saying soothingly, "Keep going. You're doing fine."

Fighting for control, Abby began reading again. "I used to humiliate Judy in front of friends. Once my husband and I brought Judy and her best friend home from a party and

I was so drunk I could barely stagger up the front steps. I fell down and Judy and her friend had to help me indoors. After that, she didn't bring friends home." Abby stopped and sat looking down at the pad, at her red hands gripping it, at her white knuckles. She could not go on. They — Fern — would know forever that she was the lowest of the low. Her eyes wide and frightened, she looked up again — and down — and up.

"It's all right," Fern said gently. "Go on."

"I can't."

"If it's so bad that you have to *decide* whether you can talk about it," Fern said, "then you *have* to talk about it." Fern leaned forward, her shrewd eyes intense. "It's a weight you don't have to bear anymore."

Abby, her face flushed, no longer looked at the yellow paper. "Evan always knew how to bait me so I'd end up being the ogress and he'd be the innocent victim. He'd say, 'Oh, you'll never understand,' and walk away. Every time, I'd be off the wall. One night — Evan was about fourteen — I'd been drinking since five o'clock and he was in bed. His report card had just come and it was terrible, and I was scared he was getting into marijuana. I told him to stop hanging around with the Harvey kids, because I'd heard they were dealing pot. I told him if I found out he was smoking pot, I'd call the police and turn them all in. Evan looked up at me with those bright round eyes of his — just waiting to see what I'd do — and he said, 'I don't have to listen to you.' "

Checking Fern's expressionless face, Abby inhaled a deep breath and said, "I went bananas. I grabbed Evan by the hair and started banging his head against the headboard with all my strength, and yanking on his hair. That tough-guy facade fell apart and he began to scream and cry, and my husband ran in and pulled me away and took Evan out of the room. I could hear him telling Evan, 'Of course you're scared. Your mother's anger is unbelievable.' They went off like some coach and the captain of the team. I was left feeling like a nothing and the worst shit in the world. I was really sore at Martin — but the idea that I would grab my son by the hair and try to bash in his head . . . I'd stone a mother who did that to a kid."

Abby looked down. She was silent. She was done. She had told it all, shared it, heard her voice say it. She felt a certain peace, a release, a pride of accomplishment. She also felt utterly transparent. Now everybody knew everything. As though removed from her body, Abby could see herself from a long distance — a pathetic, frightened little girl sitting on her hands on a plastic chair. She longed to reach out to herself and put her arms around herself and say, "It's okay. I forgive you."

Fern looked around the circle. "Would you like to give some feedback, group? Do you think Abby is aware of her powerlessness and the unmanageability of her life? Did you get a sense of the progression of her disease? Is she in touch with the disease concept? Did you get a sense of her behavior, and did she connect it with her chemical usage?"

Julia spoke. "I certainly got the sense of her progression."

"Speak directly to Abby," Fern told her.

"I thought you saw the progression of the disease, and I was impressed by the amount of feeling you showed. I certainly recognized a lot of what you said."

Abby smiled gratefully at Julia and put her hands back in her lap.

Denton spoke. "I agree. But I think you were kidding yourself about alcohol not affecting your belief in God. You said, in essence, that you'd rather drink than go to church — which tells me that alcohol has blocked your relationship with God. The bottle became your higher power, not God."

The word "preachy" passed through Abby's mind. She started to explain — "I meant . . ."

Interrupting sharply, Fern said, "Just listen, Abby. Hear what the group has to tell you."

Julia, very tentatively, asked, "Don't you have a third

child? A little boy? I wondered why you didn't mention him."

"He's untouched, thank God," Abby answered. "I made a point of never being drunk in front of him."

The room was in an uproar, several members trying to speak. But Julia's polite voice, and level, kind gaze at Abby, persisted. "I have a little girl. I always told her I was sick and assumed that's what she believed. But the older ones sit around and talk and the little one is taking it all in. She knew everything. And I think now she has been the most affected."

"But Frederick never said a *thing*," Abby answered, hot with fright and embarrassment, fingers bending and flexing the yellow pad.

"Little kids don't say anything to you," Julia continued. "Everything seems *so* tenuous to them, and they think if they complain, you might leave — and it would be their fault."

Abby felt that lump in her throat. She knew, inescapably, that Julia was right. She remembered the time, going into Frederick's room, when she bumped her shoulder against the doorjamb. He looked up sharply from his homework and said, "Mom, are you drunk?" But right now, she couldn't deal with this. She had to shut up the group, say what they wanted to hear. "You've given me a lot to think about," she answered.

Larry's big, square face was thoughtful. "What I picked up . . . I felt kind of sorry for your husband. You didn't even give the poor guy a name."

"But I . . ."

"Just listen," Fern said.

"Well, can't I tell the group my husband's name?"

The corners of Fern's mouth tugged upward. "By all means. What is his name?"

"Martin."

"Okay."

Paula spoke, her face impassive. "I thought you talked with a lot of feeling and honesty and I identified with you a lot. But I think you skipped very lightly over the effects on your husband. You gave only two examples — almost like you were telling a funny story."

Abby nodded, but thought of all the laughs she had gotten with those stories. They *were* funny, goddamn it! You had to laugh about somebody lying in a full-length evening dress on a dance floor, her arms crossed on her chest like Tecumseh.

The nurse, Marie, took her turn. "I want to give you a lot of support for the job you did. I think you really tried to be honest, and I think you are aware of the unmanageability of your life. But I got no sense of your powerlessness against alcohol. I don't think you realize on a gut level the hold the disease has on you. And I heard a lot of contradictions. You said there was no preoccupation in your first stage, but you were looking forward to drinking on weekends. You said that drinking hadn't affected you sexually, but then you wondered whether something was physically wrong with you. You said you believed in God, but you sat in church thinking about drinking."

Fern asked, "Did any of you notice a very interesting fact when Abby read the effects on Martin?"

The group looked blank.

Fern said to Abby, "In both your examples of humiliating Martin, you never said you had been drinking." She turned back to the group. "Does that tell anybody anything?"

Denton uncrossed his thin legs. "It tells me, Abby, that deep down you are still denying that your alcoholism has anything to do with Martin's hostility. You don't see that the progression of the disease parallels the erosion of your marriage. You think if Martin had been different, you wouldn't have done those things to him. I heard you giving reasons for a lot of your behavior, even the time you attacked Evan."

Abby started to say, "I don't see . . ."

Denton cut in, his voice powerful. "Abby, do you think

if you had married somebody else, you would be sitting in that chair? Be honest."

Abby was sweating. "Maybe not. Or maybe not so soon." The pulse in her forehead was agony.

"Then everything's his fault," Denton persisted. "He made you an alcoholic."

"I don't know. Maybe he made it easier. It's hard to know."

Abby heard Larry's disgusted voice across the room. "Crapola."

Denton said, "I just wondered if you were looking for someone to blame."

Abby, twisting her wedding ring around and around, tried to sound analytical. "Of course, my father was an alcoholic, so . . ."

Larry interrupted. "Did Martin actually bend your arm and lift the glass to your mouth?"

"Of course not. That's silly."

Now Larry was leaning forward, his voice eager, the veins on his cheeks bright red. "So you had a choice."

"At first there was no reason to choose. It was something Martin and I did together that was fun and companionable." Abby clung to her tone of sweet reasonableness.

"But at some point you could have made a choice."

Abby felt like crying, but forced her voice to be earnest. "I've been trying to make a different choice for at least five years."

"But plenty of people have cocktails and their lives don't become unmanageable."

Feeling swept along by Larry's intensity, Abby joined the rush of his logic and said, "But with my alcoholic inheritance . . ."

"You got hooked!" Larry half shouted. He leaned back, triumphant.

Abby was silent, staring at her knees, her hands back under her legs. Her head reeled with disappointment and terror, amazement and anger. Expecting to be applauded, she felt zapped. She could see, in a flash of reality, that she could no longer blame Martin — or her mother — or herself. But after everything that Martin had done to her, how could she let him off the hook? That bastard had hurt her too many times. He must have *something* to do with her drinking. But if it wasn't Martin, wasn't his work, wasn't his golf, wasn't her hysterectomy; if she was actually sick, then she would have to look at *herself,* and she *hated* herself.

Breaking the pause, Fern asked, "What do you hear the group saying to you?"

Abby wanted only to escape, to turn off these voices. "That I'm blaming Martin for my drinking." Abby stopped, feeling the anger she had held back rise up into her chest and throat and head. How dare they ruin that good feeling she had had, that peace. Abby remained mute, her mouth clamped closed, her body somehow shrunken. Fern sat waiting, the pressure building in the room.

"Anything more?" Fern asked.

"No."

"Abby," Fern said, "You obviously put a lot of work into your First Step, and I want to give you a lot of support for that. At times you saw the reality of your addiction. But at other times you retreated into blaming, which is your favorite defense. I don't think you have accepted how powerless you are over all chemicals. The disease is so subtle, so cunning, so malignant, and has done so much to you. I see you as a very sensitive woman who has compromised all her values. Your self-esteem has been taken away, and it is very painful for me to see how you beat yourself up as a woman. That's a real part of what alcohol does to people, especially women. Another thing alcohol does . . . you need to look at the reality that booze was your God. Everything else — your kids, your husband, your friends, your religion, whatever — came second. You must get in touch with that, Abby."

The voice was becoming almost hypnotic. "So acceptance

and surrender are still missing for you. I don't know how that comes to people. But recovery is a process, and you must allow yourself to feel the pain in family week. It can be very intense, but do not hold it off. It will help you grasp the breadth and depth and effect of your disease so you will never want to experience that again. And don't negate what you have done today. You did good work, and this group cares enough about you to give you some awarenesses. That's what we're here for. You did a *good* job. I want you to hear that."

After group, Abby sat on the edge of her bed, her hands hanging slack between her knees, the mobile mouth expressionless, the fine hazel eyes disinterested as they surveyed the green walls and gray vinyl floor. Her gaze came to rest on Annie's plant and its red fountain of blossoms. She thought vaguely, "I hope it doesn't die." A tap sounded on the door. It was Julia, asking how she was and adding, "You had a tough time."

Rousing herself, Abby smiled weakly and said, "I knew they'd find a few things wrong, but nothing like that."

Julia sat down on the small wooden chair. "I think you did a real good job. I envy you."

"For God's sake, why?"

Julia looked down at her nicotine-stained hands. "I'm stuck on dead center. You're going to make it."

Abby could remember Doreen saying those words. How could these women be so sure? Right now she felt absolutely empty, blown out. "What makes you think that?" Abby asked.

"You're stronger than you give yourself credit for," Julia answered, lifting her pale blue eyes to Abby's face. "You've already survived a lot, but you still care about people and yourself. You're still trying. You were trying this morning."

"I told things today I've never told anybody," Abby said. "I wonder what they're going to do with it all? They accepted a lot of my First Step, but are they going to accept me?"

Julia's eyes, still on Abby, were affectionate. "Everybody really cares about you. Couldn't you feel it in the room?"

Abby, pleased, nodded. "A little." She smiled, crookedly, out of one side of her mouth. "So maybe I shouldn't be depressed just because I'm depressed." The two women were silent again. Abby, swinging her legs up, lay down on her side, head propped on one hand. She let herself enjoy the comfortable quiet, the air of sympathy. Presently, she said ruefully, "Why the hell did I have to be an alcoholic — this sweet little girl from the puritan East."

Julia's gaze had disconnected again, going past Abby, out the window. "Well, at least you know who the enemy is," she said.

Abby brushed a swatch of hair back from her cheek. "The group misunderstood me on spirituality. There are people who don't believe in any god at all. I think God sent me *here.*"

Julia answered gently, "They were telling you that if you have an image of God and don't make any use of Him, then it's like He's just a picture on the wall — a decoration you look at and say, 'That's God.'"

Abby thought about this. Yes, she could understand what they meant. "I think you're really wise," she said. "Treatment ought to be easy for you."

Julia laughed without humor. "Treatment doesn't happen in your head," she said. "I used to read every book I could get on alcoholism, and in every one of them I could find something that proved I wasn't an alcoholic. The next morning I'd see the end of a glass of scotch full of decayed cigarette butts — and I'd drink it down."

Abby looked at Julia sitting there a little primly, knees and feet together; looked at the limpness of the hands in her lap, at the pale flicker of defeat in the washed-out eyes. Abby felt an ache in her heart. "I've done lots of things like that," she answered. "I guess we have to hate ourselves so much, we don't *ever* want to do it again."

Julia's eyes drifted back toward the emptiness of the window. "I just wish I could feel *something*," she said. "I'd settle for some good, solid hate."

The ache grew. Suddenly Abby could not bear Julia's eyes, which never took hold of anything. Abby wanted to shake her, rattle her into action, wanted to scream at her. The impatience, the fear, the ache, was now like a bird inside Abby, beating its wings. She sat up. "I think we should take a break from real life," she said, "and put Pandora's mess back in her box for a while."

CHAPTER

8

FOR THE next three days, Abby's impending family week dominated her mood. She was restless, and her mind kept wandering into daydreams of the past — the bad times with Martin, the good times with the children. An ache smoldered at the top of her stomach — acid — like perpetual hunger pangs.

On Friday, May twenty-first, before group, Abby received a letter at the nurses' station. It was from Martin. She stood for a moment by the curved counter and then, holding the letter judiciously, walked slowly down the hall to her room. She sat on the bed and opened it with sudden speed, tearing the envelope across its face. The letter inside was folded around thirty dollars. She smiled, warmed and relieved. It was a peace offering from the other Martin, the original Martin. The note said:

> Dear Abby,
>
> Perhaps I reacted too quickly when you asked for cigarette money. But I am fed up with supporting addictions of any kind and have never wanted you to smoke, particularly in bed. Every time I came home from work, I wondered if the house would still be there.
>
> I am, of course, glad to hear that Riverside seems to be helping you. Judy is talking about not coming to family week because of missing a week of schoolwork. Her guidance counselor agrees. I have told her it is her decision. I can't say I'm looking forward to

it, either, but as you know, I will do everything in my power to enable you to get well. My fondest hope is that alcohol will be gone from your life, and we can return to our marriage as it once was.

I love you,
Martin

Abby shook her head as her heart chilled. Typical Martin. He wanted to be nice. But even when he did the right thing, he took the shine off it, made it seem like philanthropy. Even when he was wrong, there were reasons why he was actually right. To Martin the equation was so simple: subtract alcohol, get happiness. In his head, she was the only factor that needed to be changed. The ache in her stomach was stinging now.

And Judy wasn't coming — the child she had hurt the most. The silver lining to family week was the hope of making friends with Judy. They used to be so close. Judy's sudden hugs and unexpected presents: drawings from school, hair barrettes painted with flowers. Abby could still picture the ten-year-old figure on the big bed, watching her mother dress for a party, watching the silk sliding down the grown-up body. Together they would decide on the perfume, and, emptying the jewelry box onto the bed like a pirate's treasure, they would pick a necklace. Then Abby, sitting on the bed, would let Judy brush her hair. At the end, posing with a smile, Abby could see herself in Judy's eyes — a queen ready for a ball.

Folding Martin's letter, Abby tightened her lips. Apparently Judy saw no reason to come. But why should she? After all her mother's empty apologies, all the pathetic attempts to break through the gray distance of disgust that separated them. Sitting on Judy's bed, reeking of booze and Clorets, she would say, "Oh, Judy, I so much want to stop being like this and get well."

Judy would answer, "Don't worry, Mom. You'll get better."

Then the sadness would overwhelm Abby. She would cry, saying, "I feel so unloved," and bend down, saying, "I wish I was a better mother." But the face against the whiteness of the pillow would twist away from her kiss. Judy's voice would come back, "Mom, you're drunk!"

Slipping the thirty dollars into her pants pocket, Abby moved to the bureau and put the letter in the top bureau drawer. She was aware again of the ache inside her. Why couldn't she shake it, she wondered. There would be no surprises next week. All the McGruders' agony — that was Larry's family. My God, those lighted matches. Nothing like *that* had ever happened.

Picking up her brush, she passed it through the chestnut hair. It was becoming shiny again, she noticed with pleasure. And her wrists, inside the shirt-sleeves, were no longer lean as sticks. The hollows under her eyes had filled and whitened. The skin over her cheekbones was not dull and pale as paper. Abby grinned to herself. Drinking instead of eating was not a recommended weight-loss diet. Maybe, after all, there was *something* to be said for sobriety.

But as she sat in group, the ache burned higher and a vague anxiety floated inside her. Jerold was talking about his parents and sisters, but Abby hardly listened, and in her lap, the fingers of her clasped hands wrestled against each other. Jerold finished and she felt Fern's eyes. "Abby, what's the problem?"

Abby's mind stiffened. She blurted, "My daughter may not come to family week."

"How do you feel about that?" Fern asked.

Her fingers switched to her wedding ring. "Judy's guidance counselor is saying it's too much school for her to miss. Maybe that's right. I've got enough on my conscience without hurting her education."

As Abby spoke, Fern's lips had tightened. "Do you really believe that? What is your body telling you?"

"I don't want to *force* her to come," Abby said. "It would only make things worse between us."

"Answer my question, Abby. What is your body telling you? Always listen to your body. It usually knows the truth."

Incongruously, Abby smiled. "It's saying I'm really disappointed." Her face sobered. "But I feel like I don't have any rights."

"Double crapola," Larry said. "Do you *still* attach so little value to yourself?"

"Will you make a contract with me?" Fern asked. "Will you call Judy and *tell* her she is needed here?"

"I'll try."

"There's a lot of self-pity in that word, 'try.' "

"I will do it."

Paula said, "I'm coming with you and make sure."

After group Paula and Larry escorted Abby to a telephone booth in a small anteroom off the kitchen. As they walked, Abby said, "I'm hopeless. I'm actually scared of a fifteen-year-old kid." Facing the telephone, she remembered Fern's words, "You must learn to act, not just react." Abby grasped the receiver and dialed the number. A voice answered. Abby asked, "Is that you, Judy?"

"God, Mom," Judy said, "you don't know your own daughter when you hear her?"

"I'm sorry," Abby said. "But this is a very hard call for me to make. I have to ask you to come to family week." She felt Larry's large hand on her shoulder and heard his voice in her ear — "Stop crawling and begging." Abby drew in her breath, but Judy was already talking.

"Mom, that's a whole week out of school. You want me to get good grades, don't you? I might never catch up again. My guidance counselor says we can get counseling later."

Abby's voice was firmer. "It won't be the same."

"Stop pressuring me, Mom," Judy answered. Tears were under the words. "I can't take it. I don't want to come there and have all those people dig into me and analyze me. What do they know about me! You're asking too much. I have my own life to think of. I think you're being selfish."

Now Abby's voice was steely. "Okay, here's the word. I'm

telling you to come to family week. They say it's important for my recovery and there are things you need to say to me." Abby stopped. The ache was a sharp pain. She softened her voice. "I want us to be mother and daughter again." Abby choked. There was silence on the line. Abby waited. Panic rose inside her. Suddenly, she heard her voice cry out, "Please!" Still there was silence on the line.

When Judy spoke, her words were almost strangled. "I'll think about it." Pause. "I've got to go now." She hung up.

Abby replaced the receiver and saw the damp handprint on the black plastic. "Well, folks," she said joylessly, "I want your reviews under my door in half an hour."

Paula put an arm around her.

On Sunday, May twenty-third — the day before family week — she came out of her room into the somnolent quiet and headed for the chapel to attend the service. In the elevator bank she stood nervously punching the "down" button, but suddenly turned away and went into the large lounge. The furniture was pushed at random into one end of the space, as though painters would soon start work. There had been a record dance on Saturday night — a collection taken, pizza ordered in — and Abby had gone, feeling like a teenager, relieved to detach herself in time and space. The evening had been fun. Drunks knew how to have a good time. They were, after all, drinkers who just weren't drinking.

She made her way to a far corner near the battered upright piano. Brushing potato chip shards from the seat, she turned a chair toward the window and settled down. Lifting her legs onto a coffee table, she pushed aside the empty junk-food bags and the soda cans piled like spent shell cases. She lit a cigarette and exhaled the long draft with a relieved sigh. She could not face the rah rah of the chapel service — "Let's hear it for God." The moment at the chapel door, however, the touch of the priest, *that* she had hugged to herself like a talisman. It had been a personal benediction. She wasn't ready for official Christianity. When she had needed it the most, there had been no help. Perhaps it was not God who had abandoned and humiliated her. Just his messengers. So today she would go later to the chapel — after the hustle and bustle — when she could have God to herself.

Through the window she studied the billowing clouds. Supposedly, you could find shapes of animals and things. Nothing. Except maybe white ink blots. When God looked down, did he see horsies and doggies and lambies? "Grow up," Abby told herself, laughing. But these days she did feel more comfortable about God, as though maybe He had forgiven her — a little. And she liked herself a little better. Which wasn't saying much. But it was improvement. Her shame felt softer around the edges, less slashing, less maiming. But what would happen tomorrow, facing her family in group?

"I'm stronger now," Abby thought. Three weeks she'd been sober. Two and a half weeks in Fern's group, a lifetime of living. She hadn't really flubbed that phone call to Judy. As Larry had pointed out, she didn't run away, jump out a window, fling herself down the fire stairs. She had made the call. She had *told* Judy to come. And she had glimpsed an understandable goal: an Abby who could stand her ground, be herself and maybe more.

Clearing a little more room on the table with a foot, she wondered why nobody had called to say whether Judy was coming. Didn't they think it was important? Almost certainly Judy wouldn't come. Then what? Abby stopped herself. She was projecting into the future. That was a no-no. "God grant me the serenity to accept the things I cannot change," she thought. Maybe God would help her through family week. Fern kept saying to read chapter four in the Big Book about the Higher Power. Maybe she would do that instead of the chapel.

Returning to her room, she located the heavy blue volume under magazines at the end of the bureau. The room felt oppressive and she returned to the sky view in the big lounge, picking up a coffee on the way. Opening the Big Book, Abby felt virtuous and impatient. This was, she knew, the bible of AA. Two thirds of it was stories of individual alcoholics and how AA had saved them. She had skimmed some of these and decided they did not apply to her. They were like the Saturday night AA meetings at Riverside. She'd only gone to one of these, enough to see that nobody took attendance. Maybe after treatment, AA might teach her some things. Fortunately, it wasn't a club you had to join. No dues or officers. You just went to meetings. So she wouldn't have to do it very often.

Abby opened the book to chapter four, titled "We Agnostics." It was in the first third of the book, written in 1939 when the membership was only a hundred. It was the gospel of the Program and Abby had skimmed it once and decided it was outdated and simplistic, a bit sappy. She began to read, but soon impatience overtook her, and she flipped pages, her eyes pausing on whatever caught her attention. "We had to find a power by which we could live, and it had to be a *Power greater than ourselves.*"

Abby shrugged her shoulders. It was a lot more complicated than that. She skipped ahead.

"We found that as soon as we were able to lay aside prejudice and express even a willingness to believe in a Power greater than ourselves, we commenced to get results, even though it was impossible for any of us to fully define or comprehend that Power, which is God."

Abby was getting restless. She had accepted a Higher Power. But nothing was happening. She was still on this roller coaster. There was something missing, something she didn't understand. Maybe there were answers in the next chapter, "How It Works." Picking a paragraph almost at random, she read, "Each person is like an actor who wants to run the whole show; is forever trying to arrange the lights, the ballet, the scenery, and the rest of the players in his own way. If his arrangements would only stay put, if only people would do as he wished, the show would be great. Everybody, including himself would be pleased. Life would be wonderful."

Abby thought there was something to that. She could see it in Paula, who wanted what she wanted when she wanted it. Abby's eyes skimmed rapidly ahead. "What usually happens? The show doesn't come off very well. . . . He becomes angry, indignant, self-pitying. . . . Driven by a hundred forms of fear, self-delusion, self-seeking, and self-pity, we step on the toes of our fellows and they retaliate. . . . The alcoholic is an extreme example of self-will run riot, though he usually doesn't think so. . . ." Abby closed the book. This was all very interesting, but now that she'd stopped drinking, it was irrelevant. And confusing.

Now the perpetual ache above her stomach was expanding. What was going to make her into the self-possessed Abby she had glimpsed while talking to Judy? They said it would happen in family week. But she could imagine the scene. Martin, seated in front of her in group, would self-righteously describe the terrible things she had done, and then, with enjoyment on his face, go on and list her faults. Judy would sit stonily, sending darts that said, "He's right. He's right!" Evan would turn off — so bored, so put upon because he had to sit there. And, destroyed by their contempt, she would cry and cry and cry — while everybody watched. When her time came and she told Martin how she had felt, they would fight right there in front of Fern. Martin, furious and disgusted, would pull out of family week, leaving her once again deflated, lost, helpless, deprived of any hope for sobriety. With her fingertips, Abby rubbed her forehead, looking out again into the sky. Gazing at a cloud that slightly resembled an elephant, she prayed. "If You're there, please help me. There's nobody left to ask. Nobody else has been able to do it. Please. If You're there."

But her mind wandered to Monday, to her family in Riverside, coming in each morning from their motel for their family week routine: sitting through a lecture, going to their morning family group, the counselor asking for their innermost feelings, going to another family lecture after lunch, and then into Fern's group for the fishbowl. How they would hate that! How bored, how invaded they would feel. How imposed upon! The children missing school. Martin wasting vacation time. She had already put them through so much. Now this!

That night at 2 A.M., Abby sat straight up in bed, rigid. It had happened again. Her old drinking dream. Always exactly the same. She was walking alone on a beach. The sea was calm. She was relishing the sun, the air, the sand damply firm beneath her bare feet. Then, glancing out at the ocean, she saw a towering hill of water, a tidal wave, rushing toward her — silken in the perfection of its smoothness — utterly silent, ominous beyond imagination. She stood transfixed. It loomed higher and higher, blocking out the sun as its crest curved white above her and toppled down. That was the instant she always woke in the darkness — like now — heart pounding, breath rapid, body clammy — terrified.

Her mind spun. Why, on this night of all nights, had this dream come back? Was it sent to her? A message? Was her recovery in the balance?

At lunch on Monday, Abby sat in a far corner with Larry and Paula and Garrett. "There's safety in numbers," she had decided, and wondered what her family would think of her menagerie: a twenty-two-year-old, gray-haired model, a paunchy he-man, a human fireplug. Her seat faced the door and she immediately saw the four heads in the lunch line down the hall. Judy had come! With a rush of feeling, Abby wanted to run to them, hug them, cry over Judy, lift Frederick into her arms, and she wanted to run out of the room and hide. They were at once *her* family and the enemy. They were crucial to her treatment. But they were the repositories of her sins and guilts and had terrible weapons against her. They felt to her distant and dangerous, not truly *her* people — not like the ones at this table, the ones who knew what it was like to be a drunk, knew what that meant at the bottom of the soul.

As her family moved along the cafeteria counter, Abby concentrated elaborately on her companions. Presently, with trays in their hands, the small blue name tags pinned at their shoulders, Martin and the children were looking uncertainly for seats. They had not spotted her yet. They sat down. Martin, in his gray slacks and herringbone jacket, chose an end chair. In profile, she thought, his full face with its mustache was almost handsome, despite the straight-arrow haircut. Over the tops of his half-glasses, he was sneaking glances at the patients along the table. Judy was mothering Frederick, pulling his tray closer to him, saying something. She had on blue jeans and that ruffled pink blouse she thought was so sophisticated. She must, Abby thought, be trying to impress and look grown-up, without seeming snobby. Only the back of Evan's head was visible. At least he'd combed his hair. Her eyes went back to Judy. People said they were alike and she could understand. Same chestnut hair, but cut short. Same square face with high cheekbones, but worried eyes. No lines in her skin. A normal-sized mouth. Lucky!

Judy looked up and their eyes met. Abby felt a surge of warmth. She smiled — full out — crinkling her cheeks and eyes. Judy looked away. Was that irritation on her face? Abby's eyes dropped to her plate and its watery succotash and meatball like a half-eaten cardboard baseball. How could Judy feel any friendship for a mother who said, "You're such a *grouchy* person." Judy would think that was how her drunken mother really felt. In vino veritas. It was, Abby thought, the sins of the mother visited unto the third generation. She could hear her own mother saying, "Get your hands *out of your hair*. You're so unkempt!"

Suddenly Frederick's figure in red corduroys and blue sweater flashed across the dining hall, his voice calling, "Mother." Abby had a glimpse of teeth and bright eyes before her own eyes went wet and sightless and his arms reached around her neck. She introduced him to the group at the table, and Larry held out a big hand like a bear's paw, which Frederick gingerly shook. Abby kissed his forehead and turned him back toward the family, patting him on the bottom to send him on his way.

On her way out, Abby knew, she would pass their table. What should she say? Maybe some joke about taking it easy on her this afternoon in the fishbowl. No. That was drinking behavior — pleading for mercy — saying to Judy and Evan, "Don't tell Dad. Please don't tell him.. He'll be so mad, he'll leave me." Once, after some heinous performance, she had taken Judy upstairs and given her a turtleneck shirt. Judy had thrown it on the floor and walked out.

It was time to leave. Carrying her tray, she approached the table. Martin had already turned toward her. "Hi, family," she said. "How's the loyal opposition? You ready to sock it to me this afternoon?"

"Hello, Abby," Martin answered with a half smile. "You look terrific."

"Nothing like clean living and gourmet dining," Abby answered. She reached down and rumpled Evan's hair. "Now I'll recognize you," she said. Looking again into Judy's eyes, Abby felt herself stiffen. "Thank you for coming," she said. "It's right that you be here. But I *am* grateful." She turned back toward Martin and asked, "Where are you staying? A motel?"

"Yes," Martin answered. "It's okay."

Nonchalant again, looking rapidly at the upturned faces, she said, "These are the last pearls your patient can cast before you. I am not allowed to talk to my family for the first three days. Army regulations." For the merest instant, her eyes darkened and she said, "It really is good to see you all."

As she walked quickly away, she heard Evan say, "Mom's really scared."

Abby sat in the afternoon lecture with the voice of the lecturer droning past her, only fleetingly penetrating her absent mind. She was thinking about Judy at lunch, those worried eyes dropping away. Her past impressions of Judy, fogged till now by alcohol and denial, had suddenly come into focus. Judy must be terrified. Her world, her place as apprentice wife to her father, was threatened by a sober mother. Abby remembered that cocktail party last year at home when she lurched into a table and knocked over two glasses of wine. Trying to kiss away the embarrassment on Martin's face, she had moved toward him, reaching out her arm. He ducked away from it — almost a reflex. In the heavy silence of the embarrassment, his eyes moved among the guests and settled for a second on Judy, drawing in her sympathy.

Abby shivered and escaped from that picture back into the lecture. "Alcoholism is progressive," the man was saying. "If a person continues using the chemical, there will be a steady spiritual, physical, and emotional deterioration."

This was old stuff, Abby decided, and went back to Judy. It was true, what they said. Alcoholism was a family disease. Really, Judy's life and personality had been shaped by having a drunk mother. Judy didn't seem to have any good friends. She always rushed home from school, as though the family would fall apart if she wasn't there. And maybe it would have. She had cooked a lot of dinners, washed a lot of clothes, read a lot of stories to Frederick. You had to admire her. In that morass of crap, she'd coped. She'd found a self-image: a wonderful person rising above personal tragedy. Ultraresponsible. Anything but her mother. Anything but dishonest, undependable, revolting. Sadly, Abby shook her head.

Abby turned her mind back to the lecture. "When an alcoholic stops drinking, the downward progress of the disease is halted. But it is *not* reversed, no matter how long somebody remains sober. For example, there was a man who had reached the point in his drinking where he was having blackouts, beating his wife, verbally abusing people, being arrested for drunken driving. He went through treatment here and was sober eight years. But he drank again. Within two weeks he was back where he left off — having black-outs, beating his wife, abusing people, getting arrested. So chemical dependency is incurable and irreversible. If you soak a cucumber in brine and put in spices, you end up with a pickle. And there is no way you can get back to the cucumber."

Abby's heart dropped. She was really stuck! But a week ago she would have been terrified and angry. Now she was just resigned. Was that progress?

After the lecture Abby went to her room. Feeling like a kamikaze pilot anointing himself for the final mission, she took a shower and dressed in jeans and a blue cotton shirt. She rubbed a little blush onto her cheeks. Checking herself again, her gaze took in the pictures of the children stuck into the mirror frame — Evan and Judy at two and four kicking in a plastic wading pool, Frederick at five on Santa's lap. "In happier days," she thought. Quickly she put on brown loafers and a blazer. She was too fancy, she knew. But it was very comforting.

The family was already in Fern's room and their eyes locked onto Abby as she smiled and sat down. She could feel Judy's stare, critical, resentful, and maybe a little gloating. Martin's face was expressionless. His hands, palms down, rested on his knees. Frederick, head down, had one foot jammed up onto the chair seat and was snapping a loose piece of rubber on his sneaker. Evan was reclining in his chair, legs stretched out, ankles crossed. His round blue eyes were checking out the room — the posters; the patients; Julia, tall, awkward, gray; Jerold, long-faced, pimpled; Frank Ruyter, shy behind his glasses. Abby felt defensive. Evan would be sneering inside. But these people had admitted they needed help. They were trying. He must be scared. They might get at him about drugs. She remembered a statistic: a child with an alcoholic parent has a fifty percent greater chance of becoming addicted. Eighty-five if both parents are chemically dependent.

Next to Fern sat the counselor in charge of the therapy

group attended by her family each morning. The woman's name, Abby had learned, was Margaret Raymond. She was a slender, small woman, stylishly dressed in pleated gray slacks and a white blouse with a big bow at the throat. Her face was narrow, with large brown eyes. Her tightly curled hair was what Abby called "advanced Brillo." She seemed to be in her late twenties. "Too young," Abby thought. "She'll never see through Martin."

Fern called the session to order. The introductions proceeded around the circle. When the moment came — "My name is Abby and I'm an alcoholic" — she felt awkward, self-conscious, like a beginner on the first day. When the circuit reached her family, Martin announced, "My name is Martin Andrews and these are my three children — young persons — can't call them children. Their names are Judy, Evan, and Frederick." Judy looked upset. Abby checked on Fern. Her eyes glinted, but she said nothing. Frank Ruyter in his mild voice read the reflection for that day: "Getting over years of suspicion and other self-protective mechanisms can hardly be an overnight process. We've become thoroughly conditioned to feeling and acting misunderstood and unloved — whether we really were or not. . . ."

Fern spoke. "We have Abby's family here this week." She looked toward them and smiled, saying, "I'm glad you're here. Abby needs your help." She paused and continued, "Though you have already been told this, I want to remind you why you are here and why it is essential that you be complete and honest. It is often said that alcoholism is a disease of denial and delusion. Four things contribute to the denial. Blackouts, which are temporary loss of memory. Euphoric recall of the pleasure of using your drug of choice. Repression of events too painful to think about. And families often do not tell alcoholics what they do when they are drunk and how it makes them feel. So a using addict does not have a clear picture of reality."

Fern paused for a moment. Abby pushed a lock of hair away from her face. Then Fern said, "Now I am going to ask you to move into the center of the group — what we call the fishbowl."

Obediently, the Andrews trundled out their chairs. Facing her family, Abby tried to relax the muscles knotting across her shoulders. If she unclasped her hands, she knew they would shake. She felt a pulse, like a tiny heart, beating in her right temple. As though they were acquaintances out of her distant past, she studied the figures in front of her — the firing squad. Sitting slightly behind her father in the protection of his shadow, Judy was arranging her expression, intelligent, attentive, sincere. She was set to play her accustomed role, the martyr, a little wistful, a little hurt — definitely coping — making the sounds of truth, but nothing really private, nothing that might spoil the picture, might make her father mad.

At Martin's left was Frederick, looking scared, for himself, for her. Why were they putting him through this trauma? Next to him, to the rear, Evan's round face had a faint, concealing smile. Probably guilty about judging his mother when maybe he'd had a hit of pot this morning. He'd stay clammed up. Wouldn't give anybody an opening for questions.

Martin, slightly in front of everybody, was smoothing his mustache with a forefinger. That meant he was nervous. But probably relieved. Probably thought he was going to get the management tools to solve the problem. And glad to be in at the kill. Needed at last. But he would say the same old stuff. As usual. Dial-a-litany. Abby felt the muscles at her neck ease. She had nothing to fear. Nobody would lay a glove on her.

Fern spoke. "Abby, would you like the group to tell your family how they see you?"

Suddenly her throat was tight. She hadn't figured on the group. "Yes," she said, hearing her voice slightly strangled.

After a pause, Larry uncrossed his short, heavy legs. "One thing I've picked up about Abby — she often looks out in left field for her problem, instead of focusing on her drinking. So I hear a lot of blaming. But inside her, there's a caring, warm person who can be a real friend and who wants to get well."

Julia, adjusting her shapeless dress over her knees, said, "I think Abby wants desperately to be back to her old self, and I know she used to have tremendous spark, because I see it here sometimes. I find her easy to talk to because she listens."

Paula's silver-gray head turned toward the family. "I see Abby as a strong, determined woman who has difficulty realizing her strengths. I think she's beginning to open up a little and tell the truth and let the rest of us in. But she goes just so far and then slams the door. I think she's afraid of being not strong enough to handle things."

The nurse, Marie, bent her small body forward. "I think Abby, down deep, still does not want to surrender. She always has a reason for everything she does — and I understand because I like to be in control. When you surrender, you lose everything that you think is worth keeping. But it isn't."

Fern waited through a short silence and then spoke to Martin. "I have a lot of concerns about Abby. I think there's a part of her that genuinely knows how seriously she's been affected. But what the group says is true — the strength, the defenses, the low self-esteem, the inability to surrender. I see her as a very angry lady. And somebody who has not yet accepted herself as the valuable human being she is. It is not acceptable to her that she is an alcoholic, a woman alcoholic. She needs self-forgiveness. But she's a gutsy lady and I like her."

Fern's eyes moved over the family group. "Who would like to go first and tell Abby how you see her and how it's affected you?"

"I might as well take the plunge," Martin said. He looked at Abby over his half-glasses and then pushed them back up his nose. "This is not the way I had planned to start. But to pick up on what Fern said, I simply cannot understand why you have low self-esteem. You have a healthy, loving husband. You have healthy children who are just dying to love you. We have been blessed materially. You cannot recognize the good things. I have great difficulty understanding why you concentrate on the negative instead of the positive, because I'm afraid I'm the other way around."

Fern interrupted. "I hope you'll understand by the end of the week that in alcoholism, the feelings are all negative. Go on."

"You know, dear, I have a terrible memory, so I've reached the simple device of a sort of calendar." He lifted the yellow pad from his lap.

Abby shifted in her chair. He had pages and pages — years and years of sins — in precise little writing. He wasn't going to hurt her. He was going to bore her to death.

Martin started in. "I began noticing her rambling talk at parties, and a couple of times we had to leave early. The first time I realized I had a problem was about five years ago when Judy found her passed out in the back garden. I didn't know what *kind* of a problem until Roger's birthday party." He looked at Fern. "Abby was stinko drunk and she . . ."

"Speak to *her*."

"You were stinko drunk and you just *had* to jump into the pool with your clothes on, and then, to take some of the embarrassment off, our host felt he had to jump in, too. Such things are mortifying to yourself, your husband, and to your friends." He glanced down at the pad.

Abby could feel her jaw clamping. At least he could get his facts straight. Roger had *bet* her she wouldn't jump in.

"Moving along here," Martin said, "there was the time you went to Filene's with a neighbor of ours, who told me afterward that you were rude. The reason you were rude was that you were *drunk.* And a lot of people aren't as tolerant of drunks as some of us."

Abby's cheeks felt hot. The clerk was absolutely bitchy. Nobody would have stood there and taken it! But that was all right. She could see now that Martin wasn't going to tell the *real* truth. Not in front of strangers. Too much family pride.

Martin bent down to the pad again.

Fern spoke. "Martin, how angry have you been with this lady?"

"We've done a lot of yelling and screaming. No physical abuse."

That was a lie, Abby thought. There was the time he threw her across the room into the bureau. Conveniently forgotten.

Martin was continuing, "After a while, I learned that anything I said when she was drunk didn't sink in. So I'd walk away before we got into a big, pointless fight."

Yes, Abby thought, that was one of his little tricks to put her down. She wasn't *worth* listening to.

"Martin," Fern asked. "How angry are you on a scale of one to ten?"

"Damn angry."

Fern leaned back in her chair and asked, "Well, how do you *feel* about having a wife who is an alcoholic?"

Martin answered, "I think alcoholism is better than cancer or leukemia, which are terminal."

"I'll let that pass," Fern said, shaking her head. "How do you *feel?*" There were some smiles around the room. Abby could see that Judy was upset. Poor Martin. All his life he'd trained himself to be under control, to be strong and logical, to have answers. But he'd been defeated by her drinking, and now he was failing in her treatment.

Martin pursed his lips. Abby, rather enjoying herself, knew what was coming: that tone of peremptory impatience. Martin said, "I'm not getting through. Or you're not getting through to me."

Judy leaned over and half-whispered, "She wants to know if you're angry or what."

Martin's voice grew louder. "I feel angry."

"Okay," Fern said. "So something's been missing for you in your relationship with Abby. Tell me, what was it that made you fall in love?"

Martin looked startled. He glanced at Abby and then back at Fern. He took a breath. "I loved her honesty, her vivacity, her physical and emotional beauty. She was very sensitive, very sympathetic. She gave me the feeling that everything I said and did was right. I never had to plan and think, and I could be myself and it was wonderful."

Abby's heart warmed. Damn Martin. He could still do this to her. But why didn't he do it when she needed it?

"Good," Fern said. "Now, tell Abby what's been missing in your relationship."

Martin consulted his yellow pad. "When I was writing this last night, I had two major points I wanted to make. One is that I do love you, Abby." He smiled at her. She kept her face stony. Martin pressed on. "You are the most important person in the world to me. Second, I have a deep love for the children. Third . . ."

"What's been missing, Martin?"

He raised his voice. It was curt, exasperated. "If you'd let me try it *my* way, maybe . . . there's no point in my being here if you won't let me speak."

Fern's voice was mild. "Talk about feelings."

Martin sat silent, jaw clenched. Then he said, "All right, I'll try." Looking directly into Abby's eyes, he said, "Maybe I've failed you, Abby, by not expressing love for you . . ."

"Talk about feelings. How have you been hurt?"

He'd never do it, Abby thought. Conditioned against it since birth. But Abby moved quickly to another thought. This was the man who would be waiting at home. This man, incapable of dealing in feelings. Fear — even terror — swept away her complacency. Her stomach burned again. There was no help waiting for her. No understanding. Just the loneliness again. The same enormous tide sweeping her away. Despair drained Abby's strength.

Fern leaned forward in her chair. "Martin, you have some very sensitive, tender feelings inside you. How lonely have you been?"

"Well, naturally, to be married and not have a partner for five years . . ."

"How lonely?"

Martin looked sightlessly down at the yellow pad, gripped in both hands, knuckles white. "I've been very lonely."

Abby held her breath. It was going to happen. Martin, the great stone man who never cried, was going to break down. But immediately, like a jointed wooden doll strung together with rubber cord, he seemed to snap back together.

"I've been terribly frustrated," Martin continued evenly, "trying to find out what was bugging you, 'Abby. I'd wait till you were sober and then ask you, 'What triggered your drinking last night?' And all you'd say was, 'What do you care? You don't care.' " His voice was getting louder, fuller. "I've got enough pressures and problems with my business — and then you add on the alcoholism . . ." Suddenly Martin lowered his head and covered his eyes with one hand. There was a long silence.

When Fern finally spoke, her voice was kind and urgent. "Martin, are you telling yourself, 'If I'd been a better husband — if I'd told her I loved her more often — if I'd sent her two roses instead of one — maybe this wouldn't have happened?' "

Martin's head snapped up toward Fern. His voice was angry. "No! I'm not!"

Her voice was still kind. "I'm not so sure about that. I hear you saying, 'No matter how hard I try, it doesn't work.' And when nothing works, you feel all kinds of hurt and frustration that you have to survive. So you bury the pain and build a wall. And you don't see much over that wall."

Abby's heart was beating fast. Fern saw through Martin.

Now she would understand what it was like to live with him. And now Fern might teach him to change. Teach the whole family so they could work together, so she wouldn't be alone.

Suddenly Margaret Raymond spoke. "Martin, part of the family disease of alcoholism is your reaction to it."

Martin was already speaking. "I feel very much that . . ."

Fern interrupted. "Did you hear what Margaret said? It's *very, very* important."

Martin turned toward Margaret. "Say it again, please."

She spoke slowly and distinctly, a dry clarity to her voice that made the words impressive. "I was explaining the disease process in families. To protect yourself, you withdraw and cover up your feelings. But even though you push your feelings deep down inside, where you don't have to deal with them, they don't go away. They're still there, festering, making you miserable and making you do miserable things. Martin, you are like many thousands of husbands with alcoholic wives."

Abby could feel the excitement, the adrenaline still rising. They *both* had Martin's number.

Abruptly, Evan's voice — superior, petulant, shocking — sounded in the room. "It's very irritating to be asked by you people to sit here and listen to these cheap leading questions and be expected to break down on cue." His voice grew louder. "Maybe there are things my father wants to get out, but when you . . ."

Fern whirled toward Evan, her blue eyes fierce with outrage. "Do you know what you just did here?" Her voice was like a hammer. "Do you know what you just did? For once in his life your father was beginning to get at some feelings. And you stopped that. You got so uncomfortable, you had to fix it *all* up and control it."

Abby, from a great height, watched herself lurch to her feet. The rasping clatter of the chair shivered the tension. Now she was upright, hands clenched, mouth contorted.

Tears poured over her flushed cheeks. Looking down at her astonished family, she cried out, "I'm going to have to do it *all alone*." Her wail hung, printed on the air, as she turned and fled the room.

CHAPTER

9

AT BREAKFAST on Tuesday, May twenty-fifth, Abby sat alone, preferring the company of her despair. It was an old friend, and she knew how to sink into it, drawing it about her like a warm cloak. She had stayed aloof since yesterday's disastrous fishbowl, since the moment she shut Fern's door behind her and stood gasping in the hallway. Controlling herself, she had stolled unnoticed past the nurses' station to her room, where she could give in to the vibrating restlessness that permeated her body.

Her head ached with panic as she paced the small area, ricocheting off the bed and bureau and table. If Martin and the children kept on this way, if nothing happened in family week, could she get well? And if she did, how could she ever, ever go back to that family? How could she ever stay sober without their help? Moving toward the mirror above the bureau, she glimpsed her tear-streaked makeup — next to the happy pictures of her children. Would she have to leave home, she wondered, and start a different life? In a different place? She went into the bathroom to wash, and faced herself again in the medicine cabinet mirror. She grinned mockingly at her reflection and said aloud, "Nothing like a little self-pity."

During the morning lecture Abby sat in a chair against the wall, safe from intrusion. She listened disconsolately, intermittently. These lectures were so tedious. The man was

216

saying, "The American Medical Association has long recognized alcoholism as a disease." Abby was a little surprised. She'd thought that was a relatively new development. She tuned in again. "The AMA has three criteria for a disease. There must be a causative agent. In alcoholism it is the drug of choice. There must be definitive symptoms. They are an increase in tolerance, temporary loss of memory, changes in behavior, denial, and preoccupation with drinking. Third, there must be a predictable outcome. Alcoholism ends inexorably in death."

Abby shivered. Well, she'd never been even close to that. Then the phrase "cycle of addiction" caught her attention. The lecturer was saying, "Alcoholics overcome negative feelings about themselves by drinking — which leads to destructive behavior — which causes guilt and increases the negative feelings — which causes even more drinking — which causes . . ." Abby considered this new idea, "the cycle of addiction," and had a flash from her girlhood: the wild plunges, forbidden by her mother, she used to make on her bike down the steep hill behind their house. At the top she would grip the handlebars with fear. But then, launched, the bike bucked like a horse over the dirt hummocks and her heart pounded with excitement, immune to the dangers of ditches and trees rushing toward her.

In her morning group — while her family was downstairs in their own therapy group — Abby sat picking at her fingernails. Her mouth was dry. She jumped into the initial pause, as though from a diving board. "I want to talk about yesterday in the fishbowl and why I was so upset." Fern nodded. Abby continued, "My husband just wants to stay uninvolved and let somebody else fix me. He hasn't even taken the time to think what's at stake here. He hasn't grasped . . ."

"What is at stake?" Fern asked.

Abby's words came in a rush. "My sobriety. And I feel like I'm not getting any support from anybody, from my family, from you. I know what needs to happen. I *know* I'm powerless. I don't know whether *you* believe that."

"Why would it make any difference to you what I thought?"

"Because you're the authority figure here."

"No, I'm not. I wouldn't accept that kind of power from you. What's *really* important, Abby, is what *you* feel about *you* in your heart — deep down where you live. What I think is absolutely irrelevant."

"But I've been getting feedback from you that I am not accepting my powerlessness."

"Wait. Wait. You are not hearing me. You do *not* need to convince me of anything. My function, as I see it, is to give you some awareness of what I see. What you do with that is up to you. Now, what you need to do, as *I* see it, is get into the self-acceptance — the surrender process. Intellectually, you understand it, but the process means absorbing it down into your whole being. How that's going to happen for you, I haven't the foggiest. But I hope it does, because your *life* depends on it."

Abby slumped back, mute, washed with helplessness, with desperation. How was it going to happen? When?

That afternoon, bracing herself, Abby entered Fern's office for afternoon group. Her family was not yet up from their afternoon family lecture on the first floor. Deflated, she took a seat between Garrett and Julia. Across the room was Margaret Raymond, the family counselor, who for two mornings now had been drawing out her family. "How much does *she* know about me?" Abby wondered. Presently, her family arrived, and she watched them file in the door — Martin with his face set and grim; Judy sucking in her stomach, her way of looking thin and interesting; Evan with his shoulders slouched, ultracool. Frederick peeked at her from behind Martin. She winked and he smirked. Abby smiled at them and they nodded.

Abby read the Reflection of the Day: "In my new relationships, I pray that I may not be so eager for approval that I will let myself be dishonest — through flattery, half-truths, false cheeriness, protective white lies." Paula started out the session, discussing the fact that she was *really* comfortable only with children and animals. Then Abby and her family assembled in the center of the room, arranging themselves as before. Fern turned to Evan, lounging on the end of his spine, legs out, ankles crossed, and said, "Tell us how it's been for you at home."

"Not that bad." A smile was on Evan's face.

Fern's voice was sudden and sharp. "Is there any reason why you can't sit up straight like the rest of the adults in here?" Sheepishly, Evan heaved himself semiupright. She asked, "Would you like to tell us what you saw and felt at home?"

Evan's eyes were sleepy. "I first noticed that my mother would be a little spacy some nights. But I didn't think it was a big problem. Some people just aren't wrapped as tight as others. When it got worse, I decided I'd have to put up with her. But it hasn't been that bad."

"Okay," Fern answered. "Maybe later on in the week you will feel like involving yourself in the process." She swiveled one degree to her right. "Judy, how has it been for you?"

Fear lay in Abby's stomach like sour food. Judy, exuding poise, maturity, glanced quickly at a scribbled list lying on her lap and then looked Fern directly in the eyes. "For a long time," she said firmly, "I didn't realize what the problem was, but I learned not to rely on my mother, because she wasn't there for the things you expect your mother to do."

"Speak to her," Fern said.

Judy turned toward Abby. "Having to keep the house going made it really hard to get good marks at school." Her focus moved away from Abby, toward the group. Smiling wanly, she added, "Mom was the only one who got room service."

Almost with relief, Abby felt the fear turn to simmering

anger. This was Judy's big chance. She was going to show her father — show the world — how superior she was, how beautifully she had coped with such a raw deal. The little phony!

"Were you the member of the family who took care of your mother?" Fern asked. "And how did that make you feel?"

Judy lowered her eyes modestly. "I'm learning here that I shouldn't have done that. But when she was so sick and out of it, you can't . . . she'd slop around the kitchen trying to make dinner; I couldn't stand there and do nothing. At the least, I had to keep an eye out so she didn't catch the hot pads on fire." Judy stopped.

Fern said, "Look at me." Judy turned her head toward the penetrating blue eyes. Abby, with satisfaction, watched the saintliness waver in Judy's eyes. "You are avoiding the issue," Fern continued. "Tell your mother the hurts. She needs to hear them from you, and you need to tell her. How did taking care of your mother make you feel?"

Judy's eyes dropped away from Fern's face. "I resented it," she said, and lapsed into silence.

Fern sat a long minute, lips compressed. She gestured toward a chart on the wall listing columns of emotions: alone, anxious, bewildered, calm, concerned . . . "Can you tell us," she asked, "which of those feelings you have at this moment?"

Abby knew Judy would be saying to herself, "This is really *stupid.*" And then she'd be clicking through the options. "Embarrassed" would lead to embarrassing questions. "Angry" would look bad. "Frustrated" would be flaky. Judy would know they'd like "scared."

"Scared," Judy answered.

Abby was triumphant, but felt the despair filtering through her again. Nothing was going on here that would break her loose. She was sentenced forever to helplessness.

"All right," Fern answered. "What's scary for you?"

"I'm scared, because I don't know what's going to happen this week and the rest of my life with my mother."

Fern was quiet for a moment. She chewed on the corner of her mouth. "Judy," she said patiently, "you're covering up a lot of hurts. It is very important for you to say them and leave them here forever, and your mother needs to hear the things she may not know about. Your father told us you found your mother unconscious in the backyard. Please tell her about that, in case she's forgotten?"

Abby could see Judy's expression crack, the mouth opening slackly, the startled eyes darting up to her father, who sat unmoving, his eyes straight ahead, expressionless. Judy looked at Abby, who sealed her own eyes to hide her instantaneous terror. In her stomach, the ache was sharp and burning.

Judy looked down at her lap, where her hands were clamped together into one, large, white-knuckled fist. "I was about eleven years old," she said. "I woke up in the night with a pain in my stomach and I called out, 'Mom,' and nothing happened, and I called out a lot."

Abby pushed her hands under her thighs and braced herself, tensing her chest as though that would hold her heart steady and impervious.

Judy was saying, "I went looking for Mom. I knew Dad was away. She wasn't anywhere, and I got really scared. I went out into the backyard and called. And then I saw her kind of strewn out on the chaise lounge and not moving, like she was dead. I remember my head felt like it was going to explode. I sort of shook her shoulder and her head flopped over and her mouth opened and she went, 'Aaaaaaaaaaa.' "

Now Judy's voice was trembling. "I tried to pick her up and she was stumbling, and I was sort of carrying her. After I put her into bed, I remember I felt like her mother, because I was putting covers on her." Judy stopped again, head down.

Presently, Fern said gently, "How did you feel about that?"

"I didn't like it at all, because I felt like she ought to be doing that for me." Judy was silent. Her right cheek began to quiver, and quickly she hid the offending flesh behind her hand. Fern sat waiting. Judy, the hand still pressed against her cheek, continued, "I went back out into the yard and stood there a long time crying and wondering what was the matter with my mom. And I remember I thought maybe it was something I did."

Abby was numb, her eyes inward, searching. Why couldn't she remember that? What else did Judy know?

Fern's voice was saying conversationally, "So you thought it was all your fault?"

Judy's eyes were down again, watching her thumbs wrestle with each other. Her voice was almost inaudible. "I figured maybe she didn't like me — maybe she had to be drinking to be around me."

The pressure inside Abby burst loose. "Oh, Judy, that breaks my heart. More than anything I have wanted to be your friend. But you were always so hard to get close to."

The pain in Judy's eyes flashed into anger. "Of course I was, Mom. Because I was afraid of you. If I let you get too close, you drank and put me down and hurt me. Like, you'd tell me, 'Oh, you have such a short temper.' So I tried to control my temper, which is really hard. But then you complained I was moody. So I put on a fake front and pretended I was happy. But I decided that was stupid."

"So it didn't work," Fern said.

"No."

There was another pause. Fern said, "It's been very tough not having a mother."

"Yes," Judy said, softly. She drew in a long, quavering breath.

"Tell your mother about it," Fern persisted gently.

Judy's voice was small, tight. "When I was little, you'd forget to do the wash and I'd go to school in damp clothes. And you wouldn't have my lunch packed and you'd bring it to school late. Sometimes I ate it on the bus going home. I learned that I couldn't depend . . ." She choked. Her blood rose like a thermometer of pain, reddening first her neck and then her face, finally breaking free in tears. She dropped her head and, with the backs of both hands, blocked her eyes.

Fern said quietly, "Go ahead. It's all right to cry."

Abby sat paralyzed by shame. What a crummy, crummy mother! She had lost all power or right to offer Judy comfort. Julia leaned forward and placed a box of Kleenex in Judy's lap. With blind hands, Judy groped out a white tissue and wiped at her eyes, head still down. But still the tears came, her body heaving, the drops leaving round blooms on the list under her hands. Frederick reached out and put his arm around her. Evan, impassive, stared at the air two feet above Abby's head. Martin leaned subtly away from Judy. "He can't stand it," Abby thought. "She's out of control. Like I was."

Judy, her face still huddled downward, said furiously through her tears, "I *swore* I wouldn't cry. I don't *ever* cry."

"Let it happen," Margaret Raymond said gently. "You're getting rid of a lot of bitterness from a lot of years."

Abby felt tears swelling in her own eyes, and she blinked and squeezed them out, the round drops bright in the harsh fluorescent light. Her heart, full of guilt and yearning, expanded toward Judy. Maybe, Abby thought, if I could just touch her for a second. Abby lifted her hand, but it was shaking, and she froze and shoved it back under her leg. "Oh, Judy," she said, her voice trembling, "I'm so *sorry.*"

Fern's voice was quick and sharp. "Are you sorry for having a disease?"

"Yes," Abby answered, startled.

"If you had cancer, would you be sorry?"

Abby paused, eyes dry now. "Probably," she said, ruefully. "Probably I would. And I'd apologize for it."

Fern snorted disgustedly. "Yes, you probably would." Flinging one leg across the other, she twisted toward Judy.

Abby sat amazed. She really had spent her life being a doormat, apologizing for things that weren't her fault — when she was as good as anybody.

The pause was broken by Margaret Raymond. "Judy, you told us some things this morning about looking after your mother. Tell them to her."

Judy looked at Abby, saying nothing, as though gathering strength. Abby, curling her toes in her shoes till they ached, held on to the seat of the chair and hardened the muscles of her body, tight as a spring. She could see Judy's face reddening again, and the voice, when it came, was rapid with outrage. "I kept lying for you, telling people you weren't feeling well, that you had some bug. One time I baked you potatoes, and when I brought them up to you, you were passed out in bed. I had tried *so hard* to do what I thought was good for you. I tried so *hard* to be the daughter you needed." Then, almost wailing, she added, "You were just *gone!*"

Abby sat weeping without a sound, her swollen face lifted, the tears running down her face onto her cotton blouse, her body motionless — and inside her chest, hysteria.

Judy, watching her mother, began to cry again, and this time she let the tears flow. After a while, Fern said gently, "Go on. You're doing fine."

Still sobbing, but now with tears of anger, Judy said in a rush, loudly, "I'm sick of all the crap, sick of baby-sitting you, sick of not being able to bring my friends home, sick of being yelled at and being put down, sick of thinking it's all my fault, sick of watching you tear yourself apart."

"Judy," Margaret said in her dry voice, "tell your mother what she looks like when she's drunk."

"Your eyelids get droopy, slitty looking," Judy answered, staring straight at Abby, who was still weeping, motionless and silent. "Your eyes get spacy and bloodshot. Your face sags and gets kind of dazed looking. You slur your words and you smell bad."

Abby closed her eyes to stop the tears, but felt locked up

inside herself with all her guilt. Eyes pleading, she looked back at Judy, at the anger in that face, so much an image of her own.

"How did you feel about your mother then?" Margaret asked.

"I thought she was disgusting. I hated all the dishonesty and the sneakiness. You thought I didn't know, but I'd see you take a swig out of a bottle and then hide it. I hated not trusting you. Sometimes I'd find a bottle hidden and pour it down the drain, and then I'd feel bad because maybe I shouldn't have done that. I had a piggy bank with a cork in the bottom and I never used to open it until New Year's — and one time you just took all my money." Her voice was hoarse with anger and bitterness, but her eyes were bright as though intoxicated by rage and release.

There was a momentary hush. Like a fist against Abby's heart, Frederick's voice rang out in the silence. It was a cry. A howl. "That's not my mom!"

Instantly, without thought, Abby kneeled in front of Frederick, taking his hands, looking up into his face. From her mouth came the words, "Yes it is, Frizzer. Yes, it is."

Returning to her chair, Abby sat stunned by guilt. Her mind was floating free of her body, like the time when she was Frederick's age and came home from school with a high fever, her head light and empty. Her father, she remembered, sat for hours keeping a washcloth damp on her forehead. Now, as Frederick and Fern talked, Abby listened from a great distance. Frederick was explaining, "I just thought my mom was being picked on."

Fern answered softly, "You love your mother, don't you?"

"I've got a great mom," he answered, his forefinger working on a small hole at the knee of his pants.

"I totally agree," Fern answered. "But I think you do understand that she has been sick. Did she ever do anything that made you unhappy?"

There was a long pause. The hole in his pants was getting larger. Finally he answered. "Yup."

"Would you like to tell us about that?"

The sneaker was back up on the seat. "When there'd be an open house at school, they'd say, 'Did your mother come?' And I'd say, 'No,' cause she never did."

Abby gasped.

"Perhaps you were scared that maybe Judy was telling the truth?" Fern asked, gently.

Frederick, tearing at the sneaker's sole, was silent.

"So what were you scared of?"

More silence. Now there was three fingers in the hole in his pants. "I don't want anything to happen to my mother."

Fern smiled. "I'm sure you don't. And the way you can help her is to tell her the truth, so she'll never let herself be sick like that again."

Fern turned her attention to Martin. Soon he was again struggling against Fern — against himself — protesting, "I *do* have feelings. I feel that I have failed Abby here because I have gotten things wrong."

Fern, still patiently goading and instructing, answered, "Let me give you a clue. When you say, 'I feel that . . . ,' when you follow 'feel' with 'that' — you are expressing an *idea,* not a feeling."

While Abby sat amused, Margaret Raymond told Martin that he was trying to make sense out of a senseless disease. And Fern asked him whether he got an emotional payoff from having a wife who drank and was helpless. "Think about that," she said.

Dispassionately, Abby told herself that Martin must be suffering terribly. *He* hadn't done anything wrong, just kept everything functioning, been the responsible one who cared about the family. But nobody here was giving him credit for that. Instead of supplying answers that would solve his problems, they were implying something was wrong with *him.*

Then, suddenly, Abby's detachment broke. Fern was turning away from her family and saying to the group,

"Anybody like to give Abby some feedback?" Larry looked toward her, the usually kind eyes remote. Abby's hands were wet, and she held her body very still. He said, "I feel sort of conned. I thought you'd been honest and told us everything, but now I see you didn't give us the whole story on Judy. It makes me wonder what else you didn't tell us about your kids."

Garrett followed immediately. "I agree. You certainly didn't tell us the things we heard today." Other voices sounded around the room. "Put one over on us." "Deceived." "Much worse." And Paula said, "I really am surprised. I never realized you treated your daughter like that." The bell rang. The session was over. Abby, nauseated, could hardly force herself to extend her hands and join the ring for the Serenity Prayer. Nobody in the group would ever believe her again — these people who were more important to her than her family. She was utterly disgraced. And they were all she had, the only safe friends on earth who would listen to anything from her and understand.

Abby hung back as the other members of the group crowded out the door, along with her family, who did not look at her. But Fern was already dialing her telephone and looking away out the window. Abby left the room and moved slowly down the hall, determined not to cry.

Suddenly, she switched into anger. They had betrayed her. She had tried so hard to tell the truth, and it had hurt so much. But that made no difference to them. And Judy had never told her how awful it had been, had never said those things to her. Judy must have been coached in the morning group to say the *worst* things. Because the two of them had had good times together — many laughs. If somebody had been in the house and written down a log, or taken pictures of what was actually going on, they would have . . .

Another voice within Abby interrupted. "Stop conning. You knew!"

At the nurses' station, Marie was behind the counter. "You look like you're carrying a load," she said.

"I feel like I'm going to split," Abby answered.

Marie took her behind the counter to a small, empty room, and they sat at a table in the center. "I've been the worst person in the world," Abby said. "I've let my daughter and my group down and . . ." Abby went on, alternately crying and talking, pouring out her grief and self-disgust — how ashamed she felt, how degraded. "If I could wish for anything, it would be to give those years back to my kids. They have so much pain growing up, pain you have no control over. But I was the *cause* of pain. Their own mother!" Abby stretched her arms out on the table and hung her head.

Reaching across the table, Marie gathered up Abby's hands. "Don't be so hard on yourself. Things will come out all right. Just trust in the treatment process."

With her eyes still down, Abby answered, "Judy may look like a woman, but she's a child. She should have spent her days doing the things kids do, not protecting a drunk, not making sure the drunk didn't burn the house down. And I've lost my credibility with the group, and I think they don't like me now. And that matters terribly to me" — she tried to smile — "even if they are drunks."

Marie listened calmly, still holding Abby's hands. "We do things that in our innermost depths, the most bottom part of our hearts, we don't want to do, the last things we could imagine ourselves doing. So we keep shoving those memories away where we won't have to look at them. And that's the real garbage that has to come out. When you get down to rock bottom this week — when you've admitted everything and there's nobody left to blame except yourself — then you can surrender and stop fighting and accept the fact of your alcoholism."

Returning to her room, the good feeling of Marie's arms around her in a parting hug, Abby passed Larry's room and glimpsed Garrett's outstretched legs. She turned in through the door to where he and Larry were sitting. She looked into Larry's square face with its red-veined cheeks, into Garrett's soft face with its sideburns, and was almost frightened by her need of approval from these two men, so utterly strange in her life. For once, she was going to take a risk and deal with something head-on — lay open her feelings — be honest. "I understand why you think I let you down," she said. "But I'm glad you said what you did. That's what I'm in treatment to hear. But what you think about me matters a lot, because I feel very alone without you, and I need your help. I want to get back into feeling good with you."

Larry stood up and put his arm around her, saying, "Don't worry, Abby, I'll always love you." Garrett rubbed her back. "You exaggerated it," he said. "Nobody's upset with you. We think you're a great person."

Abby turned and faced them, saying, "Thanks, you guys." Feeling wetness in her eyes, she headed for the door, and in the hall she felt warm and light, felt happy with herself. She had been in agony and she had released it by doing what they said: turning to people instead of booze. She had voiced her pain, not covered it up somehow — by getting mad — by distracting herself and helping another patient. She had not tried to manage the situation. She had trusted her strength enough to give up control and see what happened.

That night Abby could not get to sleep. Tomorrow was her turn to talk in the fishbowl, her turn to answer back. Lying in bed, she was feverish with ideas and phrases — the perfect things to say that she must not forget. Repeatedly she got up and sat in her nightgown at the little table, scribbling complaints and injuries into her stenographer's notebook. But, gradually, she began to feel, "So what!" The angers seemed empty, exhausted. She thought maybe she should be positive tomorrow, and asked herself what she wanted from Martin.

What she wanted, she knew, was intimacy. That did not mean raising children and promoting a career. And intimacy wasn't sex. She wanted Martin to trust her and care. She wanted him to *like* being alone with her. She wanted him to talk with her. When Frederick fell and scraped a knee, she wanted somebody she could tell. She wanted to *love* Martin. It was possible. She had loved him early in their marriage. But dependency then had been a relief, allowing him to take over her life. And in those days — it seemed a century ago — he had let himself be vulnerable, human, forgivable.

The tumult in her head began to subside. She flipped back through her notes, so random, so higgledy-piggledy. She really should organize them, simplify them, make a readable list. But, oh, God, she didn't want to be like Martin. All their life together, he had listed her to death — the daily duties waiting for her in the morning on the kitchen counter. She didn't want to do to him what he'd done to her: turn up with a hundred pages on the decline and fall of Abby Andrews. She'd wing it tomorrow. Be spontaneous. It would be more sympathetic that way.

CHAPTER

10

FERN'S BLUE eyes circled the room and the murmurs of conversation quieted. "Whose turn is it to read today?" she asked. "Mine," answered Abby. With feet flat on the floor, knees at right angles close together, the book held almost primly up to her face, she read the reflection for Wednesday, May twenty-sixth. "I know today that I no longer have to proceed on my own. I've learned that it's safer, more sensible and surer to move forward with friends who are going in the same direction as I." Next the procession of voices sounded around the room — ceremonially — "My name is . . . I am . . ." Finally there was the moment of nervous, expectant quiet.

Jerold straightened his tall body. As he spoke, Abby watched the play of embarrassment and relief on his long, large, hollow face. "I want to talk about my love for a girl who left me. She was the only girl I've ever had, and it's been eating my insides out." The group and Fern drew out of him a picture of his life: getting up at 5 P.M., alternating cocaine and marijuana, getting head rushes, then going to bars where he peddled cocaine, and sometimes gave it away. "I could make friends by drawing 'em out a line of coke and they were forever grateful. You'd catch eyes and draw attention from a lot of people who'd think, 'Geez, that guy must have money.' "

He would move on from the bars to people's houses "to

sit around and bullshit." The rest of the night he worked on his precious car at a friend's gas station, a friend he had "turned on to coke." Two years after his girl left him, he was so frightened one night, so lonely, he telephoned her. She let him come to her room, just to be near her in the darkness on top of the coverlet while she slept. "I just lay there," Jerold said. "I just needed somebody to be with."

When Jerold was finished, Larry asked, "In the years you went with that girl, did you ever spend any time together when you weren't on chemicals?"

"Yeah," Jerold answered. "Maybe a few days."

"So you hardly knew each other," Larry said.

Jerold was silent.

Evan dried his palms on his pants. "He should be sweating," Abby said to herself. Would Fern ask him about drugs? "He'd blame me," Abby thought. Some line about having a few hits to cool the pressure. But he wouldn't talk about stealing money from her purse. Stealing was just like a druggie — "Just like me."

Fern said, "We have Abby's family with us again. Let's see what progress we can make today."

When they were assembled in the center of the circle, Martin immediately said, "Abby, I want to . . ."

Fern interrupted him. "Excuse me, Martin, but I'd like to start with Evan." Abby saw Evan's nervous tic begin — the forearms tightening and releasing. She knew he hated being the center of attention. But he wouldn't want to be ignored, either.

Fern continued blandly, "Things couldn't have been easy for you these past years."

"Our family isn't any worse than any other," he answered. "I know lots with problems worse than ours."

"Evan, did you ever get angry?" Fern's voice was casual, almost indifferent.

"Yeah," he said.

"What did you do about that anger?"

Evan laughed. "I used to beat up on Judy."

"That was the pecking order," Judy said bitterly.

"Well, I didn't see any solution to things," Evan said, his voice defensive. "I thought this is the way the world is."

"Evan, did you ever get angry at your mother?" Fern sat at ease in her chair, hands on its arms, voice still mild.

Evan ran his tongue over his upper lip. "When I forgot to do my chores — see, I have the shit jobs like taking out the trash — when I forgot, Mom was like total wrath. I'd get mad, because why do that stuff when you get nothing in return? It was like there was a double standard."

Fern said nothing. The room was still. Abby could see the uncertainty in his round, forever innocent eyes. She knew how that silence could press against the mind, squeezing it, until words came out, any words to satisfy Fern's waiting blue eyes. He began to talk. "I remember one night she said . . ."

"Speak directly to your mother," Fern said.

Evan looked at her. Her own eyes looked back, alarmed, defended, and she could feel her jaws clench. She knew what was coming. Evan had her — and his father — trapped. He was going to grind his anger into them. Evan's voice was accusing. "You were real pleased with yourself because you'd gotten a watermelon for desert and that was, like, my highest thing. But you were on one of your big health kicks when you're suddenly caring about us and going to make us into superheroes, like we'll leap tall buildings if we have two helpings of vegetables. By dessert time, I couldn't eat any more and I tried to explain I was too full. You were bombed, and suddenly you picked up the watermelon and threw it right in my face."

Abby clenched her jaws, the muscles aching now, and narrowed her eyes. She wanted to speak, to puncture him — let him know, let everybody know, what she suspected. She wanted to ask him where he'd been every time she'd needed help. "Maybe stoned," she would answer for him. But she'd better not. He'd ask where she'd been when he needed her.

Fern's voice, urgent, was saying, "Keep going. What did you do then?"

"Well, I guess I started crying. It was like that watermelon all over the floor showed how screwed up everything was. I mean, it was good intentions that just totally fell apart and I didn't think it was my fault. I didn't understand what the hell had caused it all." He stopped.

"What were you feeling, Evan?"

"I don't know. Maybe, 'Why is she doing this to me?' Mostly I used to think, 'I gotta get out of here,' and 'Someday she'll get hers.' I remember I ran out. But I remember I stopped and said, 'I don't care if you're dead when I come back.' It was *so* bad."

Abby sat motionless. There was a pressure in her temples. Her hands trembled.

Fern's voice was quick, sharp. "Evan! What are you feeling *right now?*"

He sat straight up, his smooth face pale. "I'm really pissed off," he said.

"Look at your mother," Fern said. "What do you see?"

Abby, begging him with her eyes, met his stare. Though she felt no tears, her cheeks were wet and raw.

"A stranger," Evan said, "Or maybe a crying baby. An infant."

The room was silent. He continued to gaze at Abby. Suddenly, he leaned forward, his face only a few feet from hers. She closed her eyes and waited. When he spoke, his voice was low and level and hard. "I don't know if I can ever forgive you for what you've done to me and the way you've messed up my life." Abby, her eyes still closed, began rocking very slowly back and forth. Evan straightened and looked around the circle as though mustering his witnesses. He focused again on Abby's unseeing face and said, "It's your fault everything's so screwed up." He leaned forward again and half shouted, "Do you know that? Do you *know* that?"

Abby opened her eyes. Her voice was calm. "Yes," she said.

"Good," Fern said. The room was quiet. "Frederick, do you have something you'd like to say to your mom?"

Now it was Abby who bent forward. "Don't be afraid," she said earnestly to Frederick. "I want to hear whatever you want to tell me." But her mouth crumpled as tears welled again in her eyes. Frederick, eyes enormous, opened his lips, but no words came. Instead, his own tears ran one by one down his soft, flushed cheeks. "Mom," he cried out and braced his legs to get up.

"Don't start that!" Martin bellowed at Abby, whipping his arm out in front of Frederick. Abby flinched. Frederick snapped his frightened face up toward Martin.

"Wait a *minute!*" Fern said. "What's this all about?"

Martin retreated, his face red. Frederick, cheeks glinting wet, looked back and forth between his mother and father. Abby spoke, her mouth a tight, straight line of fury. "Because Martin is so good and I'm so bad, he can't understand why anybody comes to me for comfort."

"First things first," Fern interrupted. "Frederick, would you like to hug your mother?" He nodded. Fern said, "Okay, there she is."

Frederick got up and went to Abby, who smiled as she curved down toward him. His arms went around her neck, and her hands clasped his waist. "You're so special," she said into his hair and then, to keep from crying, clamped both her lips between her teeth. Frederick, back in his seat, smiled encouragingly. Judy was looking away, her face sour.

Fern turned to Martin. "What's going on with you?"

Martin's voice was aggressive, angry. "She will do absolutely *anything* to get sympathy — cry, get mad, smile — whatever's expected. It's all a big con. But I think she conned *herself* more than anybody."

"Anybody care to comment?" Fern asked.

Frank Ruyter took off his horn-rimmed glasses, baring his

mild eyes. "Martin," he said, "I think you're trying to cut Frederick off from Abby to punish her."

Fern nodded. Her voice was stern. "Don't interfere with people's feelings. Let Frederick experience his feelings for himself. And don't judge people's emotions. Consider the possibility that Abby might actually have sincere, genuine feelings. Think about that, Martin."

After a moment, Fern shifted her eyes. "Judy," she said, "I want to contratulate you for what you did yesterday. How do you feel today?"

Judy's face glowed. "Relieved, I guess. Like there's a weight off me. But scared."

"Of what?"

"I figure Mom may be bitter toward me for saying all those things in front of people. I kept thinking I should take it easy 'cause she's my mother."

"Believe me, Judy," Fern answered, "that was the most loving thing you could do for your mother. But why don't you ask her how she feels."

Judy simply looked at Abby.

Abby gripped the edge of the chair. "It was very good that I heard all those things. I guess I had never faced till now what a rotten life you've had because of me. That's why I wanted you to come this week, because more than anything, I wanted us to be close again." She stopped and took a breath, feeling that her next words would be the bravest she had ever spoken. "When I come home and I'm sober, how is it going to be between us?"

Judy's face was expressionless. "It depends."

"What does that mean?" Abby asked, looking directly into Judy's guarded eyes.

"It just depends, that's all." Judy's gaze was level, almost challenging.

Abby felt kicked in the chest. The two sat silently looking at each other, a pulse beating steadily in Abby's neck. Fern started to speak, stopped, sighed, and said, "All right, Martin, what did you want to say?"

Martin lifted a single sheet of paper from his lap, glanced at it, frowned, put it down, and looked up at Abby. She sat stiffly, knees touching, elbows close to her sides, hands holding her green secretary's notebook. The jaw was clamped again. Martin began to speak, his voice methodical. "First, I think I should apologize to you, Abby. My approach has been wrong, and I have not been giving you the help that you need. I have had great resentment against Fern, but I see now that she was right and I was wrong." He paused and cleared his throat. "Second, I was awake a good deal of last night trying to figure out how to get the job done to-day. I thought a lot about Fern's question, 'What's been missing?' I decided, in a general way, the word 'consistency' is very important in all this."

Fern rested her chin on her left hand.

Martin paused again, looking down at the paper. "Or perhaps 'stability' best expresses it."

Suddenly Larry slapped one of his big hands on his knee. "Martin," he said, "you seem like a pretty good guy. But this is the third day of listening to you talk about your problems like an accountant."

Martin flushed. "That is *totally* inappropriate," he said. "A cheap shot. I am working my hardest to do what is right."

"I don't know whether you're protecting yourself," said Garrett Owen, "or protecting Abby, or protecting the sit-uation. But it's like, 'Goddamn it, I'm going to keep that lid on.' "

Abby grinned inside. He was lost. His strengths — his reason, sanity, rationality — were useless. The system he had grown up in, everything he had absorbed as gospel — his standard of values, his sense of duty, in effect, his man-hood — was all betraying him. He must feel reduced, weakened, rudderless. But she didn't feel sorry for him. He was getting his own medicine.

Fern smiled at Martin. "My heart goes out to you because everything here is *so* difficult for you. You keep trying so hard and nothing's happening. Just *let* things happen. Give yourself permission. You don't have to be careful of Abby. She's very strong, or she wouldn't have lasted this long." For a moment Fern gazed quietly at Martin. Then she asked, "Have you ever been hurt by this lady?"

Martin glanced back and forth at Fern and Abby, and then at Larry. His eyes fixed on Fern. "Yes, I have been very, very hurt; very, very angry."

"Tell us, as simply as you can, about one of those times," Fern said.

Martin starting to check his notes, caught himself, and spoke directly to Abby. "An example I had was the Kiwanis testimonial dinner for George Carter. It was very important to me, both professionally and socially. I told you that, and I asked you, for once, not to humiliate me in public. You had been sober all afternoon, and when I was taking a shower and we got dressed, you seemed fine. I was really hopeful. We drove to the dinner, and when we got out of the car, you were staggering. That was a *fifteen minute* drive. I couldn't *believe* it. I just couldn't believe that you thought you could deceive me. And then you denied you were drunk. You *denied* it while you were wobbling like that. So we went inside . . ."

Abby interrupted. "I make a distinction between being drunk so I can't handle myself, and being high and well aware of what I'm doing. I talked to all the key people before dinner. Do you think it was obvious that I was . . ."

"Oh, bullshit!" Martin half shouted. "That's your old semantics game."

"I'm just asking an honest question," Abby answered innocently.

"You're still denying. I can't believe it." Martin's voice was growing harsh. "When you got inside, your hair was messed up, and you were standing with your legs apart and your shoulders hunched over. Your eyes were glazed. It was very obvious that you were drunk." A prickly red rash was creeping up from under the collar of Abby's blouse. Martin glared at her. "I never should have brought you, but it was important for me to have you there so people could see that you were sober and could do it." His voice had become louder, higher. "And then between two speeches — deliberately — when everybody could hear it — you said, 'Martin, how can you stand all these horses' asses?' " Martin leaned back in his chair and took two deep breaths. "Can you *imagine* what that did to me?"

"Tell her," Fern said. "She was drunk. She may not know."

"I was absolutely mortified. I was shocked." Martin's voice was rising again. "I was furious. I was bitter. I had been stabbed in the back."

"Martin," said Fern, "what are you feeling right now?"

Without a pause, his voice still loud, hard-edged, Martin said, "I'm mad as hell."

"Good," Fern answered. "Have you been depressed? I'm curious because of the intensity of your feelings — not just anger, but rage and helplessness."

Martin looked down at his hands clamped between his knees. He seemed oblivious of Abby in front of him. She scratched the rash on the back of her neck. "I don't know if I've been depressed." His voice was low, choked. "I can see . . . maybe I have been angry. I don't know. A lot of the time I just didn't feel anything. Just indifferent to Abby. I kept thinking, if only I could do it right, I could fix things. I tried everything. I'd be sweet, buy her presents, bring her breakfast and coffee in bed — so she wouldn't make life miserable for such a nice guy."

He sighed. "But that never prevented anything. One minute I'd be a son of a bitch and the next I'd be too perfect. Once she told me, 'You're breathing too hard.' Once she punched her fist into the bathroom tile wall. Another time she threw herself down the stairs. I never knew what was going to happen next. After one of these scenes, I'd wake up the next morning exhausted and miserable and Abby would be fresh, with no memory of anything. I never could talk to anybody about what went on at home. I'd feel ridiculous. Nobody would have believed it."

"That's why you need to talk about it here," Margaret Raymond said.

Martin continued, as though speaking to himself. "There would be periods when she would be having only one glass of wine and controlling herself pretty well and apparently had seen the error of her ways. I'd think, 'It's still possible,' and try not to disturb the peaceful status quo. Then something would happen and I'd be back on the roller coaster."

Martin stopped and looked at Abby. She kept her face wooden. She was determined not to give him the satisfaction of breaking her down. But fear hummed like a bowstring inside her and she felt her lips tingle. He was doing it to her again. Gaslighting her. Turning her truth into craziness. And convincing these people. It was impossible to make herself understood. She had thrown herself downstairs because it was the only way she could get his attention. He had zero sense of her nightmare, and zero interest in it. *His* peaceful status quo was what mattered. And that would continue until he crushed her, until he convinced her once and for all that she was deeply faulted, that she was fatally, irretrievably silly.

"Sometimes," Martin continued, speaking now toward Abby, "I would explode and go wild and do anything and say anything. One night you deliberately smashed a plate I had made in pottery class." His voice shook. "I was so angry I was in a trance — like a slow motion film. It frightens me to think about it. I got out of my chair, went to a table, and picked up the first thing I saw — a pot that was, without question, the best thing I'd ever made. And I knew you dearly loved it. I walked the length of the living room and threw it as hard as I could into the fireplace. I turned it to dust."

Martin choked. He sat motionless for a moment, his hands in fists. He drew in a deep breath and said, "I obliterated it." He paused again. Then, his voice breaking with grief and fury, he shouted, "I was goddamn sick of it all. The *humiliation.* The *battering.* Physical. Psychological. *Everything!"*

When Abby opened her mouth, she could feel the stiffness of the flesh. Her voice was low, pulsating, harsh. "You sanctimonious son of a bitch. You're no helpless innocent, abused by a big, mean woman. You sat there and baited me with all your sarcastic remarks — which are your specialty — and made me feel like some idiot child. I told you, 'If you bait me one more time . . . I don't want to break this, but if you bait me one more time . . .' And you went ahead and made some below-the-belt remark that was unbelievably hurting. I think you were just seeing if I'd do it."

Martin's face flushed. "Here we go again," he said. "Abby, you've got it wrong. In the first place you were drunk. In the second place . . ." He began to sputter, muddling his words. "I was not . . . I wasn't baiting you. You can't stand to . . . you hate the truth. Your imagination — that's where *you* get facts. Thirdly, you deliberately, with malice aforethought . . ." He inhaled again, deeply. "I remember you got up from the sofa, went over to the chest opposite the fireplace, picked up the plate . . ."

Fern interrupted. "Group. What's happening?"

Garrett answered. "I've been in thousands of those hassles. He's right, she's wrong. She's right, he's wrong."

"She throws feelings at him," Julia said, "and he beats her over the head with facts."

Larry said, "I've been thinking that it's very important to Martin to be right. Does being right really *matter?"*

Martin twisted toward Larry. "Yes, it *does* matter," he answered caustically. "There are certain things *you* don't understand. If she's right and I'm wrong, I lose my validity. Then I become what she says — a paranoiac, a person interfering with her life."

Fern spoke. "I have some awarenesses I would like to share. Abby, you have been making progress, but as usually happens in family week, you have rejoined your family system. There are three basic roles that families get into: the persecutor, the rescuer, and the victim. Martin I see as the persecutor, the lecturer shaking the finger. The underlying message is that if you would just shape up, everything would be okay. Judy and Frederick are the rescuers. Evan has gotten out of the system by being the rebel, acting out his anger. And you, Abby, are over there saying, 'Bullshit. I am mad. I'm going to punish Martin.' "

Fern waited one beat and then continued. "Secondly, there's a concept that you, Martin, should consider. Being right is a way to be one up, so that the other person is one down." She shifted her hands to the arms of the chair and waited another moment. "Martin, do you want to stay in this marriage?"

Martin did not hesitate. "Yes," he said. "Yes, I do." He looked directly at Abby. "I believe that what we used to have is worth salvaging. Before we were married, you said you wanted to grow old with me. I was very impressed by that, and I've never forgotten it."

Fern asked Abby, "Is your relationship with this man something you want to work on?"

She looked at Martin. The fire eased from her face. "That pot you smashed," she said, "was so lovely, so Japanese. I was hysterical. A really bone-crushing sadness. I looked at it, lying there in a million pieces, and it symbolized everything that had gone wrong in this beautiful relationship that hadn't been beautiful for a long time. I thought, 'This can't have happened. This can't be us.' "

"That doesn't answer my question," Fern said. Do you have *anything* to build on with this man?"

"Yes. I love him. But living with him is miserable. And I just see no point . . ."

"So what's gotten in the way, my dear?"

"He's got to be able to communicate with me. I have a real need to talk to somebody."

"I have a real need to be talked to," Martin shot back.

Abby looked pleadingly into Martin's face. "I know I've done terrible things. But for years I've been unable to come and tell you how I feel. You wouldn't accept it. And I don't know how to tell you anymore — so I've got to change."

"The message I'm hearing," Fern said, "is that you want Martin to change."

"No, I want *me* to change." Abby paused. "But he's . . . I've tried to talk to him. I've *tried*. Maybe I've got to find other people to talk to."

Martin spoke, his voice impatient. "You have a right — and I have the responsibility to give you that right — to talk to me. And you also have an awful lot of friends besides me — Lucy, Annie, Jan — people who are reaching out to you and trying to allow you to talk to them. But you just keep saying, 'I don't have any friends.' I could save your vocal cords by putting that on a tape recorder so each time you could just push the button."

Abby bent her head, and the dark hair swung forward. Her voice was jagged, halting, tears just behind it. "I don't know what . . . I have to ask you to be aware. I don't know how to . . . I'm not shifting blame."

"What's gotten in the way?" Fern asked her again.

"He doesn't hear me. I've tried."

"What have you been doing for the past five years?" Margaret Raymond asked.

Abby's eyes were red and wet. "I shut him off because of *years* of not being able to get through."

"What have you turned to?" Margaret asked.

"The bottle. I talked to the bottle. The only pipeline I found. I can't talk to Martin. I picked up the bottle. I talked to the bottle."

Fern said, "I hear you saying, 'If Martin would just change, then everything would be peachy keen and I wouldn't drink.' That's not the way it works, Abby."

Margaret Raymond spoke in her dry voice. "If you sit there waiting for Martin to change, you may be sitting there for a long time."

243

Abby's voice was half resentment, half a sob. "What I'm trying to say is: I cannot go back home to what it was and make it alone."

Fern leaned forward in her urgency. "Yes, you can!" she called out. "Yes, you can!"

"A lot of us are going to have to do that," Julia said from Abby's right.

Now Abby's voice was desperate. "How can I go back to a place where I'm miserable, where I'm so afraid that what I'm doing won't please Martin?" She was panting now. "I'm afraid of Martin. I'm really afraid to tell him what I think."

"He's sitting right in front of you," Fern said.

Abby took a deep breath. "I want you to know I am really, really scared to be back where I may take another drink. Whatever I have to change in myself to be able to come home, that's what's important now. I can't change you. I can ask you if you're willing to help. I can ask you if you're willing to give up your drink before dinner, if you're willing not to come home after you've had three drinks and can't see the difference in yourself. I can ask you to cut down on our social life, play less golf — all those things. I can ask you to say what you feel, instead of hiding behind stony silences or jokes. I can ask you to get off my back."

She wiped her eyes with her fingers. "But I've tried all that. I've tried going and saying, 'Is there any way you could do such and such? It really bothers me to have it this way.' But you just hit right back at me. You say to me, 'Why don't you clean the sewing out of your chair? Why don't you clean the hall closet? Why don't you clean the laundry room?' I can't talk to you."

"Abby," Fern said sternly, "you are communicating with 'you' messages. If *you* get the whiskey out of the house. If *you* will talk to me. If *you* will do this or that thing, then I won't drink. And in this dynamic, that gives away tremendous power to this man. And you resent that. You resent the *hell* out of it. I want you to start thinking, 'What do *I* need to do?' Take back the power. You are a dynamite woman."

Martin spoke, "She *is* dynamite when she's sober."

"You should have told me that when I was sober," Abby flashed back.

"What did you just do?" Fern demanded. "You just negated something this man said spontaneously from his heart. You pushed it away. You were *so* quick, Abby. If I were sitting in his chair, I would think, 'Oh, my God, what's the use.' " Fern sat motionless. The long, long silence was heavy, stifling, disturbing. Then she said, "What's going to be different, Abby?"

"I'm very aware that if I take one more drink, that's it. I would never stop. I know that."

"Abby, " Fern said, "there may be times when Martin is not going to be available to you. But you can have the fellowship of AA and a woman sponsor who understands your disease, somebody you can call and say, 'I'm in a bad place. Martin is away. We're not communicating.' Whatever. You can work what we call 'the selfish program' — doing whatever you need to stay sober. Do you understand?"

"Yes."

"Unless you do that, the self-pity, the poor me, the 'He doesn't understand me' will continue and be a setup that will allow you to drink again. Do you believe that?"

Abby folded her hands in her lap. Her voice was almost inaudible. "Uh huh. I know that something has to change . . ."

Fern's voice cut in, loud, sharp. "Do you *believe* what I just said?"

"Yes."

"Okay. But I hope it's not just up in your head." Fern turned to Martin. "There are some tears inside there, aren't there."

"Yes," Martin answered.

"That's okay," Fern said, "because happiness is a goal for

everyone, and it eludes us in this disease until we think there never will be any happiness. But there can be."

In the small lounge Abby sat exhausted in her favorite spot on the sofa, feet up on the coffee table, losing herself in the great vacancy of the sky. Sipping from her mug of coffee, inhaling a cigarette, she thought gratefully, "At least I can depend on *these* vices." When Larry sat down beside her, she smiled ruefully at him and he grinned back.

"Enjoying family week?" he asked.

"Not if I win the first prize, which is two weeks in Sing Sing." She laughed, and they sat companionably for a time. Then Abby said, "I feel so shot down. But I shot myself down. I can't lay the blame anywhere else. They thought I was blaming Martin and making accusations. I guess it was a classic case of trying to get my message across and not putting it right. But maybe I wasn't right. I don't even know if my motives were right. I'm back to being totally confused. It's like Fern's shifted camps, and I'm no longer . . ."

Larry interrupted, smiling. "Fern has perfect timing. She knows when to put the arm around the shoulder and when to put the knife in the gut. But she's rooting for you. The patient is always number one. Like she says, 'Stop trying to figure it out and let it happen.' "

Abby shrugged. "I just want to clam up and forget the whole thing and not talk about it anymore."

"Well, I wanted to tell you," Larry said, "that I feel a real love between you and Martin. He knows it, and he's hanging on to it." Abby's heart jumped. Larry continued, "I identify with you because my father and mother had that kind of love. But they never got to share it because they were both alcoholics."

Turning, seeing that Larry's eyes were wet, Abby felt a strange, strangling mix of sorrow and excitement. Was she hearing what she needed to hear?

Larry went on, "I have so much frustration about alcoholism — what it did to my family — the love my parents had. The love was there. I could feel it. But they couldn't reach out to each other. And I couldn't get hold of it either."

A rush of sympathy, of fellowship, swirled in Abby's head, jamming any answering words. She found herself turning, reaching toward Larry — and he to her. She felt his hard bulk against her chest, the strong arms around her, the thin hair against her cheek, and felt her own hands pressed flat on Larry's muscular back — and then, finally, the sensation of her self-pity draining away.

CHAPTER

11

THAT EVENING, entering the lecture room, Abby was amazed and disconcerted. Martin was in the back row. Their eyes met, and he smiled the embarrassed, little boy smile that was always appealing and disarming. They still could not talk outside of group, so she sat next to Julia, acutely aware of him behind her, acutely curious why he was there.

The lecture was on "Enabling" and the speaker was a tall woman, small-faced, her hair pulled tightly back into a bun. She was saying, "For convenience, I will talk in terms of alcohol, but what I have to say applies equally to addiction to all mood altering drugs, whether it is marijuana, LSD, sleeping pills, demerol, tranquilizers, whatever. In fact many patients are cross-addicted, use more than one. Women, for example, frequently use both alcohol and Valium."

Abby sighed. Maybe she'd been kidding herself. She'd always thought the Valium was just a helper to get her to sleep or to calm the shakes. But she'd kept it hidden upstairs and downstairs — so it would be handy — just like the bottles.

"When there is alcoholism in a family," the woman continued, "there are almost always one or more enablers. They are members of the family who protect the alcoholic from the consequences of the disease and pospone the day when the alcoholic hits bottom and is open to genuine help."

Abby whispered to Julia, "They sound like terrific people to have around."

"So what does the enabler do?" the lecturer asked. "The enabler thinks, 'Since maybe I made the drinking happen, maybe I can make it go away. I will take control. I will set hours, dump out pills, smash bottles. I will hide the car keys and take away the checkbook. I will cancel events, lie to people, and make excuses. I will telephone during the day to check the voice for signs of drinking. I will put people on probation, shape everything up.' "

Abby smiled grimly to herself. Martin was hearing a portrait of himself.

The woman continued, "Family members try to be the savior — 'I'm going to cry if they need me to cry, be angry if they need me to be angry, do whatever they say.' Some people become partners and drink with the patient — 'If you can't beat 'em, join 'em.' Some become victims — 'Poor me; what did I do to deserve this?' Some are martyrs — 'I'm a faithful wife, faithful husband, and it's my *duty* to stay here and take care of the person.' People can really get off on having other people say, 'Gee, you must be a saint to put up with him, or her.' "

If Judy had heard that, Abby thought, it must have been a shocker. All that nobility and sacrifice was only behavior, and unhealthy behavior at that.

The lecturer was asking, "Why do we use that word 'enabler'? Because enablers help the addict keep right on doing whatever they're doing. I once heard a young patient say in group, 'Can you imagine what Al-Anon is telling my parents? They're saying they shouldn't let me come home.' Then the young man stared into space and said, as though he was talking to himself, 'I know my dad will probably follow through because he's a lot tougher than my mom. She's a pushover. So I'll tell her, 'Mom, what am I going to do? Where am I going to go?' "

Abby felt her skin tingle. This woman was uncanny. She was talking about Evan who had threatened to leave home.

He'd do things his own way, he said. No more of his father's cliches — "Success breeds success" — "There are no shortcuts in life." No more ridiculous school, all that useless information, nothing to do with being alive. Abby stirred restlessly. She was the one who had always rushed to talk him out of it — "Where will you go? What will you do?" What else had she done automatically, out of love and motherhood, but actually enabling Evan. Her heart sank. From now on she would have to stop and think about everything.

The lecturer was talking about the effects of enabling on the family. "Enablers don't want to do anything that will make the alcoholic drink. So they accommodate themselves to the alcoholic. They don't say anything that will get the person angry. They don't say what they feel. They constantly check out the person, always wonder, modify, hedge. They are reacting, reacting, reacting. They aren't living. They aren't making decisions like a healthy person. And after a while they think this is normal. They've long since lowered their expectations. They don't expect to go out in the evening and have things okay. They don't expect their sex life to be okay. Kids don't expect mom and dad to have a warm relationship, don't expect marriage to feel good and look good."

Abby sat in a daze of embarrassment and recognition. Those times she thought she'd outsmarted Martin, those rounds she thought she'd won, were really self-defeats. It was all so sad — and sick — and frightening.

In the afternoon group on Thursday, May twenty-seventh, Fern looked thoughtfully at Abby and her family. "I think we've gone about as far as we can go in the fishbowl," she said. "Maybe, Abby, you and Martin should take a walk together and come back here after group." Relieved, self-conscious, anxious, Abby led her family out the door. She was going to be alone with Martin. She could feel her nerves stretching tight, thinning down. In the hall she stood awkwardly with the family. The unsayable between them had been spoken, the tacit family cover-up smashed, their self-protections breached.

Abby, looking at Judy and Evan, asked, "What are you guys going to do?" She did like this sense of being a mother again, of being even a little bit in charge of her children — and herself.

Frederick, taking her hand in both of his, began hanging on it, walking his feet out from under him. Judy shrugged her shoulders. "Go watch TV in the family lounge, play Ping-Pong, something."

"Okay," Abby answered, and her nerves snapped for a second and she spun toward Frederick and barked, "Stop that! You're pulling my arm off."

Frederick, abashed, let go. Abby went on, a little softer, "Maybe Judy would take you down to that TV set."

"Why don't you have TV in your room?" Frederick asked. "Because you'll see pictures of people drinking?"

Abby laughed. "There's something to that. How about ice cream bars all around?"

That treat accomplished, the family separated at the elevator bank. Abby and Martin stood silent, eating their ice cream, hiding behind the almond-covered barricades. Then, outside the building, they crossed the drive and walked along the broad bank of the river. Ahead of them, a teenage boy threw a stick again and again for a golden retriever. A jogger passed them, panting rhythmically. The sun was a warm layer on top of the cool air. The worn and patchy grass felt yielding and good under Abby's moccasins.

Martin took the small finger of her hand in his. "I'm really sorry, Abby," he said, "that all these things have happened between us."

"I know you are. I know you are," she answered. "If you want, you can hold my whole hand."

So they walked a while, hand in hand: a handsome, romantic picture, Abby thought — Martin lean in his brown corduroys and sweater, herself slender and smart in jeans and jacket — a happy picture — two fortunates free of problems. Martin, watching the ground, kicked away a paper bag that was crumpled around a can. "How do *you* feel?" he asked, and laughed. "God, I'm beginning to sound like Fern."

"Blitzed," Abby answered, unsmiling. "Sort of in shock. Empty."

"We have an awful lot going for us."

"Well, I hope so," Abby said. "I worry that I've hurt everybody so much it's going to taint everything and we can't rebuild."

Martin did not react. He seemed in a strange, reflective mood, new to Abby. "A crazy thing happened to me last night," he continued. "I was getting undressed. I'd just put my shoes in the closet when I started to bawl like a little kid. And I didn't want to stop. So I kept on getting ready for bed with the tears running down my face." He smiled almost shyly at her. "Doesn't sound like me, does it?"

"No, it sure doesn't," Abby answered. "I bet you're glad it didn't happen in the fishbowl."

"Yes."

They walked a while, and then Martin said, "The only time I ever saw my father cry — the only time he ever shared something personal — was once when he read his favorite poem, 'In Flanders Fields,' and he actually cried. I was embarrassed, but I felt close to him and it was wonderful. And then he just slammed the book shut and it was all over. And I was mad."

They were silent again and Abby tried to picture Martin last night, tears running down his face while he brushed his teeth. She could not. But maybe some clot had broken loose so that his feelings could flow again. She glanced covertly at him. He did seem better, the plump face a little younger, his voice more relaxed.

Martin stopped and checked his watch, saying, "We mustn't get too far away." He turned, and they headed back the way they had come.

"Why were you at the lecture last night?" Abby asked.

"Margaret Raymond's orders. We'd had the same talk downstairs and she thought I didn't get the message."

"What was the message?"

"I don't think you're going to like it."

"What was the message?"

"That I should learn to detach," Martin answered, looking away from her. "That I'm not responsible for you. I can't change you, but I can change the way I react to you. I can stop letting your behavior control my life." He stopped and took a breath. "I feel free for the first time in years."

"I have to detach, too." Abby's voice was sharp, defensive.

"That's right," Martin answered casually, and again he kicked the can inside the paper bag. Abby's heart contracted. He wasn't talking about change. He'd just found a good reason *not* to change.

They reached their starting point, and, after Martin looked at his watch, kept going. They came to a bench and sat down facing the river, and Abby looked down the long band of water moving calmly, at its own deliberate pace, along its prescribed course. "Do you remember our first wedding anniversary?" Abby asked.

"Sure."

"Drinking champagne and telling each other how lucky we were? And dancing to the jukebox?"

"That's what I hope we can get back to." Martin looked at her and smiled and took her hand again.

"But we've got to learn to communicate," Abby answered. "They told us in a lecture that the average American couple in the United States spends only about fourteen minutes a day in good, solid communication. I believe it. You call me every day and want to know what came in the mail, and I ask you where you went to lunch and what you ate, and then you ask me what I'm going to do this afternoon and whether I've done such and such — and tell me not to forget etcetera and etcetera. And that's about it."

"You're expecting me to talk about feelings, aren't you."
Now Martin was looking off along the river.

"Yes."

"That's not my long suit. You know that." He was still
speaking away from her.

Abby took her hand away. "Will you try?"

"Yes. I'll try. I'm sure there are a lot of things inside me,
but I've never seen any point in dwelling on them and making myself unhappy. And if you expose your feelings, you
just leave yourself wide open for future arguments and future hurts." He rose to go. "I've been hurt enough. I don't
want to be hurt anymore."

Abby looked up at him, eyes sad.

Fern's door was still closed, so they waited outside. Martin broke the silence, saying, "I think two bright people like
us should be able to figure out what has to be done."

"Stop figuring out," Abby answered, "and start feeling."

The door opened and the group straggled out, Larry
looking quizzically at Abby, who shrugged. When the way
was clear, they went inside and Fern drew up two chairs by
her desk and welcomed them. "Did you get anything settled?"

"I don't know," Martin said. "We discussed our communication."

Martin folded his arms across his chest. "Abby thinks we
can't communicate if I don't show my feelings more."

Fern asked, "What do you think?"

"I said I'd try. But if she wants that, maybe she wants a
different man. I just don't believe in being emotional. What
is wrong with being under control? Our minister asked me
to be the Junior Warden. He said they needed my stability.
And at home, *somebody* had to be stable."

Fern smiled. "I'm not convinced. You did pretty well with
feelings yesterday. How did you feel afterward?"

"Relieved. I felt good. But that happened here. At home

254

there would have been a hell of a fight and I would have felt terrible."

"Maybe so. But Abby, I hope, will be a different person. Sober, for one thing. And you will have to use the tools you've learned here to deal with those situations. And I urge you to go to Al-Anon meetings, where you can get the advice and support of other husbands of alcoholics."

"I went to Al-Anon a few times," Martin answered. "I didn't get a whole lot out of it. It seemed like a competition on a given night to see who was having the worst time. It wasn't for me."

Fern tightened her lips. "I can't force you to go, Martin. But perhaps after this week, you would listen differently and identify with those people."

Martin was silent and Fern continued, "I want to talk about change for a minute. Until now, your happiness has been largely dependent on whatever Abby was doing or not doing. She had a great deal of power over you. She exploited whatever it was that you believed about yourself: that everything was your fault, that you were a failure, inferior, no good, that you deserved to be tromped on."

Abby was restless, uncomfortable. Fern continued, "So how do you take back your power and take control of your own happiness? You change the way you think about yourself. That means analyzing your feelings. 'Why do I feel like a failure today?' 'Why do I feel tense?' 'Why do I feel guilty?' 'Why am I enjoying all the attention I'm receiving?' It means paying attention to the signals your body sends you. What is your headache telling you? What is your stomachache telling you?"

Abby checked Martin's face. Her fears were confirmed. He looked wary, doubtful, puzzled. He said, "Well, of course, I want to do everything I can to be helpful, and I certainly want to leave here and move forward. I think I really do understand about detaching."

"Good!" Fern said. "But don't forget, 'Detach *with love.*' Detaching must not be a punishment. You have to accept

Abby for what she is. And detaching includes *not* being in charge of everything. I think that may be hard for you." Fern smiled again. "Martin, if you want to work on your relationship with Abby — and I think you do — there's something I'd like you to consider very carefully. It's a little analogy I use. If you want to hold a butterfly, you must keep your hand open and relaxed. If you grip too hard, you will crush it."

Abby's heart reeled upward. "My day has come," Abby thought. "I've just been taken to heaven." She had not been crazy. Fern did understand. This woman, this counselor in a treatment center, was agreeing with her, was saying that Martin was a crusher.

Martin nodded his head thoughtfully. Then he said, "That's very nice. Like mercury. If you try to grip mercury, it runs out between your fingers."

Abby's heart fell. Martin was still up in his head. He got the image. He didn't get the point.

Fern's face was inscrutable. "Thank you," she said. "Now there is something else important we should talk about and that's plan B. Plan A is that Abby gets well and goes home and you live happily ever after. But what do you do for yourself, Martin, if Abby goes home and drinks again? If that happens and you don't have a plan, then panic takes over."

Abby, her stomach tight, stared at Martin. His face looked sad. Slowly he rubbed his eyes with two fingers. "I've already thought a lot about that. If it comes to the bottom line — and this is a tough thing to say — I think it's better that one of us goes down the tube instead of both of us. I couldn't take it anymore. I *wouldn't* take it anymore. And it's really affecting the kids. It's not just *her* disease anymore."

"Martin," Abby asked suddenly, "why have you stayed with me this long?"

He looked startled. "I've wondered why myself," he answered. "I think fear was a lot of it. The change was frightening. I was afraid of loneliness. I was such a failure, I didn't think any other woman would ever want me. And just when I'd get serious about leaving, things would be better and I'd decide to settle for that. If I left, there'd be two homes to pay for, and I'd get the children, so I was worried about being a single parent. I used to think I was a coward. But then I'd figure it was braver to do the honorable thing and stick by my wife in sickness and in health. I thought if you were alone you'd drink more and pass out in bars and get beaten up and raped. Then that would be my fault and I'd never forgive myself. And the children would never forgive me."

Abby nodded. She felt sorry for him. She had made his life miserable. That was why she half agreed with the coward part. She had often thought there was something wrong with him because he didn't leave her. She felt anger, too. He was making the marriage her responsibility. She spoke and her voice was loud and cutting. "If *you* don't change, I'll divorce *you*!"

Abby and Martin found the children alone in the first floor family lounge, watching TV. Frederick wanted to know where they had been, what they had been doing.

Abby was evasive. "Oh, we walked along the river and then talked to Fern about some things."

"No, Abby," Martin said, turning off the television. "I think they should hear."

He had a queer look, she thought nervously. He sat in a chair across from the three surprised faces lined up along the sofa.

He smoothed his mustache. "Your mother and I discussed with Fern what would happen if she came home and drank again."

Abby sat down in an end chair, gingerly, as though her body were very fragile. Frederick's eyes were wide and frightened. "Here at Riverside they ask you to have Plan A and Plan B. A assumes that your mother makes a good recovery and does not drink again, which, of course, is what we want and expect. But Fern asked me to plan what I would do if that does not happen. I told her, for my sake and your sakes, I would ask for a divorce. This is not easy for me to say, but it is important that . . ."

Evan jerked erect, his face a hot red. "I can't believe you!" he said. "You're bailing out again." His voice was rising. "This shit about helping Mom has been a big con. It's a cover so now you can run away like you always did. And leave Judy with all the dirty work. You always had an excuse: a church meeting, or "I have to have my golf." Nothing should interrupt your social life. Bull*shit!* Such a drag. If you'd stayed home more . . ."

Abby's heart was racing. Evan was defending her! Evan understood, too. But what was the truth? This or the fishbowl? Probably both. Poor Evan!

Martin looked only tired. He said, "Haven't you learned *anything* this week? Nothing I could have done for Abby would have made a difference. No amount of love and sacrifice . . ."

Evan stood up, his arms straight as sticks down his sides, his hands in fists, knuckles white. His words came in a rush, frantic. "You're *buying* that psychology shit, that treatment mumbo jumbo. I can't stand that shit. It's *panic* in that room. You're sitting there thinking, 'Oh, I can handle all my problems without booze, so you people are all a bunch of screw ups.' Fern shoots me the eyes and Mom shoots me the eyes — and I'm a goddamned hypocrite — a screw up telling Mom she's a screw up — and I want to scream 'cause I'm burning up inside, scared, physically scared of what'll happen when that reaches my head. Goddamned people messing with my insides! I don't want anybody touching me, but I'm stuck here."

Judy began to cry. Frederick's eyes shone with excitement.

Martin lowered his head and with his fingertips massaged

his forehead. "If you would stop interrupting me and let me . . ."

"Jesus Christ," Evan shouted at him. "Don't *you* interrupt *me!* I don't give a shit why you leave. Just don't think I'll come live with you. If you split, so will I. You abandoned me first. I'll be free. I'll go to California. Hawaii. I'll live with somebody who understands me, no phony rules. Your rules suck!"

Martin answered calmly, "My life is important, too, Evan."

Evan cut in, bitterly. "What about your responsibility to us?" His voice climbed even higher. "You don't care about us. You don't care about Mom. You know she can't make it on her own." He bumped into a chair, whirled, and threw it clattering to the side. He spun back, arms flailing. He was yelling now. "No matter how much . . . Mom could stab me. Anything. Physically stab me, and I'd still feel sorry for her . . . still love . . ." He whirled again, running toward the door, which he grabbed and crashed closed behind him.

On Saturday morning — May twenty-ninth — Abby at ten o'clock still had not stirred from her room. She kept telling herself that nothing was wrong. She had heard and read all that she had to know to stay sober. Family week was finished, and, one way or another, everybody had opened up. There were no more secrets. The pains and problems had been defined. So she should feel relieved, liberated, ready to move ahead into sobriety. But everything was wrong. She felt suffocated by a free-floating depression, a miasma, a gray bubble of fear and self-disgust. She felt stripped — back at the starting line — totally overwhelmed. She felt utterly alone with herself, and that was unbearable.

When Larry and Julia knocked on her door, she called out, "Go away." They knocked again, louder. She yelled, "I need to be alone." They pushed open the door, and the two of them advanced to the edge of the bed, where Abby lay, unwashed, uncombed, smoking a cigarette, staring up into the blank emptiness of the ceiling. Larry sat on the edge of the bed and rested a hand on her ankle. "Are you all right, Abby?" he asked, and held out to her an ice cream bar. "You know, there really is life after family week."

Not looking at him, not seeing the ice cream, Abby answered, "I don't like that opening line. Go out and come back with another script — the one that begins, 'Poor, Abby. You're a piece of crap, so no wonder you feel awful.'"

Julia pulled the wooden chair to the side of the bed and said gently, "We've all felt like that."

Abby rolled over to drop the cigarette into the glass of water. Larry, pushing the ice cream bar toward her, said, "Better eat this before it melts."

Abby took the bar, but held it numbly in her hand. She said, "I'm at the bottom of a hole twenty feet deep that I dug with my own sweet hands, and I hate it down here."

"After my family week," Larry said, "I felt like ten pounds of shit in a five pound bag."

Abby looked at him, eyes frightened. "What's going to happen the first time I say no to the children? Are they going to freak out and hate me — when they're really hating me because I'm an alcoholic and a horrible mother?"

Julia answered, "Having a mother who cares enough about them to say no is one of the things they've been missing."

Still listlessly holding the ice cream bar, her voice slightly choked, Abby answered, "I don't feel like I belong in the family. I don't *deserve* to be with them."

"Do you know how much you're wallowing?" Larry asked.

Her face suddenly angry, Abby glared at Larry. "I *want* to wallow," she said, and then she laughed. "I sound like a little kid, don't I?"

Larry smiled affectionately. "Yes, you do."

Abby pulled herself upright on the bed and sat leaning against the wall. Slowly she unwrapped one end of the ice cream, bit into it, and chewed reflectively. Suddenly she pounded her fist against the mattress and said, half furious, half pleading, "I'm so goddamn mad! They made me out so black. They were so brainwashed and coached. What I did couldn't have been *that* crucial because the kids never said anything."

"Wait a *minute!*" Larry interrupted.

"And Martin," Abby went on, undeterred, frowning. "We've been going round and round on that stuff for years. And everybody was buying it. But I'm not going to let him destroy me — just dissolve me into a puddle — like the witch Dorothy threw the water on."

Bending her round-shouldered body forward, Julia rested her elbows on her knees. "I know Martin can be hard to take. But he was hurting in the fishbowl. We could see it. He couldn't have made everything up. Your kids weren't faking that pain. It was shivery listening to them. I kept thinking, 'Oh, my God, I've done all of that to my kids.' We've got to face the fact that our drinking plays a big part in every problem. In fact, it's *the* problem."

Abby's anger was instantaneous. Her voice was high and harsh. "If you're such a know-it-all wizard, how come you're in a treatment center just like me?"

Julia leaned back in the chair and for a moment gazed bleakly into Abby's challenging eyes. "I'm as sick as you are," she said. "Even sicker because I've been through treatment twice and know all the answers." Her eyes wavered and moved away toward the window. "I'm a terrific patient who never seems to recover. I don't know what's missing in me." Her eyes came back to Abby. "If that means what I tell you is wrong, I'll just leave and go have a cup of coffee. But if we don't listen to one another . . ."

"I'm sorry, Julia," Abby said. "I'm glad you're here." She hesitated. "I'm just *really* scared." The ice cream had begun to melt onto her hand, and she quickly finished it and licked her fingers. Julia pulled some tissues from the box on the bureau and handed them to her. Abby wiped her hand and sat looking at the wadded ball of paper. When she lifted her head, her eyes were glistening. "Martin will want to go right on with his life — all my command performances at parties. How can I deal with those bores when I'm not high? What's going to happen the first time I'm offered a drink? If I say no, they'll think I'm judging them. I'll be the snake at the Sunday school picnic."

"Abby," Larry said, "I'm leaving on Tuesday. *I'm* scared. But I'm telling myself 'One day at a time.' "

"But it's not just the drinking," Abby said, looking from face to face. "Fern talks about honesty. I don't know what it is to be honest with myself and up front about everything. I'm not sure I can do it — or want to — or whether it's going to be worth it." Still leaning back against the wall, Abby brushed a tangle of hair away from her face. "But I can't stand the way I feel now. I want to kill myself."

Larry moved along the bed and took one of her limp hands. "This is what family week is all about. They destroy you so there's nobody left to blame and then you can put yourself together again and leave out the bad stuff."

"But suppose all the king's men can't put me together again?" Abby tried to laugh and failed.

Larry squeezed her hand. "Come on out to the lounge and we'll play some bridge."

Abby lowered her head and combed her fingers through her hair. "I feel so ashamed. I can't go out there. I'm the woman who threw a watermelon at her son."

Larry squeezed her hand again. "Like Fern says, 'Beyond a wholesome discipline, be gentle with yourself.' "

Abby came unwillingly to the lounge, but refused to play bridge. Any sounds of gaiety, any light conversation scratched her nerves. She retreated to a corner chair and hid behind a newspaper, the words moving meaninglessly past her eyes. Presently, she left and headed down to the peace of the empty chapel. Passing through the wide doors, moving down the aisle, she took her accustomed place, the first seat in the second row. Folding her hands in her lap, she settled herself, expectant, ready for relief.

Peace did not come. As though the quiet had removed all distraction, all protection, a sense of enormous sin permeated her body. Her vileness reverberated in her mind. "Unforgivable" . . . "Damaged" . . . "Violent" . . . "Wicked." In that sanctified silence, this knowledge burned deep as her soul. She put her hands over her face and thought, "That was the way it really was. I am capable of anything." The list of horrors marched through her brain: maim, kill somebody with the car, a knife, my hands, suicide — *anything!*

Suddenly a voice inside her said, "Come on. It wasn't *that* bad. Get hold of yourself. There are millions worse than you." Abby dropped her hands from her face. The anguish eased for a moment — until the terrible clarity returned. "But it *was* that bad.". She could feel tears pushing up, and she looked at the huge oak cross. "God, help me. Get me through the next few minutes." The tears arrived, and she wiped her eyes on the sleeve of her shirt. "Please, God, I've tried to be the best I can. I'm really sorry! Help me!"

Then, like a following wave: "You're being a stupid hysteric. Nothing really, really bad happened. You didn't *murder* anybody." Then the next wave. "Please God, I don't know where to go from here. I'm somebody I don't even know." And next, "I *couldn't* have done *all* those things they said." Then, "Dear God, just help me. Take away this pain."

The stillness, the unfiltered agony, became unbearable. Abby jumped up from the chair and hurried back to her room. She lay on the bed again, her head stuffed under a pillow. But the voices could not be muffled — the voices of her mother, father, Fern, Martin, the children, all her past and present, bombarding her from every direction. "Never sew in a zipper without basting it first — Every intoxication destroys ten thousand brain cells — I love you, but I don't have to prove it to you every hour on the hour — The sign of God is that we will be led where we did not plan to go — All those from A to E bring a salad to the luncheon — Where do I fit in life; nothing makes any sense — Mom, I need two dozen brownies for my girl scout meeting this afternoon — . . . when the caissons go rolling along — You are not in enough pain yet; you are not lonely enough — I don't want you necking in parked cars — Jesus loves me, this I know, for the Bible tells me so."

Tossing away the pillow, Abby put a tape of Schubert on the player, but turned it off. Too much mood, too many memories. She got a cup of coffee and stood in the hall drinking it, but fled the sounds of life. She sat on the broad window sill of her room, watching the people on the far sidewalk, wondering where she had gone off the track, wondering if anybody so fatally flawed could ever belong in that world out there. She felt totally, irrevocably defeated. Helpless. No longer able to fight back against her troubles. Stripped of every defense.

In the long hours of that Saturday, she went over and over the past week, replaying every word and image — the bitterness, the grief, the frustration on her family's faces, all caused by her. The walk with Martin, so disappointing and maddening and depressing, so distant from their long-ago walk on the beach at Martha's Vineyard. She had changed that accessible Martin; she had brought out and hardened the worst in him, not the best. The session with Fern — so frightening. The family was on the edge of breakup. And Evan's explosion. It was she who had written all that agony and chaos into him, programmed him for trouble. How could anybody ever atone for such a crime?

But when Martin and the children left on Friday, after a family group session including the patients, everybody saying the right thing, she had felt very close to Evan. He was the one who saw her with unobstructed eyes. They had pieces of the same violence, parts of the same terror. He had hugged her tight, while Frederick chattered away, wishing they had brought the puppy so she could meet it. Poor Frederick. Had he been traumatized that week, his illusions broken? But he must have learned something about the disease. And, left behind, he would have felt he didn't count, that he was not part of the family. Yet, the memory of the tears on those soft cheeks — because of her — cracked her heart.

Periodically that day, nurses knocked and insisted she leave the room. "When you isolate, the self-pity hits like a ton of bricks." Abby talked a while with one of them, also an alcoholic, who told her, "All these years you've been using your head to deny the disease, while your guts were screaming for help. Just let the pain happen inside of you."

Abby answered, "In whatever time I have left in life, I am not going to end up like this again."

Abby slept restlessly and woke early on Sunday morning. At the window, leaking around the venetian blinds, was the slight light of dawn. The depression was still there inside her, draining away her energy, dragging down her mind. She decided to skip Sunday chapel. She was afraid of it now.

During the morning, members of her group stopped by, telling her not to worry, to lighten up. Paula delivered three clover blossoms in a battered paper cup. Garrett pushed a card under the door — a donkey in a bed, captioned, "Get your ass out of bed." Julia wrote her a note — "Hang in there. It must be working because you hurt so much." Then Larry came again to the room and invited her outside into the sunshine. She said, "No." He took her by the arm and propelled her into the hall and to the elevators. She went along, too whipped to struggle, not caring. Downstairs, with a courtly flourish, Larry held open one of the big glass doors and eased her out into the afternoon.

On the lawn in front of the Center, part of her group was gathered in the sun on an orange blanket. The air was very still. The sun was warm. The grass was green. The sky blue. The lacy leaves of a linden tree were light green and dark green. Two men were throwing a red Frisbee. Life was proceeding despite the public ghastliness of her sins. Life was there, waiting to embrace her. She had only to open herself to it. She knew, suddenly, that she did have hope, she did have goodness inside her. It was fine to be herself. She was a person that people, these people, cared about. A sense of accomplishment welled up within her. She had stayed the course. A tremendous freedom raced through her, a giddy lightness, as though she could fly. In a burst of celebration, she did a cartwheel.

Her friends applauded and she joined them on the blanket. Garrett patted her on the back and Julia beamed at her. Jerold said, "I didn't think ladies your age did things like that." Abby laughed and answered, "You're only young once. And if you work it right, once is enough."

After a half hour, Abby excused herself and walked around the end of the building and sat down, leaning against the brick wall of the Center. She wanted to be alone to think, and she liked the idea of this spot where she had sat that first Monday, promising herself she would leave treatment. She lit a cigarette and with the first puff seemed to inhale a wave of gratitude. Somehow she had stayed at Riverside, and now she had this tremendous feeling in a quiet part of herself she had never touched before. Something, impossibly, had melted and jelled all at once. The inner sense of battle, the need to conceal and convince, had disappeared. Among her friends on the blanket, for the first time in her life, she had felt the inside of her — the feelings and thoughts — matching the outside of her. She finished the cigarette. Extinguishing it on the ground, she guessed that this must be, at last, the surrender they talked about. Did it always come like this? With no help from your head? When you least expected it?

PART FOUR

CHAPTER

12

MOVING THROUGH her routines at Riverside, Abby floated
in a benign state of relief. She was sure at last that she was
headed in the right direction. The sense of wrestling against
herself was gone. She felt more secure, more open. In her
daydreams she planned how to atone to her family. She would
fix everybody breakfast, bake the children's favorite brownies, take the kids to the movies, teach Judy to sew, be a pal
instead of passed out, do the things that pleased Martin —
iron his shirts just right, align the magazines in straight rows,
wipe the water spots off the bathroom chrome every day. In
the lounge, Abby no longer listened to other patients and
thought, "Poor them" or "I never did stuff like that." She
felt more than ever like an upperclassman. The senior, bat-
tle-wise patients of her own freshman weeks were gone. Many
of the new faces around her were a touch deferential, and
one woman, a stranger, came pleading for help on her First
Step. The rituals of departure were beginning. She and Larry
inscribed each other's Big Books. He wrote, "Please know
that an admiring Irishman is plugging for you, even if you
are half Wasp, half Clairol."

On Monday afternoon, Larry finished treatment. Coming
into her room, he stood smiling, awkward. "So long for now,"
he said.

Abby stood up beside the small table. "So long." They
looked at each other. "I hate 'Good-bye,' " she added. " 'So

long' is good. It sounds less permanent. I know I'll see you again." They walked together to the elevator. "I'll call you," he said. His eyes were wet.

Abby could feel the tears on her cheeks. "I'll have happy dreams about you."

The elevator door opened and he picked up his two suitcases. "Well, my bus is here." He went in and turned.

"Good luck," she called, but the closing door sliced off her words.

On Tuesday afternoon — June first — Fern said to Abby in group, "You're looking more relaxed than I've ever seen you."

Abby smiled, partly because those blue eyes were no longer frightening. "Yes," she answered. "Family week is finished and I'm still alive."

Fern's eyes twinkled. "If looks could kill, I think Martin would have gone poof."

Abby laughed. "Poor guy."

Fern nodded and said dryly, "Unfortunately, it's not over yet." She looked thoughtfully at Abby and asked, "What are you going to do if you go home and the situation is exactly the same?"

Abby was silent, then answered, "I worry about that a lot. I just don't know."

"Think."

"I'll join AA and get a sponsor."

"Okay, but that's not what I'm talking about. What are you going to do if nothing changes at home?"

The answer lit up in Abby's mind. "I'll drink."

"What *can* you do? What choices are there?"

Now Abby understood. She would not *have* to be trapped. She had choices. Horrendous choices. Abby nodded. "I can leave the family."

Fern continued. "There is the expression, 'It's a selfish program.' That doesn't mean you push everybody else aside and tell your husband to get out of your life. You just have to think about yourself and what you need in order to stay straight." She paused. "If you don't give your survival number one priority, what happens?"

"I may drink."

"And if you do drink?"

"I'll die."

Fern's grin was crooked. "That's the catechism."

Abby was elated. After all those years of drinking, alcohol had seemed her only option. But she really did have choices. That was an enormous freedom.

On Tuesday afternoon, three therapy groups, Fern's included, came together for a lecture by the pastoral care counselor, Leila Alexander. She was a thin, prematurely gray woman with kind, interested eyes who had been pointed out to Abby and spoken of with awe. Leila, they said, was an alcoholic former nun who had done everything there was to do. Everything! Leila sat in a chair in front of the assembled groups, exposed, no lectern for protection. Abby felt the voice coming to *her* alone, explaining, defining, pinning down forever where she had been and the place she had just arrived.

"An alcoholic can be sober," Leila was saying, "but still be the most miserable, godforsaken person on two feet. There has to be some rebuilding of the spiritual values destroyed by chemicals: the honesty, the humility, the forgiveness, the trust, the love, the courage. This process begins with surrender. It is surrender to powerlessness and unmanageability: I give up. The chemical is more powerful than I am. It is surrender to the human condition: I said and did things while drunk that were hurtful, painful, devastating, destructive.

"In my recovery, the hardest thing in my whole life was to reconcile myself to the fact that good, kind, gentle, caring Leila, when drunk, had been capable of terrible things. I knew in my head that God had forgiven me. People who loved me said, 'Leila, I forgive you.' But, as long as I was incapable or unwilling to forgive myself, it was very difficult to feel their forgiveness in my gut. I still carried the burden of the past around like a big boulder on my back."

Abby wondered, "If my family never forgives me, how can I forgive myself?"

"So I finally faced the reality that, running my own affairs, I had failed. Then the question was: Where am I going to get help outside myself? Is there anything in this program that I can grab hold of and hang on to very, very tightly that will make me become a healthier, happier person? Is there anything that will give me a deep sense of forgiveness? That brought me to the third form of surrender — surrender to the God of my understanding. That does not require you to believe in the God of any religion. You can believe simply in a higher power greater than yourself. It can be the unity of a group, music, nature, anything that is inspired by a force greater than yourself. Now in my daily life, I have trust. I know that the God of my understanding will give me the grace, the strength, the courage, the people that I need to get through today without drinking. I am very grateful."

Abby could feel herself pulled irresistibly. Suppose there really was a power out there, God himself, who could be relied on to keep her — even her — from total destruction, as long as she trusted or at least suspended her doubts. Leila, standing beside a record player, organized the patients, holding hands, into a circle. When Leila started the record player, the voice of Judy Collins singing "Amazing Grace" washed over Abby and through her: "How sweet the sound that saved a wretch like me. I once was lost, but now I'm found. I was blind but now I see."

The words mingled inside of Abby's head with her own voice telling her, "Come on. How can *you,* of all people, fall for something this hokey," even as she knew that she was falling for it. Then, with patients on both sides holding her hands, her body shook with sobs. It was the word "found" that unstrung her — found after years of feeling lost, of seeking something that would fill up the permanent emptiness at her center, fill the void that even alcohol could not occupy.

That night Abby lay in bed gazing, as she often did, at her sign — I'M TERRIFIC! Usually, with nighttime honesty, the words seemed like whistling past a graveyard. But tonight there was a glimmer. She could sense that there were ways, techniques, that could let her be terrific. This was, she supposed, her first, tender sensation of strength and confidence. She did not understand it, any more than she understood what had happened with Leila Alexander this afternoon, which she guessed was maybe the spiritual breakthrough they kept talking about. Something was happening. She could feel what the Second and Third Steps were all about and she recited them in her head: "Came to believe that a Power greater than ourselves could restore us to sanity," and, "Made a decision to turn our will and our lives over to the care of God as we understood Him."

She thought about the many nights, drunk, reveling in self-pity, when she had listened to her record of Judy Collins singing "Suzanne." And all that time, on the flip side was "Amazing Grace." Could she, Abby wondered, rely on the possibility that everything — what she had been through, what lay ahead — was guided by a purpose, by a plan?

She must, she decided, hold on to that when she went home. Only three more days. She felt so new. Just hatched. There was so much still to do, still to resolve. She had to prepare for her final exam, giving aloud her Fifth Step: "Admitted to God, ourselves, and to another human being the exact nature of our wrongs." Already that week she had been jotting down the buried memories and honesties that were surfacing. And there was her mother. "Talk about it here," they kept saying, "and leave it here."

In group the next morning, Wednesday, June second, a new member, a short, plump, single girl worked first. Then Abby jumped in. "I'd like to talk about the bitterness I have toward my mother." Abby told the group about her child-

273

hood, the stream of correction and rejection from her mother: the room never clean enough, the table manners never good enough, the face never pretty enough. "Don't smile so wide; you show your gums which is unsightly and later in life there will be terrible lines on either side of your face." If she showed anger, her mother answered, "All right, you won't get the thing I bought you. It's been hidden." When she desperately wanted to tell her mother that she hadn't meant whatever it was, or hadn't intended to do it, then her mother said, "I don't want to talk about that now, Abby. We'll discuss it later."

"Sometimes," Abby described, "my mother would lock the door to her room and refuse to talk to me. And I would beat on the door and pound and call out, 'Please let me talk to you. Please! Don't shut me out.' But she would not answer one word for an hour and I would be exhausted from pounding and banging and kicking the door. Then she would say, 'If you don't stop this, Abby, I am really going to punish you when I come out. I'm getting a migraine headache. Wait till your father gets home and I tell him what you have done to me this time.' And sometimes she would sneak out through my father's room, and sometimes I'd see her and run after her, crying, and saying, 'Please let me talk to you. Don't go out. Where are you going?' And she'd say, 'I'm getting away from this insanity. I'm not telling you where I'm going because then you'll get on the phone and call and call and drive me crazy.' And then she'd go."

Around the circle there were nods of understanding, and Julia said, "You've just described my mother. I could never live up to her image of me."

Fern asked, "What is your relationship now? I know she lives in California and has refused to come to family week."

"I dislike my mother very much," Abby answered. "I am angry at her for my whole life and I have as little to do with her as possible. I used to keep trying, still hoping that I could disarm her with something that pleased her. But she would always find a way to misunderstand." Abby's face flushed. "She's a domineering bitch and I hate her for the way she treated my father."

Fern asked, "Am I correct that he was an alcoholic?"

"Yes," Abby said. "A periodic."

"Then you are a product of an alcoholic family," Fern said, "with everything it implies."

Abby nodded. "Yes. But I loved him. He used to tell me he was proud of me. I just wish he hadn't been so old. I wish I had known him more and for longer and better. I wish I knew him now so I could talk to him. I wish there was *somebody* — a sister or a brother — and especially a parent because I don't have one." Abby's eyes were wet again as she added, "But he was constantly running away."

Frank Ruyter asked, "How much of the anger in you has to do with your father?"

"I'm not angry at him. I just feel ripped off."

"I think there's more than that," Fern said. "You were very angry when you said 'running away.' "

Abby answered, "He was trying to escape from her, too. He would do everything he could to please her. Of course, it wasn't possible. So he'd take off and be gone on these trips, and leave me with a woman furious at him — and the anger would come out on me."

"I'd like to try something here — a psychodrama — if you're willing, Abby."

"Will it sting?" Abby asked, grinning, and quickly added, "Okay."

Fern placed Garrett, wearing his leather suit jacket, in a chair in the middle of the circle. She stood the tall figure of Jerold in front of him, facing Abby. Jerold was a door and Garrett was Abby's father. Abby was required to knock down the door and tell her father what she thought about him. Abby, nervous, embarrassed, approached Jerold. She pushed against him and he was immovable. She tried to go around him, but a long arm was in the way. She was getting annoyed. She shoved harder and wrenched at him with her hands — more and more frustrated, more and more angry.

She pounded on his chest, her breath coming fast. She kicked at his legs, and they were like cement. She butted his chest with her shoulder and then crashed against an arm. Suddenly she was through the door, gasping, looking down at her father, anger throbbing in her head. He had always been sitting like that, doing nothing while her mother made her miserable.

She shouted, "You were so damn passive, letting Mom run you." Then, yelling even louder, "You never stood up for me! Copped out! Never lifted a finger! Ran away! Coward! Never a man!" Fern handed her a cushion. As Abby's fingers clenched on its softness, the rage roared in her head and fogged her eyes. She flailed the figure in the chair, wildly swinging the pillow — thump, thump — screaming again and again, "You bastard! You bastard!"

Finally, Jerold pulled her away and Abby stood panting, head down, sweating. She dropped the pillow and sank into her chair, weeping with relief. Instantly Fern was in front of her, taking her hands. "It's all right," Fern said. "It's good."

That night Abby began writing out her Fourth Step: "Made a searching and fearless moral inventory of ourselves." Then she would be ready to give orally her Fifth Step: "Admitted to God, to ourselves, and to another human being the exact nature of our wrongs." Working in her room, she was content. She felt locked away from the world, doing what she should be doing. It felt peaceful. It felt good. In the Fourth Step booklet, the left pages listed the classic alcoholic faults, the right pages had the virtues — False Pride facing Humility, Perfectionism facing Admitting Mistakes, Being Phony facing Being Yourself, Selfishness facing Sharing, Fear facing Acceptance. Abby, writing under these headings, saw herself taking shape — what she had been, what she longed to be. And it was happening without pain. Her transgressions were becoming a list, a catalogue.

At breakfast the next morning, Thursday, June third, Abby sat with Julia. By an unspoken pact, they ignored Abby's coming departure. They talked instead about their mothers, Julia telling her own horror stories, so awful they both laughed. And Abby repeated her mother's announcement: "I don't want you or Martin or anybody telling me when I'm senile. *I* will tell you when I am senile."

After breakfast Abby made her way to Leila Alexander's office to give the Fifth Step. Suddenly she was nervous. Would this be degrading? Devastating? For three hours, reading from her Fourth Step booklet, talking spontaneously, she looked into those shrewd eyes — no sense of time. Balancing the good against the bad, she said, "I alibied to myself, to others, and even to God for my drinking — so it is a great relief to sit in group and let out my true feelings." "I excused all unfinished jobs and then drank because I felt badly that I had not done them — so I am trying to eliminate 'I should' from my thinking." "I am terrified by a line in the AA Big Book, 'Fear of being around alcohol is an unacknowledged desire to drink' — I have to accept my alcoholism as the disease that it is and know I must keep in constant touch with this fact."

At the end, as they stood by the door, Leila smiled and took her hand and asked, "Do you feel relief? I hope so."

"Yes," Abby said. "I feel terrific."

Leila hugged her and then said, "Remember, if God has forgiven us our sins, who are we not to forgive ourselves."

That night Abby lay in bed on her back. A crack between the window blinds projected a narrow line of light across the blanket above her toes. She had not expected to go immediately to sleep. There was too much excitement. Going home. She missed her children, missed the freedom of driving an automobile, the freedom to stay up late and to smoke in her bedroom. She missed her house. She wanted to get it in order, to do the things she'd talked about for the past three or four years — wallpaper the downstairs bathroom, put new curtains in the kitchen — and wash the windows, which she'd been postponing for six months. She would get some new clothes. Martin said she had as many clothes as Queen Elizabeth, but that wasn't true. And . . . oh, God, she'd forgotten to renew her driver's license. Was it sixty or ninety days before you had to take the test again?

She wondered whether Martin would get rid of the liquor. And would he tear the house apart looking for bottles? When he came to get her, would he be glad to see her? She'd have to kiss him. Suppose he gave her one of those dry kisses. Pursed lips. He would expect her to sleep with him that night. She didn't want to do that. Maybe it wouldn't go right. Maybe he would just need the release of it, and not want *her* for herself. Were they going to lie in bed for half an hour waiting for the other to make the first move? Why couldn't they just skip it for a while? But he would take that so personally.

The next morning, Friday, June fourth — departure day — she was exhausted and nervous and sad. There were good-byes, more inscriptions in her Big Book, even by people like Kerry who were on a different floor and in a different world. At the beginning of group that morning, Fern said, "As you know, Abby is leaving us today. I am very happy for you, Abby. This is one of the moments that makes it all worthwhile." Half rising from her chair, Fern passed across to Abby her medallion. The group applauded. Abby, eyes wet, beamed at the circle of friendly faces. She looked down at the bronze coin in her hand and laughed to herself. Engraved on it was the question, "How does that make you feel?"

She told the group that she owed them everything — her life, really, which they had given back to her. Then she sat in a daze, marveling that she had been there a whole month. Now it seemed like nothing. And when she went out the front door today, she would not be drinking anymore. She had actually done it — after all her announcements that she would give up *anything* but alcohol. "And I do not *want* to drink," she thought. "I can't believe this is me."

After group she stayed behind for her private farewell with Fern, who left her desk chair and sat on one of the plastic chairs. "I think you've grown a great deal," she told Abby. "You've felt the pain you needed to feel and I trust your progress. But I think you are still on shaky ground." Abby was startled. How could she say that! Fern was continuing. "I am concerned about the support you will receive from your family. I think you want Martin to change, and he definitely wants you to change. But if neither one of you is willing to go first, take that risk, you may end up like the old joke about the porcupines. You know. How do they communicate? Very carefully."

Abby nodded. Fern went on, "I do think Martin loves you. But his need to be in control and stay up in his head will make things difficult. You may have to consider the possibility that, though you would like better communication, the poor son of a gun is doing the best he can." Then Fern looked sharply at Abby. "If you and Martin do not make it, that will not be the end of the world. Do you know that?"

"I'm hanging on to it," Abby said.

Fern's eyes were still intense. "Whether Martin changes or not, whether he ever talks to you or not — if you *want* to stay sober, you will."

"I want desperately to stay sober," Abby said.

"Okay, but I think you have some trouble distinguishing between what you want and what you need, and I suspect you don't much want to go to AA."

"Well . . ."

"Well, tough. It's what you must do to stay sober. Try different groups until you find one you like. Go to at least two meetings a week. Get yourself a sponsor. Will you make that commitment to me?"

"Yes."

They moved together toward the door. Abby opened it and they stood for a minute. Fern put an arm across Abby's shoulders and hugged her. "I love you," she said. Abby's heart bounded, and she thought, "I will not let this woman down."

Martin was coming for her at two o'clock. She still had not packed. At lunch Julia put her hand on Abby's shoulder and said, "I'll miss you."

Abby twisted and looked up. "Will you adopt my plant?" Julia nodded. Abby said, "It drinks *only* water." She tried to smile and could not.

Back in her room, tense, her head aching, Abby packed rapidly. She was downstairs a half hour early, bags lined up by the door. Unable to sit, she paced, looking at the announcements on the bulletin board, reading the newspaper through the window of the dispensing machine. Then Martin was coming through the door in his pinstripe suit. She stood paralyzed. He smiled and said, "Don't I get a hug?"

"Yes. Sure."

He pulled her to him and kissed her on the mouth — a nice kiss. In the car Abby fastened the seat belt around her, a rule of his that she had always ignored. As he wheeled the car away from the curb, she looked across at Martin and wondered whether he had a lecture prepared — the fifteen things I expect of you. At a red light, Martin told her that they'd cleaned up the house last night and it would still be clean because he'd locked the new puppy in the garage. And maybe she'd like to go out for dinner? Or maybe order in Chinese? Abby was relieved. He was trying to be nice. And they were going to stick with chitchat. She said she'd cook something simple. She wanted to feel useful. In a restaurant she might be offered a cocktail and she was too new for that.

They drove long distances through patches of silence broken by desultory talk about her last week at Riverside, about the children, their schoolwork and summer plans. It felt tense and unnatural to her. But maybe she didn't know what was normal anymore. As they rode the turnpike into Worcester and she looked out over the city again, she thought about their last car ride together from the airport after Martha's Vineyard. How good it was now to feel well, her head clear. That Abby of the past, arriving home worrying about her next drink, seemed like a black shadow, perhaps still connected at the heels, but cast behind her.

Turning into the elm-bordered street, she saw the house waiting — her house. Now she was excited to be back with everything she loved, taking up life again. But did she still belong there? Martin carried the bags up to the bedroom while Abby idly glanced at the mail on the foyer table. Martin came down and announced he had to go back to work. Would she be all right? He kissed her again, said it was wonderful to have her home, and was gone.

"It's the same old Martin, taking off," Abby thought. If it wasn't golf, it was work. But she was glad. The tiptoeing around each other made her feel even more strange and odd. Then, suddenly, the silence of the house hit her. She was alone. This was the moment when she used to sigh with relief and hurry to her private bottle. But she didn't have to do that anymore. She could be alive without a drink in her hand. And it felt wonderful. She looked at herself in the hall mirror. No bags under the eyes. No dull hair. No rough skin and red, empty eyes. She felt the old warmth move up into her — the little flush of pride and confidence. She was a good-looking woman again.

She wondered what Martin had done about the liquor in the house. She strolled into the living room and turned right. On the liquor cabinet door hung a sign obviously stolen from a construction site. In large red letters it said, DANGER HIGH EXPLOSIVES DYNAMITE. Abby smiled, very pleased. She opened the cabinet just a crack. The bottles were still there and she stared at them for a moment, fascinated, revulsion turning her stomach. "If I drink that, I'll die," she thought. But she was glad the bottles were there. Martin trusted her. She closed the cabinet door, thinking, with a thrill of accomplishment, "Well, I passed the big test with flying colors."

She turned and surveyed the long room, the furniture familiar and somehow reassuring. But somebody, probably Martin, had moved the large bowl of seashells from the coffee table onto the blanket chest. She moved it back and found herself by the wingback chair, where she had sat, oh, God, so many hours, so bombed — like that last day before Riverside, a zombie, a mechanical drinking toy. She made a mental note to rearrange the room and exorcise the ghosts. A melancholy settled over her, a dry sadness without tears. She lit a cigarette and decided to make herself a hot lemon and honey. "I'm going to start treating myself kindly," she thought.

In the kitchen, waiting for the water to boil, she absent-mindedly ran her hand along the edge of the sink, over the dent she put in the stainless steel when she pounded it with that pot. More ghosts. Was she going to be able to live in this house now? She opened drawers and cupboards and stared blankly inside. God, there was a lot of instant food. "Maybe my marriage is instant," she thought. Somebody, probably Judy, had bought new spices and here was an unfamiliar cookbook. "So my meals weren't good enough," she thought. And then, "God, they really didn't need me." Opening the refrigerator, she saw three packages of her favorite bran muffins. That was nice. But the freezer was full of frozen dinners. It seemed to Abby that a gang of strangers had been living there.

She mixed the lemon and honey and enjoyed the sweet warmth in her throat and stomach. Deciding that at least she could unpack, she meandered upstairs to the bedroom. Opening the closet door to hang her clothes, she stood staring at the mess inside. "What a slob," she thought. "I hate women who live like that." Finished with the unpacking, she stood in the middle of the room, wondering what she was supposed to be doing. "I've got to get my bearings," she thought. "Maybe if I lie on the bed . . ." She climbed up and plumped the pillows behind her on the headboard — the old nest — and looked as she always did out the window along the archway of elms. Then her gaze moved around the room. It looked different. "It must be me," she decided. "I'm different." Her eyes passed over the chest where she had kept her bottle. "It must be still there, but it's empty," she thought. "The one in the piano is half full. I won't worry about them now. I'm alone and I'm sober and it's all right."

Suddenly Frederick was in the doorway. "Oh, Mother," he called out, and ran and threw himself onto the bed. "I'm so glad you're home."

She rubbed the sinewy little back, and thought, with just a wisp of satisfaction, that he had lost weight and needed mothering. "It's so good to be here," she told him.

"Are you all right?" he asked, staring intently into her face. "How do you feel?"

Abby laughed. "I'm fine, Frizzer. In fact, I'm better than that. I'm terrific." She talked to him about how good she felt, especially now that she was home with him. But in the back of her mind was the uneasiness that she should be doing something — like changing all the sheets. "Time for the good fairy to go to work," she told Frederick, and started with her own bed. Stripping back the blankets, she uncovered the brown, burned cigarette holes in the sheet and mattress cover. Self-disgust washed through her. "How could you have been such an idiot," she thought, "risking your whole family!" Instantly she countered, "Forget it! You were sick. You didn't burn anybody up. You can buy new sheets." The first voice came back, "No, toots, you're going to keep on using this sheet. You need to be reminded."

As she stripped the other beds, Frederick followed her from room to room and trailed behind her as she floundered down the stairs, half buried in the heap of sheets. "How does that make you feel?" she joked to herself. And then she laughed at her answer, "Like four ghosts."

When Judy appeared, she and Frederick were in the basement, stuffing the first batch of sheets into the washer. "Hi, Mom," Judy said. "Welcome home." Her eyes were distant. Face neutral. "Can I help?"

"No. That's okay. I've got to get back into practice."

Still expressionless, Judy turned away. "I've got homework to do."

Watching her disappear, Abby thought, "Well, she's probably got a right to be angry. Bet she probably wishes I'd never come home." Abby followed Judy up the cellar stairs and used the small bathroom off the front hall. When she came out, Frederick was there on the seat of the coatrack, examining her carefully.

Abby looked at him and pursed her lips. Enough was enough. He was sticking to her like a tick. She could feel her nerves tightening. "Don't you have any schoolwork?" she asked.

"No. Come out to the garage and meet the puppy. His name is Bo."

Abby shook her head. She could not face that. She did not want to test her nerves. She felt skinless, breakable, unready for full immersion in this family that seemed like alien territory, hazardous, with no paths or signposts. She told him, "Frizzer, I'm going to ask you to leave me alone for a while. I've got to get used to things. I can't be an instant mother. By tomorrow I'll be okay."

The fear was immediate in his large eyes. Abby went quickly and knelt beside him where he sat. "Don't worry, Frizzer," she said, putting her hands on his knees. "I am not going to drink again. I promise you that."

Alone in the kitchen, she made coffee and sat at the table, sipping, longing to feel natural. Evan burst through the door from the garage and dumped his book knapsack on a counter. "He's so skinny," Abby thought, and was amazed at his wide smile and the pleasure in his "Hi, Mom. You're home." He was actually glad to see her. Evan poured himself a coffee and attentively refilled her mug. "How did you like my sign?" he asked.

They sat companionably and he, too, asked about the last week of treatment. Abby was surprised. He'd hated Riverside. His eruption in the TV room had been awful. But, naturally, they had all acted as though nothing had happened. "That's the way we handle things in this family," she thought sardonically. Pushing her chair back from the kitchen table, she dug her medallion from her pocket and showed it to him, smiling self-consciously, proudly.

"That's neat, Mom," he said, and asked about members of the group. Abby was mystified and a little annoyed. Something was going on. Was Evan setting her up to ask a big favor? Suddenly he was so cool he almost wasn't there.

"What do you think of Jerold Steele at Riverside?" he asked. "Kind of a jerk to get burned like that on coke."

Abby held her body perfectly still. "Are you taking it a little bit personally?"

If possible, Evan, sprawled in his chair, was even more casual. "No. No. I'd just never let that happen to me."

Gazing back at him quietly, she said, "Okay." She knew she had to detach and concentrate on what was good for her. Trying to take care of Evan, open him up, fix his problems, was not what she needed. If she told Martin her suspicions — there was no hard proof — he would overreact. He'd cut off Evan's allowance, put him under house arrest. That was just enabling all over again. After last week, Evan had the facts and could make his own choices. Nobody could give him real help until he came out and asked for it.

While the last load of sheets was in the dryer, Abby went upstairs, every bit of grime and clutter grating on her conscience, her good resolutions full in her mind. By God, she was going to tackle the hall closet that Martin had been complaining about for two years. Inside the closet was a hill of cardboard cartons. Tentatively, she lifted the flap of the top box and looked down at an old kitchen blender, a rumpled tennis dress, a pair of outgrown ice skates, a whisk broom, an ancient telephone book, and an empty beer can. "I used to be really crazy," she thought, shutting the closet door again.

Down in the kitchen, she found Frederick on the floor, wrapped like an Indian in a yellow-and-pink-striped blanket and leaning against a cupboard door. "When's dinner?" he asked.

"Okay, I can take a hint," she answered, and got down the box of spaghetti. She filled a saucepan with water and put it over the gas flame.

"Judy always uses the big pot," Frederick said.

"Don't you have something you need to do?" Abby asked.

"Yes," Frederick said, running out, leaving his blanket in a heap. In a few moments the puppy bounded into the room — barking, skidding on the floor, jumping up on her, paws and sharp nails raking her thighs. Dutifully, she reached down to pet it, and the little teeth worried at her hand, mock, miniature ferocity — "Grrrrrrr." "He's very sweet," she said.

Frederick wrapped himself again in his yellow and pink cocoon while Abby pulled out a handful of spaghetti and upended the roll of sticks in the boiling water. Frederick said, "You're supposed to break them in half. Judy always does."

When the spaghetti was done, she put the colander down into the sink. Now the puppy was attacking her pant cuffs, sinking its teeth into the fabric, shaking its head, tugging. As she dumped the steaming pot into the colander, she tried to kick her leg free and the spaghetti slumped out suddenly and tipped over the colander and sprawled into the sink. From the floor, Frederick said, "Judy always runs cold water through the spaghetti."

Staring down at dinner tangled in among the children's

welcome home present to faithful Mom — a day's worth of dirty knives and forks, breakfast and snack plates, bits of garbage — Abby cried for a moment. "Frizzer," she said, "I am not Judy. You're going to have to understand that. But right now, I need to go upstairs for a few minutes and have a cup of coffee and pull myself together. I will come down in fifteen minutes and try it all over again."

With dinner recooked, Abby began laying out the plates around the table. "Mother," Frederick asked, "why do we always have the white plates?"

"Because I like them best. Now go call everybody."

Trailing his brilliant blanket, Frederick went to the kitchen door. "Everybody!" he called.

"Comedian," she said.

Martin and Abby sat opposite each other, with Frederick and Judy to her left and Evan at her right. Almost immediately Judy complained that Evan was pigging the melted butter.

Evan answered, "Leave me alone. You're not my mother."

"Scumbag," Judy muttered.

Abby thought, "Welcome back to the land of the living."

"I did the coolest thing to my big toenail last night," Frederick said. "I cleaned it out *so* long and got all the gunk out and it got super white. And then I bent it back and it would stay there."

Smiling, Abby asked, "Didn't that hurt?"

"No. Your nails don't have very many muscles in them or feelings."

Judy looked at him. "Eat your dinner."

Keeping her face pleasant, helping herself to a little more spaghetti, Abby recognized this moment. A month ago she would have ducked out for a swig of vodka. So the thought, at least, was still there. The whole damn family was like a car after a slow-motion wreck, its members gradually bending out of shape. It would take months, years of patience to straighten them back again. She must not dwell on her guilt. If she did, she would not believe she could still make a difference here.

"Tomorrow is supposed to be up in the eighties," Martin said.

Evan chimed in. "It was really nice today."

Judy spoke about a friend at school. "Sally is having multiple spasms. Jim has been gone for a week and she can't handle it."

"She must be in withdrawal," Abby said, noticing a quick look from Evan. She wondered how long it would be like this, every little word and glance fraught with meaning. What a drag!

Martin spoke again. "Judy, a couple of weird boys appeared at our door asking for you."

Judy's eyes widened. "For me?"

"Yes."

"Who were they?" Judy asked. Abby could hear the suppressed eagerness in her voice.

"A couple of freaks. I don't know."

"What did you say?"

"That you weren't here. That you were out at a party."

Judy's mouth was open, the lips tender-looking, vulnerable. "That's all?"

"They just said okay and left."

Evan sniggered. "They'll probably never come back again."

Frederick said, "Mom, tell me something *really* naughty that you did when you were little."

"No, Frederick, you couldn't stand two years of solid listening." Abby watched the frustration on Judy's face.

"Tell me. Tell me some, Mother," Frederick insisted.

Abby ignored him. Judy was saying, "Couldn't you have asked if they'd like to leave a message?"

Martin smiled back at her. "But Judy, they were such twerps."

There was a silence. "I can't wait to get out of school,"

Frederick said. He looked toward his father. "Can we go to Martha's Vineyard?"

"We'll see."

"That's what you always say."

"That's what I always mean."

"What kind of a car did they have?" Judy asked.

"I didn't look."

Abby, hoping to change the subject, said, "What was that car I liked? An XR-Seven?"

Judy said, "A TR-Seven, Mom."

"A T.L.C.," Frederick said, laughing.

Abby smiled at him. "That would be a nice car."

"Did they have on school jackets?" Judy asked.

"I think there was a C."

Abby asked, "Was it a red letter on a navy blue jacket? It's important." She felt Judy's surprised, grateful look.

Martin laughed. "You two are really something. No, I did not take a picture of them."

Abby breathed out, letting her interior go limp. Back away, she told herself. Don't react. Don't provoke. Don't make everybody else's problems your own. Be bland. Be oatmeal.

At eleven o'clock, Abby, nervous, lay in bed listening to the shower in the bathroom. Did he expect to make love? She felt twelve years old. Utterly inexperienced. "When I'm still shaky about loving myself," she thought, "how can I make love to somebody else?" The shower stopped, and soon Martin in his striped pajamas came to the edge of the bed. He looked down at her and said, "It's going to be hard for you to believe, but I missed you."

"Nothing like TV dinners to make the heart grow fonder," Abby answered. Martin's mouth tightened. Instantly, Abby reached out and touched his leg. "I'm sorry. That was a bad joke. You've got to give me some time. I'm new at this sobriety stuff."

Martin got into bed and came across the no-man's-land

between them and put his arm across her body and his face against her neck. "I'm glad you're home," he said. "I didn't have anybody to keep me warm."

"Be gentle with me," she said.

They made love. Afterward, while Martin slept, Abby looked up at the dim tracery of her rivers in the ceiling. There was no terror at being awake — no unmanageable urge to wander about the house, a fretful specter. She was warm and grateful. Why had she been so worried about making love? It was fine. And Martin was still here for her. He hadn't kicked her out of the house, out of the family, onto the street, where maybe she deserved to be. Everything was back to normal.

Silently she prayed, "Thank you, God, for getting me through today." But then her mind went to tomorrow. Would Martin go back to his old routines, expecting her to be perfect? What about the things they'd supposedly learned at Riverside, the promises they had made? Would he give her real support? Or just a going-through-the-motions support because he always wanted to do the right thing? And how was she going to fill all that time she had spent drinking and plotting to drink?

The security of Riverside seemed unbridgeably distant — Fern, Julia, Larry, the people who understood her. But she could hear their comforting voices saying, "One day at a time" — "Beyond a wholesome discipline, be gentle with yourself" — "Give your survival number one priority." Okay. If she had to, she could leave the family. She wasn't trapped. In the meantime, she could find new friends and the same support in AA. Things really were going to be fine. Then she prayed, "Please, God, give me strength to live here again and not want to drink. Help me to be normal."

13

EARLY SUNDAY morning in late August, two months after Abby's return from Riverside, Martin's voice sounded up the stairs — that official, peremptory tone from the nightmare past. "Abby, please come down. I want to ask you a question." The old terror and shame raced through her, that instant thought, "Oh, my God, what did I do! How am I going to get out of this one!" Walking down the stairs, she could hear Frederick crying in the kitchen. "Did I take a drink and don't remember?" she wondered. "Did I have a blackout? Am I brain damaged?"

Just inside the kitchen door, she stopped. The scene froze in her mind: Martin rigid in the middle of the room, his right hand held clenched in front of him; Frederick half behind him, eyes huge with tears, face desperate and pleading; Judy lounging against one of the counters, the faintest of smiles on her mouth; Evan sitting at the table, expressionless.

Martin said again, "I want to ask you a question." Abby could see the whiteness around his lips, the signal that he was furious. Her fear felt ready to explode her chest. He demanded, "Are you living your recovery program?"

"I'm doing the best I can."

Martin opened his right hand and slammed a vial of pills down onto the counter. "Well, this is what Frederick found in the laundry room!"

Abby recognized it instantly. One of her Valium bottles. Relief swept through her. She was innocent. For the first time in years she was on firm ground.

Martin said, "I guess I knew it was too good to be true."

Jumbled fragments tumbled through Abby's brain: "Used to be defensive and overreacting — haven't proved myself trustworthy — as long as I'm okay, everything's okay." At the same time, Martin's words beat against her: "Had such hopes — lying and sneaking — never intended to stop — no difference between Valium and a drink — all that time and trouble in family week — a waste of my money." And then, "You are just going to do this to yourself until you die, and there is nothing I or anybody else can do about it. So I think we have to discuss your future in the . . ."

He was interrupted by Frederick's wail. "Mom, you promised. You *promised.*"

Abby's control snapped. "Goddamn you, Martin. You really are a stupid, cruel son of a bitch. Can't you see what you're doing?" She knelt in front of Frederick, put both hands on his shoulders and spoke directly into his frightened eyes. "Frizzer, I have not taken any pills and I'm not going to take any pills. Or drink. So don't be afraid." She stood up, holding one of Frederick's hands and facing Martin. Her voice seethed with indignation. "How dare you say nothing to me and then drag me down here like a criminal and crucify me in front of my children!"

Then her voice changed, a new tone, factual, controlled. "I am not guilty. I can't prove it to you, but I don't think there's a need to prove it to you today. There are probably pill bottles hidden all over the house, but I can't remember where and I don't give a damn." Now she felt wonderful. She was not wacked-out drunk. She could admit she did not remember. She didn't need to prove she was a good girl and justify her behavior and find a lie she herself could believe.

"There's no date on the bottle," Martin said. "I will have to check with the drugstore."

"Good. Please do." Her voice turned sarcastic. "But you

seem awfully determined, Martin. Are you disappointed I'm not drinking again? Are you losing your little, drunk marionette?" She let go of Frederick's hand and faced her family. "Who can live with you people?" she said. "Am I always going to be on trial? Am I never going to get out of jail? Everybody watches me. Frederick sticks to me like a burr." She focused back on Martin. "I put ice in a glass and right away you're in the doorway. Aren't you supposed to be detached, Martin? What you need is a good dose of Al-Anon."

Martin flushed. His voice was punishing. "You have a point there. I'm not responsible for you. Okay, Abby, you're on your own."

Abby looked around the room. Evan was smiling slightly — unreadable. Judy's face was somber, downcast. "Jury dismissed," Abby said.

Thinking, "I've got to get out of here," she stalked through the room and out the door into the garage. Thinking, "I'll show them," she flipped the switch to open the garage door. Then she got into her car and sat gripping the steering wheel with both hands, knuckles white, anger grinding in her stomach. She felt exiled, sentenced to perpetual loneliness — like a ship she had read about, sailing forever under a curse, never touching land. She reached down to the ignition. No key. Damn. Martin must have taken them. That bastard! Maybe she had extra keys in her purse. Hell, she didn't have that either. So no money, no cigarettes.

She stayed motionless, eyes closed, tears forming under her eyelids. How could she go on living in this family! Why couldn't they trust her! When would Frederick stop following her around? When would Evan talk honestly to her and stop playing games? When would that distant, formal look relax on Judy's face, and when would Judy decide she needed a mother and come out of her room? Abby smiled grimly. At least with all that reading, Judy would have a good vocabulary.

Abby sighed out loud, the breath quavering in her throat.

You didn't get any pats on the back for not drinking, for looking and acting like other people. People just assumed you were whole and well and back to the old housekeeping. But she would never be that person they remembered. She was still a nice person, just not the same nice person. She wasn't somebody now they could manipulate with guilt trips. She wasn't guilty anymore. And she had other priorities. Her sobriety. Her peace of mind. Her sense of person.

She took her hands off the steering wheel, opened the car door, got out and went back into the kitchen. The children were around the table eating dry cereal. "Where's your father?" Abby asked. Judy looked back, silent, face hard. Evan answered, "He's up in his office." Abby headed toward the stairs, but Frederick caught her in the hall. He stood very straight, his face solemn. "Mom, I'm really sorry I did that and got you into trouble."

Abby kneeled down and pulled him to her. "You did exactly right, Frizzer. Any time there's something you don't understand, you should come to Dad or me. You don't have anything to be sorry about." Suddenly her heart split with loneliness and she bent and buried her nose in his hair, as though she could draw him within her and fill the emptiness. "I love you so much," she said. Then she stood up, saying, "I have to see Dad. Go finish your breakfast."

In the little office off the bedroom, Martin put down the telephone as Abby stood in the doorway. "Do you have my car keys?" she asked angrily.

Impassively, he said, "If you were bombed on pills, I didn't want you out there killing somebody."

"Give the keys to me."

"You're not going anywhere."

Abby's face was rigid. "I see. It's your car, your house, your kids. Everything is yours and nothing is mine."

"Sit down. We've got to talk about this." Abby sank into a chair and Martin added, "Perhaps I owe you an apology."

"I don't want apologies," Abby answered, her voice strung tight. "I want understanding."

"All right, Abby, what is there to understand?"

"Maybe I'm expecting too much," she said, wearily, looking away from him. "Maybe you can't ever grasp how fragile an alcoholic is without alcohol — what's involved when you're trying to get through bad situations and feelings without picking up a drink."

"That may be true. But what do you want from me?"

Anger surged back into Abby's voice. "They said in Riverside that it's okay to want to be first in somebody's life. That it's normal. I don't want to come fourth, *after* the golf course, after your work, after the church council, after the Kiwanis Club, after the parties. I want to be number one and know that's where I belong." She looked hard into Martin's eyes. "I need to be needed. And I've got a lot of love to give."

"You *are* number one. If I had to strip everything away and keep one thing, that would be you."

"But you don't make me *feel* that way." For a second she was close to tears. "I can't live on what you're handing out emotionally."

Martin folded his arms across his chest. His tone was almost paternal. "Abby, you've always known I'm not the lovey-dovey, sentimental type."

"In the beginning of our marriage, you gave me everything I needed. You weren't Maurice Chevalier, but you were kind and sympathetic and the man I loved."

"There's been a lot of booze under the bridge since then," Martin answered. "I have some adjusting to do, too. I've put up with an awful lot of shit, more than I could be expected to put up with. I could write a book on loneliness. So it's not easy to forgive and say, 'Okay, that was just a page in my life and we're starting brand new.' I have a lot of hope and I love you very much. But you've been out of Riverside only two months. There are no guarantees, and I'm guarded. Maybe too guarded because I don't want to get hurt again."

Biting her top lip, Abby visibly stiffened herself. "I understand that, Martin," she said. "But I have to take care of *me*, too, and I don't know how long I can afford to wait to be forgiven."

Martin's voice was quick and harsh. "How long did I have to wait for you to sober up?"

Abby put her hands flat on her knees and her voice hardened. "You go right for the jugular, don't you, Martin? Whenever you're at a disadvantage, you bring up the past. Well, as much as you remember the things I did, I won't *ever* forget them. I don't need *you* to remind me. And I think it's rotten to say you may never forgive me."

"When did I say that?"

"A minute ago."

"No, I never said that. It's not the way I feel."

Abby's fists clenched. "Goddamn you. There you go again. Gaslighting me. Telling me something isn't true when I know it is true." Her body sagged slightly. "I don't know how to get close to you. Maybe we have hurt each other too deeply." She stopped for a moment. "I feel you don't really like me at all."

Martin sighed. "Abby, I like you and I love you. Do I have to say that every day?"

Abby's eyes flashed. "Don't tell me. Show me. You come home and count the trees and if they're all in place, you say, 'Did you call the plumber?' And then you leave again to take care of the world. It's never, 'How do you feel, Abby? Been busy? God, the place looks nice.' You've *never* put off a golf game for me. You've never missed a church council meeting for me. It's like I'm just a wife, and sure, sometimes I get the blues, but you don't have to sacrifice to give me what I need."

"Abby, I'm afraid to ask you how you feel, because, if you tell me you're depressed or down, I'll be terrified you'll drink." Martin stretched his legs out straight. "And anyway, if you're depressed, I'm not required to fix your self-pity. You have to fix yourself."

"Well, where does that leave me in your scheme of things?" Abby demanded. "Do I have rights? I don't seem to anymore. Evan swears at me, and you don't say a thing. If he did it to you, he'd be punished. If I tell Frederick to eat his salad, you say, 'Don't bother him. He's been healthier than ever while you were gone.' We agreed there wouldn't be any TV for Frederick on school days. I come back from an AA meeting and find him watching TV with you, and you say, 'Oh, Frederick just came in to say goodnight.' *Baloney!* When things like that used to happen, I'd think, 'Well, Martin's probably right,' and back off. But now I know I'm right and it's really a weird feeling. I'm sober and I want to be heard — and that's causing problems."

"That was not baloney," Martin said. "And I do hear you. But I don't have to agree with you."

"It's like you're always right and I'm always wrong."

Abby's voice was loud now. "Last month you told me I had the common sense of a gnat. When I suggested that I pay the bills like I used to, you said, 'No, no. It's simpler for me to do it and get through it and know it's done properly.' When I finish telling somebody something, you say, 'What Abby means is . . .' You're still putting me down. Keeping me down. You've controlled me so long, you can't let go."

Martin's voice was defensive. "That's not so. You're obsessed with the idea of people controlling you — your mother and I controlling you."

Abby smiled grimly. "You just did it to me. When you look at me and say, 'That's not so,' you negate my whole thought process."

Martin shook his head. "You want me to express my feelings as long as the feelings are appropriate. But you are the judge of what's appropriate."

Now Abby was shaking her head. "You just don't see it. All the little ways you stay in charge. Like money. When I was drinking, if a guy came and said the dishwasher needed

297

fixing, I was such a jellyfish I'd call you and ask what to do. But now, without your advice and your permission, I buy Judy a pair of earrings for fifty dollars — *with my money* — and you have a coronary because I made a decision on my own."

Martin shifted in his chair. "I was upset because that was a substantial gift, and you do these things impulsively, without consideration. I know a jeweler and I could probably have gotten a discount."

"Money is not the issue. Control is the issue."

Jabbing his forefinger toward Abby, Martin spoke slowly with emphasis. "No! Impulsive spending — extravagance — is the issue. Last week you charged a sixty dollar pair of shoes. You already have more shoes than you know what to do with. I want *no more* charging. Understand? If you want something, you come and ask me."

Abby frowned. "It's unbelievable. You're trying to control everything I do."

Martin leaned forward. "Whatever you do to yourself, I can't control. But when it affects the family finances, maybe you need a little controlling. Did you ever ask yourself why I have only two pairs of shoes, why my shirts are threadbare at the elbows?"

Abby leaned back and laughed. "Don't give me that shit about threadbare elbows. I have to throw rags away so you won't wear them. I suppose you *need* a Buick instead of a Ford. I didn't ask you to justify those two pairs of golf shoes." Martin was silent, and Abby continued with a crooked smile. "I'm going to buy Judy some Kotex tomorrow. Do you want to give me the money now?"

Martin pushed back his chair and stood up with elaborate dignity. "At least we're talking about these issues," he said, "and that's good. But I think this discussion has outlived its usefulness. And it's time to go to church." He turned and left the room.

"I'm not sure God is up to this one," Abby thought with a wild, silent laugh.

The drive to church was wordless, Judy in the front with her father, Abby and Frederick in the back. Evan no longer went to church. Abby felt exhausted, emotionally bleached, as though the anger had drained her heart. The future, the year, the day, the next ten minutes loomed unbearable. The old, familiar anxiety rippled along her nerves. She could see that bottle of Valium on the kitchen counter. Inside it was the jumble of yellow pills, the magic bearers of the soft blur that would smooth the corners of her anxiety. Or a long pull of vodka would be better yet — the warm ball of comfort in the center of her stomach — and then the next drink and the permeating, buzzing high — the delicious oblivion, nothing mattering, all her problems dissolving into a sweet fog.

But her other voice was answering: ". . . and the next drink and the next. All the vodka in the house wouldn't fill one tooth. Tomorrow, your life would be sixty times worse. Everything you've worked so hard to do — the progress you've made — the promises you've made — to yourself, to everybody — everything would be thrown away. And everything Martin has been screaming would be true. You aren't *dying* of the hurt. You can last until tomorrow. If you still feel this way tomorrow, you can take a drink. But not today." Abby felt comforted. She had an option. This pain did not have to be permanent.

Abby was looking forward to church. It was the one time and place that always gave her strength and eased her loneliness. Her thoughts moved on to AA. Was she hopelessly, fatally out of tune? This thing that was supposed to save her life was so boring, so maddening, so unlifesaving. She had done her best. She was keeping to her contract with Fern, two meetings a week. There were the big meetings, open to everybody, alcoholics or not — come one, come all. Gigantic coffee klatches! A mob clutching white plastic cups. All that smiling and backslapping and laughing. So phony, so cliquish, so alien. Everybody so blessed by the grace of God. It was just like the Riverside AA, full of program junkies who had never returned to the real world. They used meetings to fill the hole left by the booze, fill up those hours and hours they once spent planning how to get bombed and being bombed. And, of course, they all looked down on her because she had needed a treatment center. She hadn't done it cold turkey, by herself, no help.

Two or three speakers would give their "drunkalogues," the stories of their recovery, which were so repetitive and tiresome. She had much better use for her time. She ought to be home with the family she had wronged, building trust by being present and sober. How could this help her: the endless horrors — families, jobs, lives destroyed — so much worse than her own history. These people were competing for a degradation prize. After such misery, their serenity seemed inhuman, impossible, fake. But, she wondered, could such sobriety, such serenity, such comfort ever happen for her?

Then there were the weekly step meetings restricted to alcoholics — a small group that sat around a table and told how one of the Twelve Steps had functioned in their daily lives. These meetings were so frustrating. A bunch of sad sacks reciting their AA homilies, always careful to give the right answers. She couldn't get comfort from these people because she couldn't be honest. When she said something heartfelt, she got back a slogan. They weren't like her group at Riverside. They weren't feeling and honest. That guy the other night, so angry, but boasting about his serenity. Fern would have cut him off in the first five minutes.

And she always felt like such a fool when people came up to her and said, "Hi. I'm so-and-so." It seemed stilted and forced, and made her feel so new, like a colt that had just been born, the legs all flimsy and disjointed. But, thank goodness, there was Laura — a nice-looking woman, blonde, about her age, bright eyes. Two weeks ago Laura sat down next to her and said, "I haven't seen you before. Is this your first meeting?"

Abby told her, "I've been trying to be invisible. AA and I aren't close friends yet."

"I know," Laura said with a wry smile. "I felt sentenced to a lifetime in church basements. But it gets better."

"I sure hope so," Abby answered.

Then Laura had asked her, would she be willing to help for three months in the kitchen? Making and serving coffee. Laying out doughnuts and cookies. Abby, a little to her own surprise, answered, "I'd love to." Later she had thought, "That's one commitment, by God, I'm going to keep. It's a sign I'm getting better. And it's a lot nicer than taking up a chair and snarling. And I've made a friend."

Abby followed her family up the stone steps into the church — Martin in his light gray suit, Judy actually in a skirt, Frederick with a necktie and his hair combed. Martin led the way to a pew near the rear, and Abby maneuvered the children between them for insulation. She sat enjoying the old granite columns built with three shafts bound together by iron bands; the tall wooden crucifix behind the altar; and painted inside the dome above, the blue and starry heavens, blotched by water stains.

Abby sang out during the hymn, feeling, as she always did, the echoes of church in her childhood — the security and solace. This Sunday the Scripture reading was from Jeremiah, and Abby's heart lifted.

> I have loved you with everlasting love;
> so I am constant in my affection for you.
> I build you once more; you shall be rebuilt.

During the droning sermon, Abby began her own Sunday ritual, taking stock of the past week and of herself. The fight that morning with Martin. Horrible. She had to be self-assertive, but those weren't healthy, getting-well attitudes. Why did everything have to be so hard — such baby steps forward, such giant steps backward, the old lousy thoughts constantly pushing up, taking her over. She had to get back on the track, hold on to what she had heard from Fern. Let go of her anger. "It's like a cancer inside me," Abby thought, "and nobody in the family is ever going to get better until I get better."

"But I do like myself, more and more," she thought. On Wednesday, Annie O'Reilly had said how terrific she looked. "And I didn't make a joke," Abby thought, proudly. "I just said, 'Thank you.' " When the top of the mustard bottle was stuck, she had methodically worked on it, and not impatiently banged it on the sink till the glass broke. And then there was her phone call to that new woman on the block who didn't want to help in the car pool. Probably too busy putting on makeup. "I did that well," Abby thought, replaying her words: " 'I think you're being very unfair to dump your responsibility on the other mothers.' "

There was the flat tire she changed — for the first time. That had been really exciting. She had not called Martin on the phone and maybe cried. She had stood there looking at the tire, telling herself, " 'Listen, Abby, you can deal with everyday life situations without thinking of alcohol or getting yourself in a terrible sweat. So calm down and do it. You don't have to get back right away. The kids have been coming home alone for a month and they did fine. And don't think you need to reward yourself with a bottle on the way home.' "

Now the sermon was finished and the priest in his vestments was celebrating the High Episcopal Mass. The incense mingled with images from her childhood book of Bible stories —"Jacob's Ladder," "Moses in the Bulrushes," "The Coat of Many Colors." She watched with pleasure the graceful, practiced hands of the priest pouring the wine, lifting the chalice, wiping it out with oil. Behind him was the crucifix — Christ on the cross of his suffering, dying for her sins. She felt a rush of gratitude. She was forgiven. And she no longer had to drink because of every little setback and success. Abby closed her eyes and prayed. "Lord, this is another week and I am sober and I am yours."

It was time for Communion. Filled with warmth, Abby moved down the aisle toward the rail and knelt there, thinking, "I have been forgiven and I must accept that gift." Then came that moment of awkwardness. To refuse the wine but still look like everybody else, she would pretend to dip the wafer into the chalice, not quite touching the wine. She accepted the host from the priest and held it in her hand. Now the priest with the chalice was approaching and suddenly it was there at her face. The smell of the wine snaked up into her nostrils, into her mouth, across her tongue — enticing, persuading. The compulsion flamed in her body, a false high racing through her.

For an instant she fought the impulse to reach out and grab the chalice. Then, panicky, she turned from the rail, pushing the wafer into her mouth. At her seat her heart pounded. Her stomach was fluttery, her hands shook slightly. Frantically, she took two aspirin from her bag, gathered saliva, and swallowed them, wincing at the bitterness. This was the nightmare moment she had worried about — the compulsion hitting her out of nowhere, on her blind side. What had set her up for it? The fight with Martin? All those old attitudes? "Abby, it's a disease of attitudes, sick reactions," she told herself. "You've got to change them, or you'll solve them with booze. It's not Martin's fault. You'd find any reason: because it's rainy, or sunny, or you're bored. You drink! Even if you were married to Robert Redford, you'd still be an alcoholic."

The service was over. The congregation was filing past. Under the surprised, self-conscious looks of Martin and the children, Abby knelt to pray. "God, please help me. If you ever . . . if what they say is true . . . if you take care of me and watch over me . . . please give me the strength to get through this because I can't do it alone."

On the drive home Abby felt better. The chance to drink had been right at her lips, and she had chosen not to do it. She was proud of that. And now she was going to use the tools she had learned at Riverside and make her life different. She and Frederick talked about Old Testament stories, and Abby sang him part of the spiritual, "Shadrach, Meshach, and Abednego"— the three men surviving in a fiery furnace, "hotter than it oughta be." The atmosphere in the car brightened, and Martin laughed and asked where she had learned that. "The bonus of a misspent youth," Abby answered.

In the garage Abby lingered to clean up the car, throwing away the empty coke cans and plastic coffee cups stuffed under the front seat. But her good mood lasted only seconds after entering the empty kitchen. The bottle of Valium was still on the counter, a tiny, unexploded bomb. The ugliness of the morning, of that kitchen scene, broke over her. In a second she was across the room, dumping the pills down the disposal, blasting the water down full force, listening furiously to the grinding sounds. How could Martin or the children have left the Valium there! Were they putting her through another test? Did they want her to use again? Did they hate her that much?

Abby turned down the water and filled a pot to make coffee. She lit a cigarette and leaned thoughtfully against the counter. Even a sip of that wine could have triggered the whole insanity again. So what about the next time? And the next? Would she have to beat this devil every day, this thing that wouldn't let her alone? Would she have to spend the rest of her life clawing and fighting to stay sober? "And who really gives a shit, anyway," she thought, filling the coffee mug, feeling utterly alone, shut away, while the rest of the world was free, was normal. She jammed the cigarette down onto the sink. She had to get rid of this awful feeling! Maybe if she could talk to Fern. No, it was Sunday. What about Larry? No, a man wouldn't understand. Laura. She would know about these demons.

The phone number was in her purse on the square of paper Laura had thrust into her hand. Abby reached for the kitchen telephone and stopped. Laura was probably too busy. Or at lunch. Or not there. Probably Laura wouldn't remember her name. Or would think she was looney. Too emotional. Exaggerating. "No," Abby thought. "For once, you're going to do the right thing." Her hand quivered as she dialed the number.

On the line Laura's voice sounded pleased, a touch surprised. "Hello, Abby," she said. "It's good to hear from you."

"I hope I'm not interrupting anything," Abby said and stopped.

"You don't sound okay," Laura said. "What's happened?"

"I just dumped a bottle of Valium down the disposal, and I should feel good about it. But I'm still mad and scared."

"Did you use any of it?"

"No. But at communion this morning I wanted to grab the chalice and chug-a-lug it. I panicked and ran."

"Yes, but you didn't do it. That's the important thing, and you can take a lot of pride in that. Was there a setup that led to it?"

"Well," Abby answered, "it has not been a good morning. My younger son found an old bottle of Valium and my husband, in front of the children, accused me of using again. If I'd had a gun, I'd have shot him." Abby poured out the whole story: ". . . standing there with the Valium in his hand — son of a bitch took my keys — so rigid and unyielding — trying to control me — no more charge accounts — like he has a club over my head — I'm always number four — we're back to square one without the booze." Abby was almost crying. "I feel so rotten."

"Of course you feel rotten," Laura said. "You're only human. And you don't have to be superhuman. You're doing the best you can."

"Did you have fights like that with your husband?" Abby asked.

"Sure. My husband was hostile for a year. I think he only

305

stayed with me because it was socially better to be married. There was no way he was going to forgive me. I had done those terrible things to him, and he was going to pay me back. Beside his bureau he had a wastebasket. Sometimes after I emptied it, I'd forget to put it back. He'd look at me and drop his trash on the floor."

"Can you beat it?" Abby said, laughing. Then, after a hesitation, she continued, "I want this marriage. But sometimes I can't stand to be in the same room with my husband — his name is Martin. And then sometimes I get a really warm feeling for him. He's such a good person, basically. He tries so hard to do the right thing. That's very rare. But I just don't know about love anymore."

"You're lucky," Laura answered. "You've got something to build on. But right now you need to work the Program, have faith in it. 'Walk the Walk.' "

"I don't get any nourishment from those slogans," Abby said. "They're fast food."

"They're just shorthand for the things we were taught all our lives and didn't do." Laura laughed sardonically. "Like, 'Everything in moderation.' "

"But how am I going to live with all this distrust?"

"You did a lot to them," Laura said, "and you have to earn back their trust. It takes a lot of time and good behavior. But *you've* got to show some trust, too."

"It's very hard for me to trust anyone, especially Martin," Abby answered. "There's such a risk of rejection. And trust is just as hard for Martin as it is for me. He doesn't know how to deal with a woman who's insisting on her rights. He's been trained since boyhood that the husband is king of the hill."

"Abby, your well-being does not have to depend on Martin. You have given him an awful lot of control over your emotions — which is what makes you and me drink *at* people. Do you want to give him that much power? It's within *your* power to make that decision."

"Yes. Yes. You're right," Abby answered, her voice rueful.

Laura continued. "I don't know how else to say this without using what you call fast food. But you've got to let go and let God. Easy does it. Act as if. All the things. Do them and you'll feel better. That includes going to meetings. There's one at the Baptist church tonight. I'd be happy to meet you there."

"Okay, I will," Abby said, thinking that Martin would be furious. She'd promised to go to the Sanderson's tonight for dinner.

Abby lit another cigarette. She felt reassured. But like it or not, she was being drawn into the AA program. She could hear Fern saying, "To what lengths are you prepared to go?" All right, she would ask Laura to be her sponsor — her mentor, sounding board, confessor. A little voice asked, "Is she worthy of me?" Abby turned it off. The old intolerance! The point of AA was not what she thought of the people or the slogans. The point was that it kept those people sober. She put out the cigarette. Martin would be leaving soon for golf. She'd better go tell him about the meeting.

But first she had something to do. Swiftly, purposefully, she walked through the hall, down the length of the living room to the piano. In one continuous motion she slid open its front and pulled out the half-full bottle of vodka. Around its top, on the glass, was lipstick. Her stomach twisted with self-disgust. Holding the bottle away from her, she marched back to the kitchen and the sink. Unscrewing the top, she held her nose with one hand and emptied the bottle with the other, then ran hot water to rinse away the traces. Now she hesitated. She did not want to sneak the empty bottle out of the house. That would be old behavior. If she just put it in the trash, she'd keep seeing it and there would be questions asked. She wrapped it in a brown paper bag and stuffed it into the garbage bucket. The bottle that was up in the bedroom chest was empty. She'd leave it there. To keep her memories alive.

When she came into the bedroom, Martin, in shirt and

sweater, was holding his golf pants in one hand. Abby's heart was pounding. She sat down on the bed and plunged ahead. "I know how important this evening is to you. Bill Sanderson is a big client. But I can't go tonight. I have to go to an AA meeting."

Slowly, incredulously, Martin shook his head. Carrying his pants, he sat down in the straight-back chair, set his jaw and said, "It is with the greatest regret that I accept your decision."

Abby almost laughed. "Martin, this is not a board meeting."

Martin's voice was defensive. "For once in my life I'm trying not to start a fight."

"Okay, tell me what you're thinking. I can take it."

He metered out his words, slowly, carefully. "You've been gone for five years, and now you're sober and you're still not here when I need you."

Abby marveled at the calm inside her. She said, "I'm doing what I have to do to stay sober. It's both as simple and as complicated as that."

Martin gazed at her a long time, then stood up and put on his pants and sat down. He said, "What I wanted most in the world was for you to stop drinking. And now it's the thing that's causing me to lose you."

They looked at each other again through the stillness. Abby drew in a long breath and said, "Just today I'm getting a glimmer of where I am. I don't want to be melodramatic, but I feel at last in the right place. I'm on a long road and can only sense where it leads. I want to go there. But there's a paradox. If you try to keep a grip on me, I'll end up going alone and we'll always be apart, even if we're living in the same house. If you cut me loose, you will be able to come along and we'll be together. That's what I want." Her eyes were clear and straight.

Martin was again silent, impassive. Then he said, "I'll go to the Sanderson's alone. Who'll call them? I will if you want."

"Do they know I've been in treatment?"

"I didn't tell them." Suddenly Martin's eyes turned sharp. "No. You call. I'm not taking care of you anymore. Remember? I'm not responsible for you." He paused. "What are you going to say?"

Abby felt irritation rising. But he was right. She had to take responsibility for herself. "I don't know what I'm going to tell them," she said, standing up. "But I won't lie. I'm sick of all the lying that's gone on here." She went into Martin's office, assembling words in her head about treatment and anxiety, the fragility of early sobriety and the need for AA meetings. But that would be so unclassy. That stuff was so intimate, and, ultimately, so shameful. She dialed the number. At Riverside they had said to keep it short and sweet; don't go into elaborate explanations that nobody will really understand. Clara Sanderson answered the phone. Abby said, "Clara, it was extremely nice of you to invite me tonight, but at this last minute I cannot come. I hope you can forgive me. But Martin would like to come alone, if that's all right."

Clara said the right things: so sorry; delighted to have Martin. There was an awkward pause. Abby said, "I hope we see each other soon."

"Yes."

"Good-bye." Abby was pleased with herself. She had kept it simple. Grinning inwardly, she thought, "I wonder what she's making of it."

Martin, ready for golf, was waiting. "Okay?" he asked.

"Yes. Fine. Probably relieved. No. Erase that. She was sorry."

"Will I see you later?"

"I'll leave for the meeting at six-thirty."

"Then I'll see you." Martin came to Abby and kissed her on the forehead. She patted him on the shoulder.

Alone in the room, Abby enjoyed a sense of relief. Dinner parties were such hurdles now. She always wanted to arrive at them just in time for the food and leave early, although desserts helped quiet her nerves. She despised being one of the guests who stood around sipping cokes. At her own parties she used to think, "How square. What could I talk to them about? They must be so bored, deprived of the fun of drinking." Nowadays, with no alcohol in her own hand, she felt excruciatingly boring. And frightened. What if somebody she didn't know talked to her? They would both shrivel up in dead air.

And there were always well-meaning people who didn't know what to say to somebody just out of treatment. They groped for words, awkward and curious, studying her, waiting for her perhaps to turn brown. "My dear," they would finally say, "you must be so proud, doing that for yourself." It was such a drag being treated as though you had one leg — hostesses saying self-consciously, "There's just soda in the glass," or asking you in advance, "Would you rather we didn't drink tonight?" The last straw was her mother-in-law — "No. No, thank you. I haven't drunk scotch since Abby went to Riverside."

Coming out of her reverie, Abby checked the bedroom to see if anything was out of order, and looked at her watch. One o'clock. Would anybody, besides her, be wanting lunch? Was anybody around? Judy would be holed up in her room, avoiding her mother. But don't try to eat with her. It would be one more rejection, like the disaster with the earrings. That had seemed a nice gesture — buying Judy something expensive she coveted, a thank-you present for running the house during treatment, perhaps an atonement for offenses committed — though only a pittance against that national debt. Judy had taken the earrings with perfunctory thanks. Then, suddenly, she had burst out, "Mom, I hate it when you do this. It's like a bribe."

Frederick, Abby knew, was spending the afternoon with a friend who had a new Atari game. Evan, she assumed, would be off somewhere enjoying his leisure time activity of getting zonked on pot. She wondered where that was going to end. Was he addicted yet? Had he crossed the line? She had tried so hard to detach herself. But detachment seemed like not caring, and she cared desperately. Well, there was nothing she could do about it now. Maybe this was the moment to be nice to herself — a sandwich, the Sunday paper, and a bracing cup of coffee. Heaven!

A half hour later, Abby, astonished, looked up from the paper as Evan pulled a chair to the kitchen table. She waited, saying nothing, watching that challenging light in his eyes. But it was mixed with something. A pleading? Or maybe fear? His voice, however, was conspiratorial. "Did you really not use the Valium?" he asked.

Abby leaned back in her chair. Her face was unruffled, voice conversational. "I really didn't," she answered. "But I guess I can't blame you for wondering."

Evan's face was now open and interested. "How did you get your Valium?" he asked.

"From doctors and a psychiatrist friend. Told them I couldn't sleep, was nervous."

"What's a downer like?"

Abby laughed lightly. "It's like wiping your nerves with rabbit fur," she answered, feeling uncomfortable. Why was he asking this stuff? They were like two druggies talking shop. But at least they were talking. Evan nodded and Abby went on. "But Valium is sneaky. Before you can turn around, you can be hooked. Same as booze. I always thought junkies were people lying in doorways with needles sticking out of their arms, so *I* couldn't be a junkie. I was a housewife. I already had a title."

Evan grinned, seemingly against his will. "Come on, Mom. Don't slip in a lecture." But his words had no heat. "I'd never use Valium. I know guys who drop acid and they're frybrains. God, stay away from that stuff. And angel dust. Pot's different. Have a few hits and you just mellow out."

Abby was amazed. It was happening. Evan was admitting he used marijuana, and he was asking for help. Keeping her tone easy, she said, "But when you can't get high on pot anymore, what do you do? You want that good feeling, so you use pot with other things. Like booze. Or maybe you try a dusted joint and end up in the fetal position in a mental hospital."

Evan leaned forward onto the table. Abby watched him, wondering what he would do, noticing his hands shake slightly. With the bravado still in those round, innocent eyes, he was saying, "Guys offer you a hit, it's foolish not to take a drag. With the guys I hang out with, it's almost unethical." Abby still said nothing. She did not know what to say. Now he was rubbing the flat of his hand across the tabletop. "But I'm getting scared — just a tiny bit. It isn't as much fun anymore — but I've still got that joint in my hand. I'm sitting there alone smoking and all my friends are asleep and I'm saying, 'Hey, let's go out.' "

Abby decided she had to say something. "How can I help you?" she asked.

Evan smirked. "Judge me. Tell me I'm okay."

Abby answered sadly, "I'm in no position to judge anybody. I'm scared even to judge myself." They looked at each other across the table. Then Abby got up and came around and sat in the chair beside him. She took his hand. "I'm in such a turmoil with my own feelings. But I know you're really precious to me. I miss knowing you. We've wasted a lot of years and I feel responsible for a lot of your troubles. But I'm beginning to see what is the right way to live. I don't know what lies ahead, and I'm frightened. You have to choose, too. It is you who will have to live with you. You are the one who has to decide what your life will be."

Abby reached over and began rubbing his head, something he had loved as a little boy. "If you hurt so bad, this life must not be the right way. If you get straightened out, you've got so much to go for." Evan dropped his head under her hand and luxuriously closed his eyes. Then Abby stopped and moved her hand back to his. "I want you to understand," she said, "that if you keep on using marijuana and there is a lot of druggie behavior at home, that will be too painful and would jeopardize my sobriety. I will tell your father that you must either go into treatment or leave home. I know too much now about enabling to see any other options."

Evan turned his head and looked at Abby and she could see the fear, the astonishment in his round blue eyes. She nodded her head and added, "It's your choice." Evan was silent, eyes staring. She said, "If you can't do it alone, let somebody help you. Do you need to go into treatment?"

Evan jerked his hand away. His voice was loud in the small room. "No! Hell, no!"

Abby's heart contracted. She had gone too far. The moment was broken. Evan stood up. "I guess I'd better go," he said.

Looking up at him, her face relaxed, her voice reflective, Abby said, "I've been thinking a lot today about what I learned at Riverside. Part of my recovery is to try to be honest and say what I really think and feel, and stop covering everything over with anger." She smiled. "And here's a piece of truth. I still love you."

Evan stared at her. "Sometimes I'm scared of you," he said.

Abby looked up at him. "Don't forget," she said. "Chemical dependency is hereditary."

"I've got to go," Evan said. Abby watched him leave, grateful that she didn't feel helpless anymore. The two of them had come a long way in a short time. But she could not tell Martin about this talk. Evan's trust would be destroyed forever. And then she noticed that his pot smoking no longer made *her* feel guilty.

At seven-fifteen Abby sat with Laura, coffee cup in hand, waiting for the AA meeting to begin. Coming tonight had been different, nice, a relief. Her family could never know what it meant for an alcoholic not to drink; what it meant to lose the medicine of alcohol, to change the circuitry of your reactions and overhaul your most intimate relationships; what it meant, after forty-two years, to feel like a baby. Looking around the roomful of people in rows of chairs, she thought how odd this all was. It was these people, these strangers, who cared enough to help her stay sober.

Laura turned and asked, "How did things go after we talked?"

"Okay," Abby said, and told her about Martin and the Sanderson's dinner party. "I think I understand better," she continued, "about not letting others define me and my feelings, and about its being a selfish program."

"That's wonderful," Laura answered. "That's a big step."

Abby noticed again the brightness of Laura's eyes. There was a depth in them. She knew very little about Laura's drinking history and recovery — mainly that she was two years sober, still married, and had two grown children. Her husband was a lawyer. "Are you happy in your marriage now?" Abby asked.

"I am," Laura answered. "And I'm very grateful."

"If your husband was so hostile — that's what you said — how did you handle that?"

"Well," Laura said, putting out her cigarette in the ashtray in her lap, "I was determined I wouldn't live in limbo, not knowing how life was going to be, waiting for some happy, beautiful, understanding marriage that might never come. I had to live enthusiastically and not dwell on what I didn't have and might never have. So I decided to run my own life and let my husband go — let him be angry and hurt and resentful, and let God take care of his hostility. There was a particular line: 'Your need is God's opportunity.' I really held on to that."

"Did he change?" Abby asked.

"Finally. After I did. He almost had to. It was very important when he understood that I was going my own way." Laura laughed. "He'd lost his fighting partner."

"I don't know whether Martin will change," Abby said. "He may be incapable of it. Or just unwilling." She paused and added, "Martin and I are like two needy, lonely old people, beating each other with crutches."

At that moment the leader called the meeting to order. After a few announcements, he read the ritual preamble. "Alcoholics Anonymous is a fellowship of men and women who share their experience, strength, and hope with each other that they may solve their common problem and help others to recover from alcoholism. The only requirement for membership is a desire to stop drinking. There are no dues or fees . . ."

The first speaker was standard fare to Abby, and soon she was sighing inwardly and glancing furtively at her watch. The second speaker was a slender, fortyish woman with curly brown hair framing her wide face. She was dressed in a blue denim skirt and a tailored blue striped shirt. Abby thought, "This is more like it." The woman said, "My name is Lillian and I am an alcoholic." The crowd answered in unison, "Hi, Lillian." She told her story, and soon Abby was listening closely, tingling with recognition.

There was the college partying, the ritual cocktails, the therapeutic drinks, the gradual accumulation of symptoms. Abby nodded as Lillian described her nighttimes: "lying there awake, wheels spinning in my head, and a little fire burning deep inside that means, 'You haven't had enough and you have to get some more,' a fire that can't be reasoned with."

Abby's lips parted as Lillian described the trip downstairs and the long pull from a bottle, and then back to bed, head clear now, roaming into fantasies. "I had this personal soap opera to entertain myself," Lillian said. "I'd become a singer. I was on stage, six feet tall, effortlessly thin, black silk dress with little spaghetti straps, my naturally curly hair straight and silky and blond, no glasses — totally gorgeous — lit by red, yellow, and blue lights — adoring faces visible in the first rows. And when I opened my mouth, out came the voice of Ella Fitzgerald."

Abby laughed out loud. She had done things like that, believing she was happy and fine.

Lillian described her first AA meeting, the feelings of detachment and superiority. Afterward, at home, she told her husband, "You know, these people are very interesting. They may be on to something." And then she poured herself a drink. However, she had kept going to meetings and did stop drinking. "I was in a jam," Lillian said. "I hated AA. I hated all those people. Yet I didn't want to drink anymore." She descended into a depression and began planning her suicide. She'd do it with sleeping pills, accumulated from several doctors so nobody would suspect. But in a taxi on the way to an AA step meeting, a thought came to her. Everybody would mourn for a time and then life would go on. Her husband would remarry, and probably be happier. The kids would grow up. And she would miss everything.

She arrived at the meeting. Its subject was the Fourth Step — "Made a searching and fearless moral inventory of ourselves." Lillian said, "Here I was in a smoky room, listening to a group of people discuss with great seriousness the pros and cons of writing the Fourth Step on legal-sized paper. And would a pen be better or should you use a pencil so you could erase and make changes? One fellow said, 'I'm a writer so I do the Fourth Step on my typewriter.' Another guy asked, 'Do you think it's too arrogant if I ask my secretary to correct it?' "

Abby laughed with the rest of the crowd, and Lillian continued. "I had the same realization as in the taxi. Years from now this group would still be sitting there exchanging ideas on how to write down the Fourth Step. But I saw that I had to make my choice. Did I or did I not want to join these people — in effect, join life. AA had not promised to entertain me, but it had promised to keep me sober and I believed that. I chose life. I chose to cast my nets on the right side."

When Martin arrived home from the Sanderson's, Abby was reading in bed. She could smell alcohol on his breath, and her stomach turned with nausea. He asked mildly, "How was the meeting?"

Abby smiled, half to herself, and answered, "I think those people may be on to something."

Later she lay calmly waiting for sleep, looking up at the cracks in the ceiling — her rivers — the Mississippi, the Shenandoah . . . She thought about Lillian. How extraordinary that *this* woman had spoken on *this* particular night. Into Abby's mind came the voice of the nurse at Riverside — "You will hear what you need to hear" — and then the words from Jeremiah — "You shall be rebuilt." Maybe Lillian was one of those coincidences they talk about, the ones that are not coincidences.

Abby smiled, thinking of something Lillian had said: "It's really a laugh. Here's this wonderful, huge planet, with all the stars and the oceans and endless grains of sand and the seasons, and it all works together in harmony. But the alcoholic stands there and says, 'Count me out.' " Abby rolled over to concentrate on sleeping, but behind her lids, her eyes stayed awake. "God, Almighty," she thought. "I'd kill for some ice cream. Rocky Road. With jimmies."

14

IN MAY, almost a year after leaving Riverside, Abby stood alone and angry in the backyard. In front of her was the apple tree, a presence in the darkness, its filigree of limbs and leaves black against the gray suburban night. The sweet air of the blossoms was in her nostrils. "We've been through a lot together, in sickness and in health," she said to herself, remembering her spring ceremonies of first rum collins. "Ugh," she thought, sitting down in a garden chair. Her year had been sectioned by drinks, not seasons. Rum in the spring, vodka tonics in the summer, scotch in the cold weather, and, be honest, vodka all twelve months.

She tried to look at her watch in the darkness. It was a black hole on her wrist. Well, it must be 2 A.M. For an instant she allowed the fear to stir her mind again, and then it was too late and the visions had rushed back: Judy drunk on some floor, Judy being raped, Judy in a speeding car crashing like a bomb, Judy bloody and dying. Abby shook her head, trying to rattle these images from her mind. She was being ridiculous. Judy would be all right. After all, Judy had her own Higher Power. But what would it be like, standing in the morgue, looking down at her dead body? Would this weight on the heart go on forever, this emptiness in the stomach? And what would happen if Judy got pregnant? Would there be an abortion? An unwed pregnancy? Abby could taste the anxiety, sour in her throat.

She stood up and began pacing across the patio bricks. "Let go and let God," she murmured. That was so good, so pure in its simplicity — and so *hard* to do because you *care*. You want so much to keep your child safe and happy. Judy was only sixteen. Still in high school. Between twelve-thirty and two, what could she do, besides hang out with the wrong kids. She could get terribly hurt. "Detach with love," Abby reminded herself. Judy had to learn independence, make her own mistakes and accept the consequences. But she needed limits. She wanted limits. "Let go and let God," Abby told herself again. But she missed terribly that little, dependent Judy, the thin, hugging arms, the moist, butterfly kisses.

Abby paused by the open door to the garage, seeing in her head again a smashed car, the red, rotating police lights, a white ambulance arriving, siren wailing. Should she drive around looking for Judy? That was silly, chasing kids in the middle of the night. She could only wait for the phone to ring. She began pacing again, feeling her self-control loosening, the anger taking over. How could Judy be doing this to her? Causing her such agony. It was pure defiance. And revenge. And no concern for others. Ground her till she's thirty! Then Abby answered herself, "You're taking it personally. That's your old drinking reaction."

But where were the payoffs for being sober? For being a good mother? Judy treated her like a bitch who had no right to discipline anybody. Maybe Judy liked the good old days and nights when she ran her own show. Maybe, subconsciously, Judy wanted to get back her freedom, wanted to make her mother drink. "But she's only testing," Abby answered herself again. "She's proving to herself I won't drink. She doesn't want total freedom. That's frightening. And it means I don't care."

An image of the liquor cupboard indoors, waiting, pushed into her agitation. But the alarm that swarmed through her was half anger — anger at Judy. That kid was making her violate her most central commandments: Sobriety came first ahead of everything. Remember that she was addicted, not to alcohol, but to changing her mood. Beware of moods that might weaken her vigilance. Remember H.A.L.T. — "Don't get hungry, angry, lonely, or tired."

Then to Abby's mind, as it did almost daily, came Larry's phone call a month ago. He had said he was fine, still chugging along sober. She told him how bad she felt for not calling him, how often she thought about him, how grateful she was for his help and comfort, how special a man he was. She explained that maybe this was why she hadn't called: she wanted to keep the experience untouched in her memory. But as she talked, she had sensed an odd embarrassment in Larry. Probably she was laying it on too thick.

Suddenly Larry had cut in. "Abby," he said, "I'm sorry to have to tell you some bad news, but I thought you'd want to know. I was back at Riverside seeing Fern, and she told me that Julia Waugh died in a car crash. Ran into the abutment of a railroad underpass. She was drunk."

Every time she thought of those words, Abby relived her gasp and strangling choke, as though she had taken the last breath of air in the room. Again her body tingled with shock. Again, "It could have been me," flashed in her head. Again the sadness washed through her. Poor Julia. A nice, smart woman. The terrific patient who never got well. Almost in the same instant, Abby was trembling with fury and frustration. How could Julia have done that! The dumb shit! To *know!* To be an educated drunk, to know the odds and continue to death! So senseless. So futile. Such a waste. Well, Julia knew the choices. Damn it, she *chose* to drink. "Better her than me!" Abby thought.

But the fear stayed inside her. Even two minutes ago thoughts of liquor had returned, though she was no longer bothered by the presence of alcohol, and was sometimes even nauseated by the sight of it, by the smell on Martin's breath. That old friend had come knocking on the door, saying, "Remember me? I can take care of your anger and loneliness." And here she was again, answering, "Oh, boy. A drink *would* let me sleep, let me avoid Judy's transparent excuses, let me deal with this mess in the morning."

Now, thank God, she understood about AA; that it kept you awake to the price of drinking, kept the flow of healthy attitudes continuous. You could not control the things that came into your mind, but you could control what you did with them. You could push away sick thoughts with healthy thoughts. To herself, she said, "That little twerp, Judy, isn't going to make me take a drink."

She went back to the chair and sat down, trying to relax her body and concentrate on healthy thoughts. She reminded herself of a line from treatment — "To 'let go' is not to be protective; it's to allow another to face reality." "So why," Abby wondered, "am I here at this god-awful hour, working so hard to detach?" She replied to herself, "You're sitting here because you've chosen to be here." She *wanted* to be the one waiting up, responsible enough to cope. Abby rose and wandered about the patio, gathering odds and ends of gardening tools, flower pots, fertilizer bags, and putting them away in the storage cupboard. She went back indoors and began tidying kitchen drawers, until at two-thirty a car pulled up in front of the house. Instantly, Abby was outside. She glimpsed a pale, nervous face behind the steering wheel. Judy was coming around the car, dressed in a short white skirt and a man's black jacket, two sizes too large. "Okay, Mom. Okay," she said.

"I'm really angry," Abby answered, her voice a flat statement.

The car pulled away from the curb, tires screeching.

"I'm sorry," Judy said.

"Sorry isn't good enough. This is the second time, and I thought we had an understanding."

Judy's face was wreathed with innocence. "I tried to leave, but my date was sick and I . . ."

Abby interrupted. "I'm not a fool and don't treat me like a fool. Go to bed, and in the morning we'll try for another understanding." Judy, head down, walked rapidly up the walk and disappeared inside.

Later, when Abby climbed gingerly into bed, Martin, one quarter awake, asked, "What's going on?"

"It's okay," Abby said. "Everything's under control." Then she wondered why she hadn't told Martin. It would upset him so that he couldn't sleep. But maybe that wasn't the truth. Maybe this was the old game—I won't tell Dad about you, if you don't tell him I was drunk at dinner. Maybe she wanted to win Judy. She needed her kids. She felt so alone.

The next morning, getting out of bed, Abby had a hangover. Too little sleep, too much adrenaline, she decided. It wasn't fair. A hangover after no drinks. But she had done well last night — with Judy, with herself. Now, if she could just get through their little session today . . .

Abby put on a robe, brushed her hair, and went downstairs to organize breakfast while Martin finished his jogging. After breakfast, he would be off to his Saturday golf. They sat together at the kitchen table, Abby with her boiled egg, Martin with a bowl of Wheatena, supercharged by a heaping tablespoon of bran. He asked no questions. He was preoccupied with the barbecue they were giving the following Saturday on the patio, and together he and Abby composed the guest list. Then he kissed her on the cheek, rubbed her shoulder, said, "I'll see you later," and was out the door. Abby, with a tinge of irony, called to his back, "Have a good time."

Abby stayed clear of Judy till noon, giving her time to have breakfast and get over her morning mumbles. Then Abby knocked on her closed door.

"Who is it?"

"The big bad wolf."

Silence. Then, "Okay. Come in."

Judy, in white painter's pants and a blue sweat shirt, sat on the unmade bed, a book in her hands. Abby stood for a moment, taking in the scene. An expensive sweater and skirt were tangled with the rumpled blankets and sheets. Along the floor, as though they had collapsed, exhausted, on the way to the almost empty hamper, lay a bathrobe, pants, bra, one dirty sock, shorts, yellow tee shirt, underpants, more socks, a shirt. In the rear corners of the room were drifts of clothes — more socks, a crumpled blouse, tee shirts, underwear. On the flat surfaces were dark glasses, pins, cards, hair clips, a shampoo bottle, dirty coffee cups and glasses, date book, panties, pictures. The drawers of the bureau were half open. Abby thought, "The bureau is like me. It's puking at the sight of this room."

"If I'm going to keep my temper," Abby said to Judy, "I'm not sure I can do it in this setting." She led Judy down to the kitchen and poured them both a cup of coffee. They sat across from each other at the table. Abby lit a cigarette. Judy's hands were folded in her lap, and her face, stiff and unreadable, was turned toward the window. "How was the party?" Abby asked.

"Okay."

"Just okay? Doesn't sound like the extra two hours were worth all this stink." Judy said nothing. Abby continued. "What's going on, Judy? It doesn't make sense to me. Twice in two weeks." Abby paused. "What do you get out of it?" Judy remained silent, looking away. Abby frowned. "I know you're still angry at me. But how angry are you?"

"I'm not angry at you," Judy said, her tone sullen.

"I don't believe that," Abby answered. "For five years, I was not there when you needed me; you couldn't have friends home; you had to take up the slack running the house."

"But, Mom," Judy answered, her face suddenly animated. "I told you. I really tried last night, but there was nobody to take me home. Do you think I'm lying?"

Abby leaned back in the chair. "That doesn't wash, Judy. You know if you'd called, I'd have come in my pajamas to get you. The issue is: are you going to abide by the rules of this house?"

"They're only *your* rules." Judy's voice was confident now.

Abby's heart clenched. These kids always knew your weak spot. "Whether you like it or not," she said, "I am sober and the mother in this house. If the household is going to be a good place to live, everybody has to work together and cooperate."

"I'm sorry I'm not perfect," Judy said. "But that's the way life goes."

Rage rose like bile in Abby's stomach. The little snot. Abby went on, keeping her voice even. "I am very pleased that you are having a social life. And a twelve-thirty curfew is not cruel. You are only sixteen. You have your whole life ahead to enjoy the fleshpots of the world. But right now you are in my care and I believe you should get your experience gradually, without being badly hurt — and without turning into one of those thirty-year-old teen-agers."

Now Judy's face was flushed. She brought her hands up from her lap and held on to the edge of the table. "You're just saying that because you think you have to be the big parental figure." She glared into Abby's calm eyes. "How am I ever going to be independent if I don't have the freedom to use my own judgment, without a lot of stupid, stifling restrictions."

"I think you can make plenty of free decisions between breakfast and midnight," Abby said tartly. "But you have to accept the consequences — in this case, my reaction. Now, at the risk of boring you, I want to say that I am trying very hard to get well and put the past behind me. I think you're stuck in the past, and I cannot afford to let your old behavior bring mine back. Pacing the floor at two-thirty in the morning is an attack on my serenity, and that makes me very angry."

"Then don't pace," Judy said.

"If I didn't care about you, I wouldn't pace," Abby answered. Her face had turned eager, her voice firmer. "You are one of the people I love *so* much, whose welfare is *so* important to me — I can't help myself." Abby leaned forward. "Judy, I really do know what it's like to be your age and angry and lonely and want to get people's attention any way you can. But unless I have hurt you since I have been sober, such behavior doesn't apply anymore, and I have to unhook from it. You remember at Riverside all the talk about detaching with love. I love you very, very much, and I want to build a new relationship with you. I want mother and daughter things to happen between us. But I am not going to snap to attention anymore and get upset and try to fix everything."

Abby stopped and Judy looked back to her. There was a long silence. Abby asked, "Do you want to say anything?" Judy shook her head. Abby continued, "This is the second time in two weeks you've stayed out late. Evidently I have to hit you over the head with a two-by-four to get your attention. I'm grounding you for the rest of the weekend."

Judy stood up. "Okay. Fine. I don't care. You can lock me in my room for the rest of my life."

Abby shrugged her shoulders again. "You *chose* not to come home when you knew you should."

Judy's voice was loud, vibrating with anger. "I hate all that psychology." She plunged toward the door, half turning, quivering with injury, yelling back, "I can't believe the shit I take from you."

Abby sat still, both hands on the table, her stomach churning. She needed *something.* A cigarette. Thank God for this buffer, this permissible addiction. "Take it easy," she told herself. "You said what you had to say. It's up to her whether she chooses to listen. You did your best."

Late that afternoon Abby was in the basement moving clothes from the washer to the dryer. She heard Martin coming down the stairs and she turned to face him, a tangle of wet clothes hanging from her right hand. He stopped in the middle of the room and said, "Judy was waiting for me when I came in the door."

Abby threw the wad of laundry into the dryer and sat down on the straight-back wooden chair beside the washer. Her chest tightened and she bit her bottom lip. Her eyes were unwinking. Martin continued. "Judy said she was a little late getting home last night and couldn't help it. And that you're being unreasonable and acting like it's the end of the world. What happened?"

Abby could feel her heart thudding against her chest. "Martin," she said, "this is between me and Judy. I am not going to give you my story and then have you play ·judge and decide who's right." Abby braced herself and waited for his inevitable reaction — "Now, Abby, don't you think . . ."

Martin sat down on the old, rump-sprung sofa across from Abby. "What makes you so sure I'll take Judy's side?" he asked.

"You always do. It's a historical fact. Check in the library. Under M."

Martin laughed. "You know, for the past couple of months, I've been wondering who my wife is."

Abby's heart still pounded. "Do you like her?"

"I don't know."

"What sort of a woman is she?"

"She's not my mother."

"That's a break."

Martin leaned back and smiled. "My mother lives to please me."

"Maybe you're married to Gloria Steinem," Abby said.

"I'm not sure I could handle that."

"When are you going to decide?"

Martin got up. "I don't know that either."

Abby asked, "What are you going to tell Gloria's daughter?"

Martin laughed ruefully. "I guess I'll say it's between her and her mother."

Listening to Martin climb the stairs, Abby felt warmed, relieved. She would take her little breakthroughs any way they came, even in a messy basement, probably surrounded with forgotten bottles and pills. She finished loading the dryer, returned upstairs, and filled the dishwasher with the day's accumulation of sandwich plates, milk glasses, butter knives. "Pretty soon," Abby thought, "the help in this hotel is going to rebel."

The phone rang and it was Annie O'Reilly, asking her to come to lunch next Wednesday. Abby accepted, pleased, reluctant. It wasn't the same these days — not for her, anyway. She had become a different person. Maybe the bond had always been the drinking, the jokes about Martin, the chance to pour out her "poor me's." Now their intimacy could not include alcoholism and the Program. And it was difficult at Annie's little luncheons, sipping Perrier, laughing, while she envied the others, not for their cocktails, but for their highs.

But she had her sponsor, Laura, who understood. When they talked, three, four times a week, Laura always said the same thing, "I'm glad you called." Abby went upstairs. The kitchen was empty. She dialed Laura's number, and the six year old answered. Abby asked, "Is your mother busy? Please don't get her if it's inconvenient."

"Mom!" bellowed the child, like a hog caller. *"It's for you!"*

Laura came on the line. Abby described the events with Judy and how Martin had actually cooperated: "That's not a declaration of undying love and trust, saying that we'll go side by side into the sunset, forever together. But I'll take it. It's progress. And I didn't grovel with a lot of thank-yous."

"I think you can feel terrific," Laura answered. "You stood your ground. You felt strong enough to handle Judy yourself. You had the courage to speak the truth. And Martin showed some different behavior because you're changing. From what I gather, he married you because you were strong and funny and an independent spirit — and you're turning back into that woman."

"Well, I'm trying," Abby answered. "And, you know,

I'm not afraid of him anymore. I've figured out it's because I'm not doing anything wrong. I don't have anything to hide. So today I feel a little hopeful."

"Today is all that matters," Laura answered.

That evening, with the whole family home, Abby decided to serve dinner in the dining room. She fetched a sullen, reluctant Judy and made her set the table. As Abby checked the pot roast, buttered the broccoli, stirred the rice, she could hear the sounds of plates and silver being slammed down onto wood. Deciding there had been enough crises between them, Abby told herself, "Detach. With love. Not the urge to kill."

At the table, Martin sat at one end, Abby at the other. Evan and Frederick were together, across from sulking Judy. Abby spooned out the pot roast, and Martin, looking up from his plate, grinned and said, "You remembered my onion."

Abby smiled back. "You have a few privileges around here."

Frederick dribbled gravy on his shirt. Immediately, his eyes wise and appraising, he told his mother, "Don't worry. It looks like an alligator." She laughed and said, "You'll get through life all right." This little boy, she thought, was reason enough to fight to repair her family.

Evan bent toward Frederick and stared with mock intensity at the gravy spot. "That's not an alligator," Evan said. "That's a cockroach." He lifted his hand. "I think I'll smash it."

Up came Frederick's hand toward Evan's head. "That's not a face," he said happily. "That's a pile of doo-doo, and I think I'll squish it."

Judy spoke. "Evan, that's certainly a mature, responsible way to behave." The entire family stared at her. She flushed.

Martin said, "I've been watching you, and if anybody's being immature around here, you are."

Judy clamped her jaws tight, and her face looked hot.

Martin bent forward slightly. "We would like to have a pleasant family time, which is hard when you are sitting there like a thundercloud. Now, either cheer up and participate, or take your plate upstairs to your room so we don't have to look at you."

Judy's eyes, staring at her father, were startled, then angry. She stood up, lifting her plate. "Okay, I know when I'm not wanted."

As Judy stalked from the room, Abby glanced at Evan, but his face was unreadable. What was happening to him? He was so close to her heart. But he seemed to have holed up inside himself. He still did not bring friends home. He was still pals with the Crawford boys. But he was nice to her, even sometimes companionable, though never confiding. She had not seen any of the usual drug signals: his pupils huge in his eyes, trouble sleeping, personally filthy, trouble at school. He seemed reasonably normal — for a teenager. Once, he had come along to an open AA meeting, but dismissed it as boring, no connection with him. Time would tell. Abby sighed. Parenthood was the pits.

The meal finished pleasantly with talk of a weekend on Martha's Vineyard when the weather warmed up. Evan said he had friends there with summer jobs and maybe he'd like to do that, too. Abby got up to clear the table. "Do you want to go to an AA meeting with me?" she asked Martin.

"No," he said. "They might think I was the alcoholic."

Was he trying to be funny? Abby wondered. Probably not.

On Sunday morning, Judy came downstairs, whistling and chirping, wearing a sun visor with a bear printed above the inscription BEAR WITH ME. Abby thought, "Butter is not melting in her mouth." Exuding cooperation, Judy cleaned up the kitchen and loaded the dishwasher. After church, she disappeared into the basement, almost smothered by the laundry in her arms. Abby went upstairs. Judy's door was open — a rare event. The room was shining clean.

An hour later, taking Frederick to the church fair, she

heard Judy's voice in the kitchen saying, "In some houses toast doesn't taste good. This is a toast house." Abby smiled. That was nice. Home was getting a vote of confidence. Then Abby heard the voice of Judy's new friend, Margie, saying, "Put in another piece for me." A part of Abby was thrilled. Judy wasn't afraid to bring somebody home. Another part was furious. Judy was being punished. More defiance. Abby called her out into the hall. Judy's eyes were full of innocence. "Oh, Dad said it was all right, " she explained.

Abby sat down on the seat of the hall coatrack. Could Judy see that she was trembling? Inside her, even the healthy self stuttered with rage as it said, "Take it easy. Take it easy." Her sick self said, "That son of a bitch Martin. That shitheel." Fighting to keep her voice calm, she said, "I don't mean to be rude to your friend, but you are being punished and Margie will have to go home."

"But you only said I had to stay in the house," Judy answered, "and Dad thought because I'd been so good . . ."

Abby stood up. Her voice was icy. "This is between you and me. Please explain to Margie. I'm sure she'll understand."

Judy looked at Abby's clenched face, turned, and went back into the kitchen. Abby walked out to the car with Frederick, but waited until Margie came down the front walk. Then she pulled away from the curb, thankful that tonight she had an AA meeting, one of the small step meetings. Maybe it would calm her down so she could tell Martin exactly what he had done.

That evening, as she drove to the meeting, turmoil still steamed inside Abby. Ringing in her ears was Frederick's wail: "Oh, mother, don't go tonight. Come on. Do you *have* to go? Are you going to have to go to these meetings forever, for the rest of your life?" And Martin. Was this as good with him as it would ever be? Martin giveth; Martin taketh away? Why couldn't they be on the same side? In the same uniform. Not looking at each other across the trenches.

"Face it, Abby," she told herself. "You can't take a donkey and make it run in the Derby."

She wrenched her thoughts toward what lay ahead. The topic was Step Nine, making amends to people she had harmed. How ironic! Martin and Judy should be making amends to *her!* But what should she say in the meeting? She wanted to sound wise and deep and healthy. Maybe she could use what somebody else had once said — that her amend was to be the best possible Abby. She *ought* to talk about the phone call last week with her mother — the hurt and frustration. But she might dredge up a new pain, a new failure. Or somebody else, asking questions, might surface something inside her. She'd had enough trauma for today.

The meeting was in the basement of a Methodist church, and Abby felt her usual relief at the sight of the dozen or so familiar figures assembling around the long table. Each week, for two hours, as though entering a decompression chamber, she could come to this room and step outside her life at home. Only recently had she switched to this new step group, Laura's group, where she liked the people better and could respect them. These men and women shared not only her disease, but her purpose, and when they went home, they shared the same struggle. If the meeting did hurt tonight, it would hurt good — and settle her, quiet her, move her into positive grooves.

She approached the big, rectangular table, wondering which person was the leader, so she could sit several chairs away and not talk immediately. She took a place, as the almost ritual greetings passed across and along the table. "How's it going?" "I see you're back again." "You're looking good." Laura arrived and smiled at her. Abby answered, "Hi, Spons," and was aware again of how much she admired the sparkle in Laura's eyes, her air of composure.

The meeting began, everybody around the table introducing themselves. The leader read the preamble — "Alcoholics Anonymous is a fellowship of men and women who share . . ." From the book *Twelve and Twelve,* each person

331

doing a paragraph, the group read aloud the chapter that discussed in detail how to carry out Step Nine.

Then the leader, George, spoke. He was a shortish man in his fifties, with thin blond hair and a stomach visible beneath his blue shirt. He was a dentist, she had found out, who drove in from the country to preserve his anonymity. He talked about the courage the Ninth Step required, his fear of the people he had lied to, stolen from — family, friends, everyone. "I was petrified of the mailbox," George said. "When I walked out to the road, I thought every car going by was looking right at me: 'There he is.' 'He owes people money.' 'He's a drunk.' " But then he made his amends. He went to his creditors and admitted he had lied and had no money. And the more he did it, the stronger he got.

Abby knew what he was talking about — her fear of meeting the garbage man, the one person who had known how much she was drinking. There were just so many empty bottles you could hide in cereal boxes or stuff into vacuum cleaner bags. Last month, looking him in the eyes and feeling good, she gave him a bag of home-baked cookies. "Was that an amend?" Abby wondered.

Next Carrie spoke — a young woman in her late twenties, pretty, large brown eyes, dark curly hair cut short, frilly clothes, a nervous smile that annoyed Abby. She described her fear that her amend would not be believed. All her drinking years she had been saying she was sorry — "Sorry Bill that I made an ass of myself at your wedding; sorry Steve that I got sick all over your car; sorry Dad that you were always giving me money because I couldn't pay the rent. I'm sorry. I'm sorry. I'm sorry. So many times and always hollow."

Abby thought, "I'm never going to say 'I'm sorry' again. I'm *me* now, and I don't have to apologize for that."

Mary spoke next — a large, solid woman, a housewife with a square face and the bright smile of a young girl. Her married daughter had answered the amend with a stream of grievances. "So I told her," Mary said, "that I didn't like me either when I was drinking. But at this point, I had to turn her over to God. So when she was willing to accept me the way I am, she should let me know. Four months later she walked into the house and said, 'I accept you the way you are, Mom.' I guess if you can find the strength, things do get better."

"That's wonderful," Abby thought. "That's great. Keep telling Judy, 'Take me as I am.' Look after myself. And wait."

Now Carol spoke — a woman in her forties, tall, slender, granny glasses, straight blond hair pulled back, divorced, designed sweaters for a living. Abby admired her independence, her fortitude. "The most difficult amend of all," Carol said, "was my husband, because I was still blaming him for my drinking. I remember some fellow in a meeting telling me I ought to pray for my husband. I said, 'I'll pray that he drives over the next cliff he comes to.' "

Abby chuckled and nodded.

"But," Carol continued, "I couldn't sleep at night and was uncomfortable and angry, and didn't know why because I was enjoying my sober life. I was asked in a meeting, had I made amends? I couldn't imagine doing that, but gradually I became honest with myself and could look into parts of the marriage and recognized how much I really was at fault, how I had made my husband sick. And I saw that I couldn't live with guilt or resentment. So I had a meeting with him —I was very shaky — it was very painful — but I sat and made amends. I couldn't believe the burden that was lifted."

Listening, staring sightlessly at a saccharine engraving of Christ hanging on the wall, Abby wondered: Would amends to Martin take away the anger? The sadness? The loneliness? But how could she make an amend to Martin? How could she act as though she was all wrong and he was all right? So demeaning. Putting her head on the block. And he'd cut it off. Besides, maybe she didn't feel all that sorry. When she was drinking and needed him so badly, he hadn't heard her. Too busy with himself. Too busy being the head of everything. Abby caught herself. That was the old blaming. What was the truth? How sorry was she? No answer came — nothing except sadness.

But now the faces around the table were turning toward her, and she had to speak. "My name is Abby and I'm an alcoholic," she said.

"Hi, Abby," the group answered.

She licked her lips. She was going to risk it after all. She said, "I was on the phone with my mother and I told her I was sorry I hadn't been the daughter she expected me to be. Pretty soon we were in an argument, and she told me she wasn't sure she could ever forgive me. It was like I had been kicked in the gut. I was crying and I felt so alone and so hollow, like I was in the middle of the universe all by myself. The thought came to me, 'There is no forgiveness anywhere. If I can't get it from my own mother, it doesn't exist.' "

Abby stopped and took a deep breath. She had shared this and nothing had happened inside her. Just a big anticlimax. So she would go into her prepared spiel. "But one of the things I've learned in AA is that everything has to start with me. By staying sober, by becoming the best Abby I can be, I'm making an amend to myself, to my higher power and to whoever I come in contact with, including my mother. So I think Step Nine for me is a change in attitude and a change in my whole way of being."

Several more people talked, a lawyer, an electrician, a secretary. Then it was Laura's turn. She spoke toward Abby. "I really hooked into what you said. I think the key idea here is forgiveness. And the readiness to take full responsibility for our past acts. At first I thought Step Nine was so boring. In reality, I was terrified of it. After I was sober about a year, I went to a meeting on Step Nine and afterward told my sponsor that my mother was sick and dying a thousand miles away. She said, 'Promise me tomorrow you will pick up the telephone.' I knew I had to obey the Program — that if I worked the Twelve Steps I would stay sober.

"So I did dial the phone and asked my higher power to start speaking through me. My mother sounded very faint and far away, and I didn't know if she could hear me. Suddenly, a voice seemed to come from behind me. I almost turned to see who was speaking. I heard the voice say, 'Mom, I love you.' The voice was mine. I was so full of resentments, I had never said that to her before. But I wasn't making the call to fix a relationship. I was obeying the principles of this program. The next morning she died. But I had done what I needed to do for myself. I went on a better high than J&B ever gave me. So now, when I feel discomfort, I turn to the steps of the Program."

Abby wondered, could she ever say I love you to her mother and not have it a lie? But in Abby's imagination was a picture of her mother's face, cardboard gray, on a hospital pillow, dying. What would she want to say to her mother, to Martin, on their deathbeds? What if the amend was going to be *that* important?

When the circuit was completed, murmurs passed around the table — "A really good meeting." The group rose and held hands and said the Lord's Prayer. Then Carol turned to Abby and said, "I once bared my soul to my mother, and it was excruciatingly painful. And at the end of the whole thing, she said, 'Now what kind of cookies did you want for that meeting you're going to tonight?' "

Abby laughed. "That's my mother in a nutshell. I think she believes I'm an alcoholic because she wasn't a good parent."

"Well?" Carol asked. "So?"

Abby was mystified and annoyed. She hated people who talked in coy riddles. And now Carol was saying good-bye and leaving. Then Abby understood. "So?" So whose problem was it? It was her mother's problem. "If she can't understand and forgive me, it's not my fault," Abby thought. "And certainly no reason to drink."

Driving home, Abby tried to blank out her mind, give her emotions a rest. But the meeting forced itself into the empty spaces and she finally gave up and faced the question: should she make a formal amend to Martin? She'd done a sort of out-of-town tryout with Annie while having tea, apologizing for all the trouble she had caused. And then Annie had deflated her, saying, "Oh, it wasn't that bad." So the amend she had decided on for Martin was to remain sober, be emotionally present for him. Amends didn't have to be formal. They could be a continual process, done gradually, growing out of the moment.

At home, Martin was watching television. He smiled at her and asked, "Was it a good meeting?" She said, "Yes." She did not have the strength, the heart, to tackle him about Judy's friend. And would anything she could say make a difference? Other matters were more important right now. She wanted to think, not fight.

For a few minutes she sat with Martin, watching the end of the news. Then she followed him up to bed. But she could not sleep. Eyes open, trying to distract herself, she lay there reviewing her rivers. Martin's foot rubbed against her calf. She moved her leg away and went back into her head — "Mississippi, Shenandoah, Missouri . . ." Damn the amends meeting. It had stirred up the mud at the bottom of her consciousness. But her higher power had brought her to those people. Well, what had she heard? That her discomfort could be lifted. That she had to forgive. But what if she wasn't sorry?

The turmoil was like an itch, and the muscles in her legs and arms ached with the need to move — and move again. She rolled to one side and then the other; pulled the pillow over her head, tossed it to one side; and envied Martin's regular breathing. After making a fool of her with Judy, how could he make a pass with his foot and think the welcome mat would be out! Especially when they played that sad game night after night: Are you tired, or are you going to watch TV? I think I'll watch something. Well, I think I'll go up and read.

Abby pushed one of her pillows onto the floor and asked herself, "How much do you want this marriage? Don't forget what the man in AA had said — 'If you hurt enough, you'll drink.'" But how would she support herself alone? Martin could probably get the children, and she'd pile her guilt even higher. Abby rolled onto her stomach and hugged a pillow to her chin. She might have a business relationship, you go your way, he goes his. But she had too many nerve ends for that. She *had* to react to people.

Abby turned on her side and pulled her knees up toward her chest. Could she find somebody better than Martin? Maybe. Maybe not. He really and truly tried to do his best. He was a good guy, or she wouldn't have married him. They had many more similarities than differences. She believed in the sanctity of marriage. Maybe what she built now could be better. Real love. But what's that? It's sharing, trust, respect, companionship, fun. They used to have *some* of that.

Abby stretched out her legs, moved onto her back, and put one arm over her eyes. Okay, she would commit herself to this marriage. For now. If it was too hard on her sobriety, she'd know. And she'd be strong enough to leave. In the meantime, knock off the poor me's.

Abby began rubbing the back of her neck, hoping to soothe her restlessness. "Live those phony words you said at the meeting," she ordered herself. "Make yourself the best Abby you can be. You got this family sick. You get healthy and they can get healthy. It's already begun. Maybe for anybody else they're baby gnat steps. For you, they're gazelle leaps."

Abby slipped out of bed. Martin, under the blanket, was unmoving, breathing quietly. She padded into the bathroom, shut the door, and turned on the light. She lowered the top of the toilet, sat down, and leafed through a magazine from the rack on the wall. She could not concentrate. She got up, studied herself in the medicine cabinet mirror and was pleased. The flesh was firm around the high cheekbones, the skin pink. Her hazel eyes had their old clarity and levelness. With her wide mouth, she gave herself the panorama smile. She'd gotten off lightly.

Still looking at herself, she wondered again. "How sorry are you?" Why was the question bugging her so? Maybe because Laura had reminded her the key was forgiveness. Nothing could happen until that happened. She thought of a line from this morning's church sermon — "What you do for the least of my brothers, you do for me." Suppose the least of her brothers, who needed her love, concern, and forgiveness, was Martin. Abby sat down again on the toilet seat and stared blankly ahead at the white tiles. She thought, "If I live to be a hundred, I can never make it up to him."

Abby sighed. Yes, that was the bottom-line truth. She sighed again. Would a cup of hot milk put her to sleep? She went silently down the stairs, intensely aware of the hundreds of sleepless trips she had made to find a hidden bottle. And as she stood by the stove, occasionally testing the milk in the saucepan with her forefinger, the unanswerable questions still pressed in upon her. Was she trying to have everything the way *she* wanted it? Were her expectations too high? She longed now to make peace with Martin. To make peace with life. Maybe if he got some help. Abby's mouth twisted with involuntary anger. "No," she thought. "He'd be terrified of letting down his guard and finding out he was just as screwed up as the rest of us. And who would ever have the nerve to tell Martin Andrews, the sun god of the world, that everything he believes about himself is wrong."

Suddenly, as though on cue, Martin, wearing pajamas, his face plump with sleep, was standing in the doorway. She looked at him amazed, then understood. He sat down at the table and she said stonily, "You thought I was drinking again, didn't you?"

Martin nodded. His voice was quiet, reluctant. "Yes."

"Martin, what's it finally going to take for you to trust me?"

His tone was placating. "It's not that I think you're going to drink. It's that I can't stand the thought of it happening. So I worry when anything is the way it used to be. If you're grouchy in the morning, or unusually tired at night, I worry what that means. If I'm in bed and hear the tap running, is she taking a pill?"

Abby felt herself softening. "I know. When Judy was so late, I had her dead in a ditch." Then her voice stiffened. "But you know it hurts a lot, wanting to be trusted and knowing you can't be. If something doesn't change, this is going to be a miserable, miserable house."

"Do you think I'm happy with the way things are?"

"No. But when are you going to get off dead center and do something for yourself? I can't live with all your bad feelings hanging over my head."

"What do you suggest?"

"At Riverside they said to go to Al-Anon. I can't help you; I'm too busy helping myself. Or we could go to the groups for couples at Riverside."

Martin folded his arms. "I play golf with a fellow who's in Al-Anon and he's been talking to me about it. But I don't know."

Abby drank the last of the milk and put the empty mug in the sink. Still with her back to Martin, she braced her arms on the counter and said, "Sometimes, like right now, I just don't know if it's going to be worth it."

"What do you mean?"

"All the work it's going to take to get us back in shape. The emotional trauma in fixing this wreck."

Martin's voice was urgent. "Anything worth having is worth working for."

"That's the stockbroker in you," Abby answered, still facing away.

Suddenly she felt his body press against her back, his arms around her waist, his hands spread out across her stomach.

In her ear he said, "I can't imagine life without you." He paused, and then, "When did we last make love?"

Speaking toward the faucet, Abby answered Martin, "Two months, four days, twenty-two hours, sixteen minutes ago."

Instantly his body was gone and a chill came over Abby. She heard his voice saying, "That's what you do, Abby. You make a joke and slam the door in my face."

She turned quickly. He was sitting at the table, arms folded, his face sad. He looked boyish to her, vulnerable, and she thought that he did not deserve all this. She moved quickly to the chair beside him and, half turning, put her hands on his arms. "I'm sorry, Martin," she said, and then caught herself and added, "I've said that too many times before. It feels like sand in my mouth. But I am sorry for so much, even if you can't believe it."

Martin was silent, staring down at her hands on his arms. Abby's mind was racing. She had begun the plunge without meaning to, and the thump of her heart was loud in her ears. In her head, "You'll be sorry," collided with Laura's voice — "When I am upset I follow the principles . . ." — and Carol's voice — "I couldn't believe the burden that was lifted" — and her own voice again — "If he was going to die tomorrow . . ." But, more a sensation than a thought, she knew she would do this terrifying thing, do what they said to do. She began to speak, her voice and face earnest, intense. "I know my drinking caused you a lot of pain, and I can see I must have been the bitch of the century, because when I'm really hurt, I fight like a tiger. But you still nursed me and took care of me and endured me and I want to thank you for that."

Martin turned his face toward her, eyes startled.

Abby's mind whirled with feelings, but no words matched them and she froze and then blurted whatever came first. "It wasn't your fault. It was mine."

She fell silent, the beating of her heart still sounding in her ears. Martin looked stunned, then confused. After a moment he answered, "I don't know how to respond, but that's very nice of you to say." He paused and when he spoke again, his voice was reflective. "It's true. It was really bad." He stopped and seemed to look inward. "You know, I used to think it was totally inconsiderate of you to go off and get involved with an addiction that jeopardized everything we had worked so hard for. I'd think, 'Why the hell is that bitch sidetracking me?' "

Abby bent her head and closed her eyes. The knifing pain was there again. He had done it. He had turned her confession against her. He had jabbed into her shame, breaking the film of skin just forming. But, also, more than anything, she felt a profound satisfaction. She had gone to any lengths. She had been equal to the terrifying task. She could stand this pain.

She looked back again at Martin and felt separated by acres of emptiness. He was over there. She was here. But his eyes were earnest. He didn't understand what he had done. He thought he was being honest, explaining, sharing feelings the way he was supposed to. And maybe he had that right. She must remember that his reaction to her was irrelevant. Her amend had been for herself alone.

He was saying thoughtfully, "I used to worry what would happen if you were in a serious auto accident and became a total invalid and an added burden to me. I thought maybe that final responsibility would do me in. Those anxieties don't go away quickly."

Abby was silent, empty.

"I'm not a machine that's always there without feeling," Martin went on. "I take my responsibilities very seriously. I worry that there won't be money in the checking account. I worry that the kids' needs at school won't be covered. There's just me, you know. And I feel like I'm the only one who worries." He was leaning away from Abby, and his voice was growing strident. "I haven't been the sort of man who gets into trouble and causes grief to his family. I've worked hard and become a success and provided for my family and that makes me feel good. And I don't seem to get any points for that." Suddenly his voice faltered. "But I've been taught all my life that regardless of how bad things get, you have the strength if you can call on it."

Martin bent his head and put his right hand over his eyes. Abby reached her arm across his shoulders and felt them quivering and knew that he was crying.

Talking downward, eyes still covered, Martin went on. "I have all these feelings that seem right to me and everybody makes me feel like they're wrong. And the person I want to depend on does it the most. I need to be wanted and listened to and cared for."

Abby could feel tears pushing up behind her own eyes. Poor Martin. So covered up. So choked. So impacted. And breaking open, even a little, was so hard and hurt so much.

Martin dropped his hand, and Abby could see the wetness on his cheeks. He did not look at her. "I love you, Abby. I'm proud of you. I love to show you off. But I'm afraid of you. This is the first time I've been able to tell you this. I'm afraid of your anger. I'm afraid to show any weakness because you'll use it against me. I've always been that way. Always clammed up. I wish I wasn't that way."

For just a second, Abby put her cheek against his, feeling the prickly stubble. "I know," she said, impressed, excited. If this controlled, sealed man could feel so deeply about *something,* if he had a chink in his armor, there was real hope.

"I've never wanted to be weak," Martin continued. "As a boy I was skinny and funny looking with a chubby face, and I didn't have much strength, so I was always one of the last ones chosen for everything. I always wanted to be Mr. Popular. I always strived for the A's but I got B's or C's.

Abby kept her arm on his shoulders. "Martin," she said, "we're both lonely. All my life I've felt different and isolated. I can go to AA meetings and feel very, very comforted. But when I come home, that's where you want somebody to hold you and give you a squeeze and say, 'Don't worry. You're going to be fine. You'll always have me.' "

Looking away across the kitchen, Martin said, "It's going

to seem crazy, but it's all hooked up with wanting my clothes laundered and ready and clean so when I want to reach in there, I've got what I need. Or having the dishwasher emptied and the dishes in their place. It makes me uneasy when nothing is in reserve. And if I don't have things orderly, it implies that I need somebody to do something for me — that I'm dependent."

Abby bent her head toward his. "I draw a lot of security from you, Martin. It's a very important thing for me to lean on." She bent over to put both arms around him, but it was too awkward, and she stood up behind him, hands on his shoulders, thumbs gently rubbing the base of his neck. "When you tell me how much you hurt, I can help and take my share. If I don't know what you're feeling, we can't work things out together."

Martin cocked his head back, enjoying the luxurious touch of her fingers. "If I'm complicated for *me* to live with," he said, "what must it be like for you?"

"I always want to know when you're crying inside," Abby answered. "Then it doesn't seem so one-sided — like I'm the only one whose guts are ripping apart."

He stood up and faced her, and they held each other and kissed. Abby said, "Let's always be good to each other." She kissed him again and said, "I think I can get to sleep now. That hot milk is great stuff."

Martin laughed and steered her toward the door. "Is it addictive?" he asked.

In bed, Martin's foot came across no-man's-land and rubbed her leg, and she turned toward him and said, "If you were a real swinger, you wouldn't send your foot over to make an indecent proposal. You'd come yourself."

She could sense him smiling in the darkness as he answered, "You're right. I was sending a boy to do a man's work." They met in the middle of the bed. "I love you, Abby," Martin said again.

The answer — "And I love *you*" — stuck inside her. This was too soon. It would be the biggest breakthrough of all.

But she felt a deep and searching warmth, and she let that pour out through her body.

Martin left the house early the next morning for a breakfast meeting. Abby came down late to the kitchen, yawning, feeling wrung out but relaxed. As usual, the puppy, released from Frederick's room, was waiting to jump on her. "You're obnoxious," Abby scolded. "And you're not even a good dancer." She headed straight for the coffee pot and poured herself a cup. Ugh! Dishwater! Goddamn Martin! Okay. Take it easy. Make another pot. Abby opened the can on the counter. It was empty. Not to worry. Alcoholics never run out. Two more cans in the cupboard. She got one and took off the plastic lid. The can was already open and empty. So was the other. Her grease cans! "Oh shit!" Abby pushed the dog away with her foot. Well, she wasn't going to drink instant! There was only one thing to do. Drive to Dunkin' Donuts.

Turning to go upstairs to get dressed, Abby noticed a white sheet of paper on the other counter. On it, in Martin's hand, was written:

> Abby,
> Don't forget to have the car greased.
> Take gray pinstripe suit to cleaners.
> Get roll of stamps at P.O.

Abby picked up the list and read it again. Compressing her lips, she crumpled the paper and threw it in the trash. "He must be thinking of some other woman," she joked to herself, grimly.

That afternoon Abby was vacuuming the living room in preparation for the party on Saturday. She felt restless, uneasy — and haunted by Julia's death. Almost daily, it seemed to settle on her mind for a time, oppressive, agitating. "Booze really does kill," she thought. "And suddenly, not always inch by inch." One more drink and she could be dead. You never knew which drink would do it. She thought about Fern's words: "The disease is cunning, baffling, powerful — and patient." Then she thought about something Larry had said on the phone: "They tell us that these examples are given us so we may live."

The living room seemed stifling, and Abby went out into the back patio. She sat in the same chair where she had waited for Judy on Saturday night, imagining *her* dead in a car. Teenagers were so lucky, believing they were invulnerable. She looked at the apple tree and thought about the childhood Abby, running to her apple tree for comfort, hugging the limb and sobbing. But even in those moments, she had somehow believed that her promises to herself would never be broken.

"Well, this Abby," she thought, "who is about a century older, knows different." Years of her short life had been squandered. But that was fate. The cards she was dealt. And fate had also given her back her life. A resurrection. Like a miracle. A day without a drink used to be total heroism. And now the obsession, the tickle in the mind, was gone. Her amazement, her gratitude, was entire, but she believed it had not been her doing. It had been a gift.

Her eyes still on the tree, she admired the powerful trunk supporting the branches on its shoulders, spreading its power out to the intense green of the furthest leaves, the whiteness of the tiniest bloom. "I *do* have worth," she thought. "I'm *here*. I've been kept alive for some reason. No single reason. I'm here for all reasons. I want to create some good in my life." She laughed to herself. "Something white and green with a big, shining light." She closed her eyes and prayed. "Dear God, allow me to go on. Allow me enough time to find a little serenity and to enjoy it — one day at a time."

She heard Frederick's voice. "Mom. I'm home!" She went inside and he delivered the news bulletin of the day. "Mom, do you know that *everything* is made of atoms?" He decided they should go roller-skating, and dug out Judy's skates from the hall closet for Abby. As a special treat, they went onto the forbidden tar street, smooth as toffee. At first, uncertain, Abby held Frederick's hand. But then the feel, the balance, came back. Reveling in this sense of control — of her legs — of herself — she struck out on her own, laughing, doing crossovers, while Frederick said, "Oh, Mom, you think you're so terrific."

Abby laughed again and said, "Yes, I do," and thought about her sign from her room at Riverside. She had brought it home, and it lay in her bureau drawer, face up on top of the gloves and handkerchiefs and necklaces and mementos. Each time she opened the drawer and came upon it unexpectedly, she felt a lift of encouragement, a new steadiness, an interior balance — like the skating. She felt a confidence that — no matter what might happen in her family, no matter what Martin might do, no matter how many lists he might leave — she was going to be all right.

Abby skated to the curb and sat down, gasping from her exertions. It was time, she told Frederick, for his homework. After prodding him upstairs, she decided to be dutiful, too. There was still the garden to get ready for the barbecue Saturday. Fetching her kneepads and a trowel from the outdoor cupboard, she knelt at a border and began digging a row of holes to receive the blue pansies. The air was quiet. Two honeybees were busy in the tulips beyond her hands. One bee followed the other to the same bloom. With the trowel in her hand, Abby sat back on her heels. Was there enough nectar for both, she wondered. Or was the second bee buzzing because he was mad?

She felt entirely concentrated in that moment. No past. Everything finished. She felt immaculate. She felt herself joined to the bees, to the damp earth and the pink of the tulips, to the flowering tree behind her, the warm sun on her neck. All life — the universe itself — was in tune. And now she belonged to that vast perfection. Happiness flowed through her. "This is wonderful," she thought — and the awareness broke the moment. She smiled inwardly and dug the trowel into the earth and went back to work.

AUTHOR'S NOTE

LIKE EVERYTHING else in this book, Julia Waugh's death really happened. It was a dramatic, personal shock. During my research, I interviewed Julia. At one point she disappeared into her kitchen to make us both coffee. Soon afterward, she again left the room. Suspicious, I checked her coffee mug. It was half full of scotch — despite her weeks of treatment, despite her terribly damaged liver, despite her intelligence and knowledge, despite everything imaginable and rational. My heart felt squeezed in a fist.

Some months later I received the same phone call as Abby. Julia was dead. I experienced the same sorrow and disbelief and anger. But I knew by then that I could not hope to understand what had happened. I knew that alcoholism — this disease that is the third biggest killer in America — cannot be comprehended by the intellect. It can only be grasped emotionally, in some internal region below thought. The same is true of the process of treatment and recovery, which can save alcoholics from their slow-motion catastrophe. And that is the goal of *Broken Promises, Mended Dreams:* to tell a classic case history in terms of deeply interior feelings so the reader can vicariously live — and emotionally understand — the journey from alcoholic drinking to healthy sobriety.

I chose alcoholic women because their problems in recovery are especially complex, and have been pinpointed and taken seriously only in recent years. I began by interviewing on tape some twenty women who had become sober through Alcoholics Anonymous. I spent a week at one treatment center observing and interviewing, and at a second center, went through a four-week course of treatment. With the permission of the patients involved, I joined their therapy group, participated in their sessions with their counselor, sat with them in the lectures on alcoholism, relaxed with them at meals and in the lounges — and interviewed them at great length.

During those months of self-education, I realized that, while every story of drinking and recovery was different, there were consistent threads, universal ingredients. I began actively searching for a woman who could be the subject of a book. Aware that alcoholism is a "family disease," profoundly affecting spouses and children, I wanted a woman who was still in her family — and somebody both feeling and expressive whose story included most of the classic moments of recovery. With the help of the counselor in my therapy group at the second treatment center, I did find such a wife and mother, who had successfully passed through that same group. She and her family agreed to work with me, provided their anonymity be preserved.

I chose a name for her — Abby Andrews — and there followed many, many hours of intensive, often emotional, always affecting talk on tape. But no person can remember every feeling, thought, and word from a rending period a year in the past. So I found five other women graduates of that same therapy group, scattered about the country, who became my consultants. After I wrote each scene in Abby's story, I discussed it with several of them by telephone, exploring their feelings during similar pains, triumphs, despairs, angers, failures, breakthroughs. Their husbands and children also gave me advice.

I used this material — plus my other interviews and my own experiences — to jog Abby's memory, to fill out the crucial moments in her saga, and to supply missing pieces.

From time to time a crucial element in the recovery process had to be dramatized in a way more explicit, more telling, than Abby's actual story. In those cases I felt free to use episodes from my other sources. So, though all names, places, and physical descriptions have been changed, all the moments in this book were experienced, said, felt by a real person. And, along the way, every chapter was read and checked for clinical validity by the director of counseling at the treatment center I joined.

All the women I interviewed spoke to me freely and with profound honesty. I am everlastingly grateful to them. And I am in special debt to my five consultants. Month after month, at a moment's notice, they interrupted active family and business lives to dig unsparingly into themselves and their anguished pasts. They are unable to breach their anonymity so I must thank them only as Pat, Jerre, Leslie, Sandra, Ann. During my research I had many teachers — busy, dedicated people who trusted me, gave me access to their professional lives and expertise, and guided me through the intricacies and pitfalls in alcoholism treatment and recovery. My appreciation to: Maureen Dudley Piekarski, June Qualy, Rachel Easton, Marion Mann, David Hiers, Wynne Schroeder, Jim and Pat Crisman, Dan Kunehardt. And absolutely vital to this book were St. Mary's Rehabilitation Center and Beach Hill Hospital, whose staffs gave me their unstinting confidence and cooperation. Lastly, of course, there is Abby, her husband, and children, without whom — in the words of the cliché — *Broken Promises, Mended Dreams* would not have been possible.

The three-and-a-half years spent on this book have left me with a horror of the disease of alcoholism and an abiding respect for all those involved in the process of recovery. Treatment centers have their individual programs, some very different from the one described in this book. But the programs work, and the centers produce success rates of up to seventy percent. Alcoholics Anonymous knows how to keep men and women sober for the rest of their lives. Al-Anon gives support and techniques to husbands and wives of alcoholics. Alateen does the same for the children. But my special admiration is for the amazing women who take their lives in their two hands and rescue themselves from the physical, mental, emotional, spiritual netherworld of alcoholism. They bring about, really, their own resurrection. And their return goes beyond their original person, to a fuller, deeper being. Again and again, women with a clear sparkle in their eyes have said to me, "It was a terrible way to get where I am now, but I'm actually glad it all happened."

Richard Meryman

THE TWELVE STEPS OF
ALCOHOLICS ANONYMOUS

1. We admitted we were powerless over alcohol — that our lives had become unmanageable.
2. Came to believe that a Power greater than ourselves could restore us to sanity.
3. Made a decision to turn our will and our lives over to the care of God *as we understood Him.*
4. Made a searching and fearless moral inventory of ourselves.
5. Admitted to God, to ourselves, and to another human being the exact nature of our wrongs.
6. Were entirely ready to have God remove all these defects of character.
7. Humbly asked Him to remove our shortcomings.
8. Made a list of all persons we had harmed, and became willing to make amends to them all.
9. Made direct amends to such people wherever possible, except when to do so would injure them or others.
10. Continued to take personal inventory and when we were wrong promptly admitted it.
11. Sought through prayer and meditation to improve our conscious contact with God *as we understood Him,* praying only for knowledge of His will for us and the power to carry that out.
12. Having had a spiritual awakening as the result of these steps, we tried to carry this message to alcoholics, and to practice these principles in all our affairs.